"From one of the most innovative (and ethical) financial advisors in the country, Dale's views on the world of public finance should be resource No. 1 for any and all public officials."

Ron Bennett, CEO
School Services of California

"Packed with information, yet easy to read. A Win-Win for concerned taxpayers and citizens across the state."

Donald P. Wagner, Member, Orange County Board of Supervisors
Irvine, CA

"Win-Win is filled with insights about a business far too few citizens and school district officials understand. Comprehensive, thorough and well-organized."

Tatia Davenport, Deputy Executive Director
California Association of School Business Officials (CASBO)

"This book demystifies school bonds for taxpayers, parents and school board members. A must-read for every school board member."

Haney Hong, President and CEO
San Diego County Taxpayers Association

"An essential resource for anyone involved in school district finance."

David Gomez, Executive Director (retired)
California Association of Latino Superintendents and Administrators (CALSA)

"Taxpayers and school board members looking for a blueprint on how to ensure that more of their tax dollars are used to improve schools and less to pay interest, need to look no further, Dale Scott's Win-Win is the best resource they will find."

Frank Gornick, Ph.D, Chancellor Emeritus
West Hills Community College District

3rd
EDITION

—

win-win

....

An Insider's Guide
to School Bonds

3rd
EDITION

———

win-win

··

An Insider's Guide
to School Bonds

Improve Your Schools and Protect Local Taxpayers

Dale Scott

DALE SCOTT & CO

DS&C PUBLISHING
SAN FRANCISCO

Win-Win: An Insider's Guide to School Bonds
Improve Your Schools and Protect Local Taxpayers

Third Edition
Dale Scott

First edition published 2013.
Second edition published 2017.
Third edition published 2019.
Printed in the United States of America

Published by DS&C Publishing
650 California Street, Suite 2050
San Francisco CA 94108
415.956.1030

ISBN: 978-0-9897374-1-8

Library of Congress Control Number : 2019917242

Ed-Tech Bond(s)®, GO Reauthorization Bond(s)®, CAB Restructuring
Bond(s)®, and GO Flex-Bond(s)® are registered trademarks of
Dale Scott & Co., Inc.
Teacher-Staff Housing GO Bond(s)™ is a trademark of
Dale Scott & Co., Inc.

Cover design: Adam Elwell
Editing, Third Edition: Barbara J. Barr, Impeccably Edited
Book design: Adam Elwell and Chris Shults
Photographer: Drew Alitzer

DEDICATION

In memory of Ron Bennett—client, mentor, friend.

TABLE of CONTENTS

Table of Contents

FIGURES AND TABLES

PREFACE

"Experience is not what happens to you; it's what you do with what happens to you."

~ Aldous Huxley

The purpose of this book is to demystify the complex, often challenging process that goes on "underneath the hood" in developing a General Obligation (GO) bond measure, placing it on the ballot, putting together a campaign for its approval, and, once it is passed, structuring and issuing the bonds for California school and community college districts. *Win-Win: An Insider's Guide to School Bonds* is designed to deliver a balanced understanding of this process, enabling elected school district board members, educational and civic administrators, and members of the public to become more active and involved in that process.

My "research" for this book is the sum of everything I've learned in the past three and a half decades of work in the field of municipal finance as an investment banker (on Wall Street and in California at Wells Fargo Bank), financial advisor, and participant in scores of bond campaigns.

I know from experience that not everyone – including the participants themselves – shares my enthusiasm for the unique combination of local politics and public finance that makes up the K–14 bond process. This hit home early in my last year of graduate school, when I sat down with my faculty advisor to discuss possible career paths and job opportunities.

Even in the 1970s, my advisor, with his shaggy silver-gray hair and turquoise bracelet, stood out as a flamboyant character for a Harvard finance professor. He didn't hold back on his opinions, either. When I mentioned

I was interested in working for an investment bank in the field of public finance, a pall of both horror and boredom came over his face.

"Listen," he sniffed. "Nobody actually wants to work in munis. People only take those jobs in the hope of transferring to corporate finance."

I bit my lip, but it was clear my "advisor" didn't know the first thing about me. If he'd read my file – which was sitting, obviously untouched, in a stack of newspapers atop his typewriter – he'd have seen I'd spent the previous summer traveling around the country interviewing city finance officers as part of a federal consulting project to analyze the impact of federally funded public works projects on local economies. Before that, I worked first as an intern and then as a speechwriter for a (badly losing) Boston mayoral candidate. And before that, I'd worked as a largely unpaid staffer for a newly elected member of the San Francisco Board of Supervisors as she tried to learn the complex navigation around the city's bureaucracy. Looking back, it seems pretty clear that my career path was headed toward a confluence of local politics and finance – though it was apparently not so clear to my advisor.

"The problem," he said, leaning back in his chair, "is that once you're hired into a muni finance department, you're branded, and it's impossible to get out. Sooner or later, you're going to be at a cocktail or dinner party and someone will ask what you do. When you say, '*I work in muni finance*,' the conversation will just stop. Dead. Why? Because muni finance is boring. Utterly boring and nobody, nobody cares a thing about it."

Although my advisor missed the boat on me, I have to admit he pretty much nailed muni finance. There's a lot about it that is boring, and I've never met anyone at a cocktail party who got excited about tax-exempt bonds. There are thousands of rules and regulations – federal, state and local – that form a potential compliance straitjacket. Board meetings are almost always held at night and, more often than not, run far too late. Politicians are, well, politicians. The business of public finance can be cutthroat and is filled with its share of – shall we say – less-than-noble characters. And *nobody* – and here I include even my own late mother – nobody likes to hear about any government plans for yet another tax increase.

And yet ... The ability of local voters to decide how their tax dollars will be spent and what improvements should or should not be made in their community is at the core of American politics and, at least for me, verges on the sacred. I am always thrilled to work with local parents, seniors, business people, teachers, and former students as they organize and ultimately succeed in passing a local bond to improve their neighborhood schools, and I urge everyone who has the opportunity to get involved in their own communities.

When put together correctly, the work done to pass a bond measure has a transformative effect on people's sense of their role in their community. And when the work starts on the voter-approved projects – be it a new school, improvements to an athletic facility or the installation of wireless computer technology – a community's excitement and pride erase all the negatives, the arguments, the long nights, the frustrations and the sacrifices. At least for a day or two.

THE K–14 GO MARKET: UNCHARTED WATERS

When I first started thinking about this book, I remembered Stephen Rappaport. Stephen was my first boss back in 1980, when, with my freshly-minted master's degree, I joined the Municipal Finance Department of the now defunct Wall Street investment bank Bache Halsey Stuart & Shields. With his firmly-buttoned blue pinstripe suit and blue polka-dot tie, Stephen was pure Wall Street. He'd even written a book that became about as close as you could get to a best seller in the field of public finance. *Municipal Bonds* (1980), by David Lamb and Stephen Rappaport, was for years widely thought of as the definitive text on the municipal bond market.

As I began writing *Win-Win: An Insider's Guide to School Bonds*, I pulled Stephen's book off the shelf and flipped to the table of contents, scanning for the section on school- and college-district debt financing. Nothing. Not a single mention. Incredulous, I flipped back to the index. School districts? Nope. Community college districts? Not there. General obligation bonds? Only a discussion of state and municipal GOs, but not a word about school districts or community college districts.

I was stunned. K–14 general obligation bonds are today one of the largest sectors in the U.S. municipal bond market. And, yet, just 35 years ago, in what was then touted as the most comprehensive guide to public finance in print, K–14 GOs didn't even get a mention.

This fact, I believe, speaks volumes about what has taken place in the K–14 debt market over the past three and a half decades. Consider this: From 1985 through 1989, California school district and community college district bonds made up less than 5 percent of long-term tax-exempt debt sold by California local governments. But between 2008 and 2012, K–14 debt shot up to nearly 35 percent of all new long-term debt sold by local governments in the state.

Amazingly, until now nothing has been written to help participants navigate this enormous – and enormously important – marketplace. Outside of a handful of financial advisors, investment bankers, underwriters, rating agency analysts and bond lawyers, almost no one understands the hundreds of steps that go into putting a bond measure on the ballot, running a bond campaign and selling the bonds to investors. *Win-Win: An Insider's Guide to School Bonds* is designed to meet this obvious need.

This book is not intended to be a deeply technical guide to K–14 GO bonds, nor a juicy tell-all exposing the dark secrets, grudges and feuds (and, believe me, there are plenty) among the small cadre of professionals who dominate this market.

Rather, it seeks to provide enough insider information to school district administrators, elected officials, journalists and interested citizens (as well as anyone considering a career in *decidedly not boring* public finance) to help them deal intelligently with the hundreds of decisions and actions that go into issuing a school district or community college district bond in California.

HOW THE BOOK IS ORGANIZED

Win-Win: An Insider's Guide to School Bonds starts with a review of the three most important state judicial and/or legislative actions that have shaped and continue to shape this market:

- The 1971 *Serrano v. Priest* decision by the California Supreme Court, which required that education funding be equalized among school districts

- The 1978 passage of Proposition 13, which limited total real estate taxes to 1 percent of a property's assessed value, and restricted annual increases of a property's assessed value (the basis of real estate taxes) to 2 percent

- The 2000 passage of Proposition 39, which reduced the required voter threshold for the passage of general obligation bonds to 55 percent from Prop. 13's two-thirds

After that, the book is organized chronologically, starting with the initial planning process that goes into placing a bond measure on the ballot and continuing through to the actual issuance of the bonds and the various ongoing regulatory filings required after they are sold. These sections include:

- How to get ready for a bond election, including who needs to be on the team, figuring out what type of election works best given the needs of the district, and how to select an election date

- The steps needed to call for a bond election, including how to craft the ballot language, the required back-up documentation and how to manage the passage of the resolution

- How the district can best communicate with voters about the bond measure (without breaking any laws)

- An overview of the different strategies and techniques used in putting together a bond campaign

- The steps, procedures, decisions and actions required before issuing the bonds

- The filings and notifications required after the sale of the bonds, why no one wants to do them and why it is critical that they be completed anyway

Preface

By the way, Ed-Tech Bond(s)®, GO Reauthorization Bond(s)®, CAB Restructuring Bond(s)®, and GO Flex-Bond(s)® are registered trademarks, and Teacher-Staff Housing GO Bond(s)™ is a trademark of Dale Scott & Co., Inc. However, I'll spare you the use of the ® and the ™ symbols from now on.

INTRODUCTION TO THE THIRD EDITION OF *WIN-WIN*

When the second edition of *Win-Win* was published in October 2017, I figured I had at least four to five years before there would be any reason to even think about starting work on a third edition. Eight months later, my firm's long-time client, Jefferson Union High School District in Daly City, California, passed Measure J – the first teacher-staff housing general obligation bond in the country – and blew that plan out of the water.

Serving as Jefferson Union HSD's financial advisor on Measure J was among the most exciting and gratifying programs I have worked on in my entire career. But I have to admit that my original sense was that the need for affordable workforce housing was mainly a problem for a few high-income counties in Northern California. As I began to discuss Jefferson Union HSD's teacher-staff housing project with clients around the state, I soon learned that this issue is being grappled with by communities – small and large, urban and rural – across the state.

Designing, financing, and building teacher-staff housing is a vast subject and one that probably deserves a book of its own. For this reason, the teacher-staff housing section in this new edition of *Win-Win* focuses more narrowly on the advantages that can be obtained by funding these programs with general obligation bonds and an overview of the challenges that come with the implementation of these programs.

This third edition of *Win-Win* also includes a description of the significant legislative changes in the required general obligation bond ballot wording that dropped out of the sky with a thud at the beginning of 2018. These new requirements amount to the biggest change in general obligation bonds since the passage of Prop. 39 in 2000. The fact that almost no one saw them coming is a story unto itself, even if their overall impact remains unclear. And while many continue to try to repeal these new wording requirements, they are – as of the date of this writing – still legally required and should be given careful attention when drafting a ballot measure.

Chapter

ONE

....

OVERVIEW OF THE CALIFORNIA K–14 GO DEBT MARKET

....

"By our holding today we further the cherished idea of American education that in a democratic society free public schools shall make available to all children equally the abundant gifts of learning."

  ~ Serrano v. Priest (1971) 5 Cal.3d 584

In November 2000, California voters narrowly approved Proposition 39, which lowered the required percentage for approval of a General Obligation bond measure to 55 percent from the previous high hurdle of 66.7 percent. Prop. 39 triggered an enormous shift in the K–14 debt market, creating both opportunities and headaches we're still sorting out today.

To really understand California's current system of funding improvements in school and community college districts, you have to go back more than 30 years before voters approved Prop. 39 to a single conversation between two men at a neighborhood elementary school in eastern Los Angeles County.

THE *SERRANO* DECISION

In 1968, a young parent named John Serrano, Jr., wondered whether his local neighborhood school could meet the educational needs of his son, a promising young student. Serrano set up a meeting with the school's principal and asked for advice as to what he could do to improve his son's opportunities.

The principal's answer was simple and direct. The best possible thing John Serrano could do for his son was move to another town.

School district funding, the principal explained, depended on local property taxes. The wealthier the community, the more money for its schools. By moving out of their East Los Angeles neighborhood to a more affluent community, Serrano would be able to find a school with more resources to apply toward his son's education.

The idea of having to move in order to find a better school infuriated Serrano. But, in the end, he knew he had to do what was right for his son. He moved his family out of East Los Angeles, heading farther east to the San Gabriel Valley.

But even though the schools there had better funding, he couldn't stop thinking about the children back in East LA whose families couldn't afford to move. And the more he thought about it, the angrier he got. And he wasn't shy about letting people know it.

One night at a dinner party, he was again telling his story about having to move because of the way schools were funded and how unfair it was. A lawyer from the Western Center on Law and Poverty happened to be there and, as the party was breaking up, pulled Serrano aside.

The Center, the lawyer told Serrano, had been looking for a way to challenge this exact disparity. Would he be willing to lend his name to a class action lawsuit, the lawyer asked? A lawsuit that challenged how education was funded in California?

This simple conversation produced a seismic shift in California education funding. The legal argument behind *Serrano v. Priest* (Ivy Baker Priest was State Treasurer when the lawsuit was filed) was simple and straightforward. The State of California oversaw a public school system that relied on a system of local funding based on property tax revenues. Because of this, the plaintiffs argued, there were "substantial disparities" among school districts as to how much funding was available for an individual student's education.

For example, based on the taxable value of the homes and commercial property within the Baldwin Park Unified School District (a K–12 district located within the San Gabriel Valley), the district could spend $577 per student per year. However, in the Beverly Hills Unified School District, less than 30 miles to the west, the district could spend $1,232 per student per year because the assessed value of property in Beverly Hills was much higher. Put another way, the residents of Baldwin Park would have had to tax themselves more than twice as heavily as the taxpayers in Beverly Hills to produce the same amount of funding for their children.

In August 1971, after three years of legal wrangling, the California Supreme Court ruled that education was a fundamental constitutional right and remanded the case to a lower court for trial. Two years later, the Supreme Court upheld a lower court ruling that disparities in per-pupil spending based on wealth violated the equal protection clause of the California Constitution.

PROPOSITION 13

The *Serrano* decision invalidated California's previous system of funding school districts solely from each district's property taxes. The state Legislature responded to the court's ruling by designing a highly complicated formula that mandated a certain amount of funding per student across the state.

In most districts, local property taxes contributed only a portion of this revenue target. In order to equalize per-student funding statewide, state government revenues would be used to backfill whatever funding was needed to bring a district up to the required level. The idea wasn't to "take" funding from the wealthy districts and redistribute to the poor ones, but rather to add state revenue to low-funded districts. This was a hugely expensive proposition and one that would be highly dependent on the health of the state economy and the political willpower of the Legislature (so much so that, three decades later, large inequities – although not as widespread as pre-Serrano – remain between wealthy and low-income districts).

Also, California property values began soaring in the 1970s, and real estate taxes soared along with them. The real estate boom was incredibly beneficial to many school districts around the state. But there was a downside. Many longtime residents, especially elderly ones, found themselves taxed out of their homes as their homes' values rose and the homeowners could no longer afford the higher taxes.

School funding was not a central focus of the anti-tax campaign that arose as a result of the 1970s real estate (and real estate tax) boom, but it was a major casualty of that campaign. Proposition 13, organized by Howard Jarvis, an Orange County businessman, and Paul Gann, a Sacramento political consultant, proposed amending the California Constitution to limit property taxes to 1 percent of a property's assessed value, and increases in assessed value to 2 percent per year – regardless of the real market value – until the property was sold. (When a property was sold, it would be re-assessed at its sale price, but from then on, the same 2 percent annual assessment increase limit applied.)

In June 1978, Prop. 13 passed with a 62.6 percent "yes" vote.[1] Its impact on school district and community college district general obligation bonds was devastating. Here's why: As originally drafted, Prop. 13 limited the maximum amount of tax on real property to 1 percent. This left no margin for levying property taxes to pay principal and interest on voter-approved GO bonds. As a result, from 1978 to 1986 – eight years – local GO bond measures were effectively banned from the ballot throughout California.

Finally, only the most rabid anti-tax crusaders could fail to see the need for a change to protect the state's rapidly deteriorating educational infrastructure, and in 1986, Article XXXIII of the State Constitution was amended to allow the levy of additional *ad valorem property taxes* (i.e., taxes based on a property's assessed valuation) to pay bonds approved by a two-thirds majority of voters – a hurdle which, ironically, Prop. 13 itself failed to achieve eight years earlier.

....

1 Although there has been much current discussion of trying to close some of its corporate tax-reduction loopholes, the essence of Prop. 13, absent statewide voter approval of any revisions, appears to be here to stay. In 1992, the U.S. Supreme Court upheld Prop. 13, finding that the state of California had a legitimate interest in local neighborhood preservation, continuity and stability, and could therefore structure its tax system to discourage rapid turnover in ownership of homes and businesses (*Nordlinger v. Hahn*).

THE DARK YEARS

Even with this constitutional change allowing GO bond elections, the years from 1986 to the end of the 20th century remained difficult for the school bond market due to Prop. 13's two-thirds majority requirement. The need was so great, however, that after Prop. 13 was amended in 1986, bond measures began to creep back onto the ballot. Modesto City High School District passed a $43.2 million bond in 1987 by 72 percent. Oxnard Elementary School District passed a $40 million measure the next year by 71 percent.

But the elections were slow in coming because two-thirds was a high hurdle. For the first five years after the constitutional amendment allowing bond measures on the ballot, only slightly over a hundred bond measures went before the voters, and half of these failed to win the required two-thirds majority.

Driven by dire need, the pace of bond measures began to pick up in the '90s, with more than 700 measures on the ballot between 1991 and the end of 2000. But the win ratio barely improved, to 57 percent.

While a 57 percent win rate might not sound that grim, statewide statistics hide significant regional differences. Districts in Bay Area counties and certain parts of the Los Angeles region saw increasing bond successes – even at the two-thirds approval level – but districts in conservative regions fared much worse. San Bernardino County, for example, passed just 34 percent of its bonds, Shasta County just 21 percent. And San Joaquin County districts managed to pass only 18 percent of proposed bonds. California, once the national leader in education and education funding, was rapidly heading toward the bottom.

PROPOSITION 39

Clearly, something had to change. Enrollments across the state were surging. Starved of funding, schools were going to ridiculous lengths trying to make space for new students. Some instituted year-round schedules and staggered student vacations throughout the year to expand the number of available seats. Many schools went to "multi-track," meaning two children would be assigned the same desk. One would use it while the other was at recess or lunch, then they'd switch and the other child would get to sit down.

In March 2000, voters were offered the chance to end Prop. 13's restrictions on general obligation bonds. Proposition 26 (the precursor to Proposition 39) proposed lowering Prop. 13's two-thirds hurdle for GO bonds to 50+ percent, a simple majority. It failed by less than 90,000 votes, just 1 percent shy of the required 50+ percent for passage.

Having come so close, reform proponents knew victory was possible, especially if new, finely retuned legislation was placed on the upcoming presidential election ballot of November 2000. (Presidential elections bring out more liberal voters.) A new proposition – Prop. 39 – was drafted that avoided a call to repeal Prop. 13's two-thirds requirement; instead, school districts would be given an alternative: approve GO bonds with a 55 percent "yes" vote and accept tighter public oversight, such as an annual public audit of bond funds.

Before the November 2000 election, the Legislature enacted Assembly Bill 1908 to establish procedures for the issuance of bonds in the event Prop. 39 passed. Among AB 1908's provisions was an absolute, ironclad limit on tax rates to be levied to repay bonds passed under Prop. 39: $30 per $100,000 of assessed valuation (the value of the property as listed on the tax rolls) for elementary and high school districts, $60 for unified districts, and $25 for community college districts. Although it sounded good on paper, imposing these caps caused a major problem: a hard tax rate cap on a GO bond made the ballot proposition close to worthless.

A general obligation bond relies on an *ad valorem* pledge to repay bond-holders *no matter what*. As soon as the "full faith and credit" of that pledge is taken away – as it would be with a hard cap – it's no longer a *general* obligation but rather a *limited* obligation bond.

Would investors buy these limited obligation bonds? Probably. There's an investor for anything at the right price. But what AB 1908 did, in effect, was transfer the risk of declining assessed valuations – a serious risk that would result in the need for higher tax rates – from a district's taxpayers to bond investors; if the tax rate was capped, it was conceivable that there wouldn't be enough money to repay investors in certain situations.

Junk bond investors are used to this kind of high-risk trade-off for higher yield. But in the world of general obligation bond finance, such a shift in risk was a major no-go. AB 1908 essentially gutted the intent of Prop. 39. Remarkably, in an industry where very few people agree on anything, the entire California K–14 bond industry rose up as one to oppose AB 1908. Even more remarkably, the authors of the legislation actually listened. Within three months, a post-cleanup of the pre-cleanup legislation – AB 2659 – was enacted, and the hard-cap language for tax rates was shuffled off the stage.

Enter the "Soft Cap"

In its place was one of the more creative inventions of the financial/legislative mind: the *soft* tax rate cap. A *soft* cap? How can a tax rate be capped but at the same time not be capped? Although it was never acknowledged at the time, what AB 2659 essentially did was toss the entire concept of capping GO bond tax rates out the window. In its place, rather brilliantly, was a cap not on *actual* tax rates but on **projected** tax rates. Here's the language of the bill:

"The bonds may only be issued if the tax rate levied ... would not exceed [the tax rate cap] when assessed valuation is projected by the district to increase in accordance with Article XIII A of the California Constitution." (Emphasis added.)

Okay. So, the obvious question is, if a district's GO bonds can only be issued if the *projected* tax rate doesn't exceed the cap, what's the maximum increase allowed (in accordance with Article XIII A of the California Constitution) in assessed valuation *projections*?

The answer? There isn't one. Although the percentage increase in an individual's property tax can be no more than 2 percent per year, according to Prop. 13, there is no limit whatsoever on the increase in total property taxes collected within a school district or community college district. For example, if no new housing is built within a district and no one sells their home for more than they bought it for, then the maximum increase in district-wide assessed valuation will be 2 percent. But if the number of homes in a district doubles in a year, then the total increase in property tax could, theoretically, increase by 100 percent or more.

AB 2659's invention of a cap on tax rate *projections* shaped the future structure of Prop. 39 GO bonds and led to explosive growth of California's K–14 bond market over the decade following Prop. 39's passage. But at the time of the November 2000 election, the potentially confusing question of how a cap could be a cap even if it wasn't a cap got pushed aside in the face of the overwhelming need for school improvements that would be enabled by Prop. 39.

Even with the increased voter turnout of a presidential election, Prop. 39 still barely squeaked by with 53.4 percent of the vote. Thin though the margin was, Prop. 39 was now law, and within 30 days of the election, three districts had placed Prop. 39 elections on the March 2001 ballot – Fresno USD for $199 million; Clovis USD for $79 million; and Exeter Union HSD for $4.3 million – and we were off to the races.

Looking back, it's hard to call Prop. 39 anything but an overwhelming success. Before Prop. 39, the statewide approval rate for K–14 GO bonds stood at 57 percent; after Prop. 39, the rate has leapt to around 80 percent. Even more amazing, in the 14 years prior to Prop. 39 (1986 through 2000), new California K–14 GO bond financings equaled about $11.1 billion. But from 2001 through 2014, that amount grew to more than $68 billion – a 513 percent increase.

Chapter
TWO

....

THE BASICS

....

"The Congress shall have power to lay and collect taxes on incomes, from whatever source derived ... "

~ Amendment XVI to the United States Constitution

WHY IS A TAX-EXEMPT BOND TAX-EXEMPT IN THE FIRST PLACE?

The professionals in the municipal finance industry are often so immersed in its rules, requirements and regulations that we all occasionally lose sight of how obscure and downright quirky the field of tax-exempt finance can be. But every once in a while, I'll get a whack on the side of the head that reminds me that not everybody lives, breathes, and dies over this small corner of the nation's financial markets.

A few years ago, I was making a presentation to a midsized school district in the Central Valley about the steps required to sell the district's first series of GO bonds. Everything was going fine until I mentioned that the bonds would be tax-exempt. The face of one of the newer board members, who up until that moment appeared to be following everything, suddenly clouded over.

"Excuse me, but …" she hesitated. "We're a public school district and don't pay any taxes. Why do we care if the bonds are *tax-exempt*?"

It was a good question, and a reminder that tax-exempt finance remains an obscure and murky area for most of the world – including many school board members. So, first to the board member's question:

When a bond is tax-exempt, interest payments to the investors are exempt from federal (and, in most cases, state and local) income taxes. Tax-exempt bonds are attractive to both school districts and investors because the interest rate on a tax-exempt bond can be significantly lower than on a *taxable* bond and still result in an equal or even greater after-tax return to the investor. A tax-exempt school bond paying, say, 3.5 percent a year can actually be more profitable for an investor than a 5 percent taxable corporate bond.

This is the underlying math that allows local governments, such as school and community college districts, to borrow at lower rates than private companies. Of course, if you're able to buy a tax-exempt bond and avoid paying income taxes on the interest, that means the federal government is not receiving the tax revenues it would be getting if you owned a taxable bond. This is why the Feds are not terribly keen on the tax-exempt market and would love to find a way to shut it down.

Then why don't they? The answer lies in the legal relationship between the federal government and the states. A series of court cases over the years has developed the concept of "intergovernmental tax immunity," which prohibits the federal government from interfering with a state's right to borrow by taxing the interest on the state's securities. While this concept has been chipped away at over the years (and the elimination of tax-exempt bonds is regularly proposed during federal budget negotiations), it remains at the core of tax-exempt financing.

SO WHAT, EXACTLY, IS A GENERAL OBLIGATION BOND?

In its simplest form, a general obligation (GO) bond is a voter-approved loan (the bond) to a local or state government in order to build, improve, repair, remodel and/or equip its facilities. When the bond is sold to investors, the industry refers to it as having been *issued*. The interest rates paid to investors are locked in on the date of sale and cannot be changed unless the bond is refinanced (or, in industry parlance, *refunded*).

For school and community college district GOs, the repayment of the bond is made through an annual assessment on all the taxable property in the district. This includes *secured property* (mainly buildings and land) and *unsecured property* (mostly equipment, but also including a wide range of items, from boats and airplanes to farm equipment). The levy is commonly referred to as pledge of the *"full faith and credit"* of the district, which means the county controller **is required to set the tax rate at whatever amount is necessary to repay the bonds.** GO bonds, it's important to note, must be repaid by the district's taxpayers, not by the district itself. (States and certain other local governments can also issue "general obligation bonds" that are secured by their general funds rather than a pledge to levy a certain amount of taxes on property. For example, the State of California regularly sells GO bonds secured only by legally available revenues rather than a pledge to raise specific taxes.)

The repayment of the bond's principal is referred to as the amortization of the loan, and the combination of the annual principal and interest payments is called the *debt service*. As with a fixed-rate home loan, the repayment of principal accounts for a small portion of annual payments in the early years of a bond, with interest making up the lion's share of the amount due. The principal-to-interest balance slowly increases over the life of the loan as interest payments decrease.

In general, the *debt ratio* (the total amount of debt service divided by the principal) of a bond is about 2:1 – that is, district property owners pay about $2 in taxes for every $1 borrowed – although, as we'll see later, this ratio can change quickly, for better or worse, depending on the structure of the financing.

Bonds are generally sold to investors in what is known as a *public offering*. Until 1983, municipal bonds were sold as *bearer bonds*. These were unregistered securities, and ownership was dependent on having the actual printed bond in your possession. Interest payments were made when the owner of the bond removed one of the interest coupons from the bottom of the bond – hence the term *coupon clipper* – and presented it to a bank for payment.

Today, each bond maturity is a *registered security* and is given a unique tracking number known as a CUSIP. In this way, bonds can be easily sold before their maturity in the *secondary market*. (Occasionally, bonds will be *privately placed* with an individual investor. In these cases, there is typically no registration of the bonds.)

CIBS, CABS AND BANS: A QUICK PRIMER

In structuring a bond financing, the financial analyst can draw on a number of different techniques and structures. This may appear complicated to non-financial people, but all that is happening – as one of my old Wall Street bosses used to say – is people figuring out different ways to make change out of a dollar bill. Regardless, it's necessary at this point to provide a relatively simple explanation of these structures – and the sometimes-enormous differences among them – so readers can better understand how GO bond deals are put together. (A more detailed, in-depth review is provided in a later chapter.)

Current Interest Bonds (CIBs)

The bedrocks of the traditional bond deal are *current interest bonds (CIBs)*. The simplest type of CIB is structured as a *term bond*. Going back to our home mortgage analogy, a term bond – like a home loan – will have a fixed rate of interest and a single maturity date (for example, 25 years). However, every year a certain amount of the bond's principal (the amount that's been borrowed) is repaid. This is known as *mandatory redemption*. (By the way, GO bond principal payments are almost always made annually, while interest payments are made semi-annually.)

Because GO bonds tend to be multi-million-dollar financings, a more common GO bond structure is for a certain amount of principal to be paid in each individual year or maturity with its own interest rate. These are known as *serial bonds*. You'll often see term bonds and serial bonds used together in a single financing, depending on investor demand, current interest rates and the overall size of the financing.

In its simplest form, each annual debt service payment is roughly the same, producing a structure known as *level debt service*. As shown in Figure 1, such a structure requires that payments in the earlier years be composed mostly of interest, the amount of which slowly declines as the principal is paid down.

While level debt service is the most conservative structure and produces the lowest level of interest payments, annual CIB debt service payments can also be structured to rise slowly over time, as shown in Figure 2.

This structure, known as *ascending debt service*, can be useful in trying to stabilize the tax rate by matching the amount of annual debt service payments with presumed increases in assessed valuations.

Capital Appreciation Bonds (CABs)

CIBs work well for first-time issuers with plenty of capacity beneath their Prop. 39 tax cap, as well as for districts with very large assessed valuations. However, consider a district that has previously issued one or more series of bonds from its voter authorization and is projected to be at the tax rate cap for several years to come. A CIB structure on a new series of bonds for this district would push the bond's tax rate over the Prop. 39 tax rate limit, so it cannot be used.

In these cases, financial advisors and investment bankers will use *capital appreciation bonds (CABs)* to jump over the debt service from the previously issued bonds in order to issue new ones, deferring debt service payments into the future in order to avoid exceeding the Prop. 39 tax rate cap.

Although much has been written about the complex nature of CABs – and the troubles some have caused – they are actually fairly simple in structure. If you are of a certain age, you might remember receiving Series E or Series EE savings bonds from your grandparents or an aunt or uncle for your birthday. Even though the bond would have a face value of, say, $100, it was purchased at a deep discount from this face value, let's say $65. When the bond matured (for example, in five or 10 years), you could cash it in for the full $100.

FIGURE 1: Level Debt Service on a $42.3 Million Bond at 5% Interest

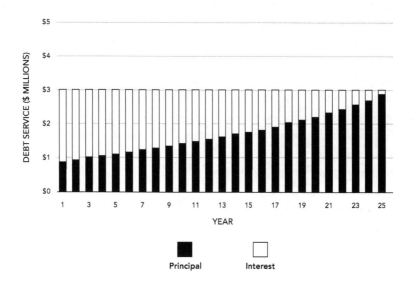

FIGURE 2: Ascending Debt Service on a $51.6 Million Bond at 5% Interest

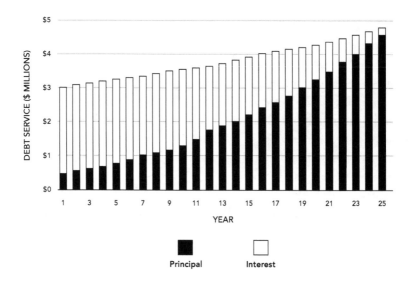

The difference between what your relative paid for the bond and what you cashed it in for was determined by the rate of interest being earned by the bond. This is the same with a CAB. Take an investor who spends $400,000 to purchase a CAB that matures in 20 years with a value at maturity of $1 million. During the next two decades, the investor will receive no interest payments. However, when the bond matures, the investor receives $1 million, which is composed of his original $400,000 investment plus $600,000 of what is called *accreted interest.*

Because they are in essence short-term fixes with potentially large long-term costs to a district's taxpayers, CABs have been at the center of many school bond controversies. (See the discussion of the Poway USD CAB controversy in *Special Topic #1.*) Used judiciously and in the right situation, however, CABs can actually work well with Prop. 39 bond programs. By including short-to-medium-term CABs in a financing structure, a district can continue to obtain project funding while skipping over those years when its CIB payments have pushed the tax rate to the maximum, allowing the bond's repayment to be deferred.

Having said that, let me repeat that CABs, because of their explosive potential for taxpayers, must be part of a well-thought-out long-term strategy and not just a tricky way to game the Prop. 39 tax cap.

Convertible CABs – A Rose Is a Rose Is a Rose?

A few years ago, just after the CAB controversy started hitting the press, I had a phone conversation with a chief business official (CBO) of a large unified district in the San Francisco Bay Area. She'd told me she planned on selling the district's next series of bonds and wanted us to review the financing plan prepared by the district's investment banker. "The board is adamant that we avoid the use of CABs," she said. "There's just too much negative publicity."

I gave our staff's research report another look. Even using liberal assumptions regarding future assessed valuation (AV) growth, this district was at or over its Prop. 39 tax rate limit for many years to come. There was no way it could issue any type of bonds other than CABs. "You know you're at your tax rate limit, right?" I asked her.

"Of course," she replied. "Our bankers have laid out all the numbers for us."

"But then," I said, still confused, "how do they propose to fund this next series of bonds without using CABs?"

"Oh, they're recommending that we use 'convertibles'!"

I had to hand it to the investment bankers. Somehow they'd convinced their client to avoid issuing controversial CABs by instead issuing "convertibles." What they appeared to have left out of the explanation was that convertibles are CABs. The only difference is that after a certain set number of years, the CAB converts into a CIB.

Used properly, convertible CABs can be excellent tools to help build a debt service structure that meets Prop. 39 tax rate restrictions. But they are merely a variation of a CAB, and carry the exact same risks.

....

Special Topic #1
THE LAW OF UNINTENDED CONSEQUENCES

A $105 million bond financing with a $1 billion price tag. There may be more egregious CAB deals out there, but it's hard to imagine any will achieve the notoriety of Poway USD's 2008 general obligation bonds and the CAB controversy that followed.

The story, first reported by a Detroit-based Internet blogger and then picked up by the online daily newspaper *The Voice of San Diego*, sent much of the school finance community running for cover starting in the summer of 2012 and on into 2013. Its repercussions continue to this day in school districts across the state.

In November 2002, Poway district voters approved a $193 million Prop. 39 GO bond. By 2007, those bonds had all been sold and the district began to consider a new bond election to continue with its school improvement program. The board approved a voter survey to test the viability of a new $179 million bond election. The results were less than promising, with voters balking at the idea of another tax rate increase. Faced with continuing project needs but lukewarm voter support, the district needed a solution.

No problem, said the bond consultants. We'll have another bond election but not raise people's property taxes. Instead, we'll just "extend" their current tax rate. How could that be possible, you might ask? Well, as already discussed in this chapter, tax rate projections must only be in "accordance with Article XIIIA of the California Constitution," which essentially means you can make any projection you want. That's just what the district's advisors did, using an aggressively liberal assumption that assessed valuation in the district would grow by nearly 60 percent over the following eight years.

But even a 60 percent increase in AV wasn't enough. To live up to its promise of not increasing the current tax rate, the district's advisors needed to find a way of avoiding any payment for more than 20 years. That led it to the use of capital appreciation bonds (CABs), which led in turn to a final bill of *more than $1 billion on a sale of only $105 million of bonds.*

Poway wasn't the first to use this method of financing and its deal wasn't the worst. If we're looking for culprits, it might be wise to start with whoever thought up the idea of the soft cap in the first place. My inner contrarian suspects that if it were not for AB 2659's illusory tax rate cap-that-wasn't-a-cap on Prop. 39, the Poways of the world would never have happened. After all, while kicking the can down the road by using CABs may be bad fiscal policy, no laws were broken. Rather, the plan Poway's advisors came up with was enabled by the soft cap embedded in Prop. 39 allowing free rein to push future AV growth projections to the levels needed to make the deal fly.

....

Bond Anticipation Notes (BANs)

Bond anticipation notes (BANs) are short-term securities issued in advance of a GO series in order to obtain immediate project funding. Their term is limited under state law to no longer than five years (including any rollovers). BANs can be highly effective at protecting a district's *authorized but unissued* bonds if, for example, a bridge loan is required to complete a project but some other form of funding is slow in arriving.

Warning: BANs can also be one of the most dangerous and toxic funding alternatives if incorrectly structured, and can result in the school district itself – and not district taxpayers – being on the hook for repayment if a district has hit the tax rate cap and cannot issue a new series of bonds.

Interest on BANs can be paid out either periodically or at maturity (essentially turning the BAN into a Capital Appreciation BAN). If requested by the district, counties can allow the interest costs to be added to the annual tax levy, allowing for periodic interest payments.

The repayment of the BAN (and any interest due) is guaranteed through the issuance of a district's authorized but unissued GO bonds. Typically, there are significant restrictions on the issuance of any GOs if a BAN is outstanding. If a district is unable to issue a GO to repay its BAN, it is required to repay the BAN from any other available fund, such as the general fund. This would, in most cases, require the issuance of some other form of debt, such as a certificate of participation (COP).

HOW TAX RATES ARE CALCULATED AND WHY THEY KEEP CHANGING

GO bonds are *fixed income securities*, which means that once they are issued and the interest rates are set, they pay a pre-determined amount of interest and principal year in and year out until maturity. While the amounts on the repayment schedule may vary from year to year, once the schedule is agreed to (e.g., once the financing "closes"), these annual payments are set.

This is where the estimation of tax rates begins to get difficult. Because even though the dollar amount of the repayment on a bond never changes, the underlying assessed valuation from which the payments are raised – and tax rates calculated – changes every year.

The Honeymooners

Here's how I explain this fixed-yet-floating phenomenon to clients. Think of a young newly married couple buying their first house. In order to buy the house, they sign a 30-year fixed-rate mortgage. Both spouses have jobs, and they calculate that the monthly mortgage payments would equal 20 percent of their take-home pay.

The next year, they both get salary increases so the percentage of their take-home pay dedicated to the mortgage drops to 18 percent. The next year, one of them gets their hours cut back, so the percentage of their wages it takes to pay the mortgage rises to 22 percent. And so on. Every year, as their financial situation changes, so does the *percentage* of their income that is used to make the mortgage payments. But – and here's the point – because it's a fixed-rate mortgage, the *actual dollar amount* of the monthly mortgage payment never changes.

It's exactly the same with a bond's repayment. Even though the amount of a bond's annual repayments is fixed on the date the bonds are sold, as a district's assessed valuations rise or fall, the annual tax rate will need to be adjusted – up or down – in order to produce the annually required payment.

Sizing a Bond Issue

To better understand the long-range impact of this concept, let's start by looking at a simple example that assumes zero percent change in the underlying assessed valuation. Imagine a district with a current assessed valuation of $5 billion. Applying a $60 tax rate per $100,000 of assessed valuation would yield $3 million per year in tax revenue. Again, assuming a zero percent increase in assessed valuation, the total amount of tax revenue that could be raised over 25 years would be $75 million.

TABLE 1 LEVEL DEBT SERVICE		
Principal	$42.3m	56%
Interest	$32.7m	44%
Total	$75m	100%

ASSUMPTIONS Assessed Valuation: $5 billion | AV Growth Rate: 0% per year | Tax Rate: $60 per $100,000 of AV | Amortization: 25 years | Interest Rate: 5%

Of course, the whole point of issuing a bond is to have the ability to borrow against this future stream of revenue to make funding for construction or rehabilitation available today. And, in order to borrow money, you have to pay interest. How much interest you pay will depend on the bond's interest rate, the term of the bond (the number of years of repayment), and how the repayment of the bond is structured (as described below).

Table 1 shows how this $75 million of tax revenues (which, again, derives from a $60 per $100,000 tax rate being levied over the life of the bond) would be divvied up, assuming a 25-year bond with a 5 percent interest rate and a level debt service structure (i.e., each year's payment of principal and interest is roughly the same). As shown, under this scenario a district would be able to borrow $42.3 million of the $75 million in tax revenues or 56 percent of the total, with the rest of the tax revenues being used to pay interest. (*This breakdown of level annual payments of principal and interest is displayed in Figure 1*).

Factoring in Growth Projections

In most districts, however, it's unreasonable to assume that assessed valuations will remain unchanged for the next 25 years, though the rate of growth is going to differ from district to district and area to area. For example, property values took quite a hit in many districts in the years after 2008. But even without increases in overall property values, people are still going to make improvements to their existing homes, new residences will be built, and new businesses will be created.

FIGURE 3: Relationship of Tax Rates to Assessed Valuation

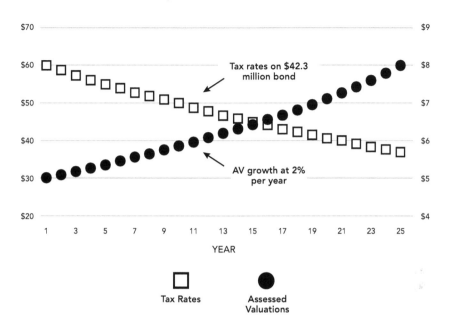

The question then becomes: What's the impact on a bond if you assume an increase in assessed valuations? As with so much in the field of tax-exempt finance, the answer is "it depends."

Figure 3 shows the relationship between assessed valuations and tax rates. Using the earlier example, we imagined a district with $5 billion in assessed valuation. If that AV grows at just 2 percent per year, it will grow to over $8 billion within 25 years. Because the tax base (i.e., assessed valuation) is growing, the required *tax rate* will decline, in this example down to less than $40 per $100,000 of AV. (The average tax rate over that period, by the way, would be about $48.)

But, as with the case of the newlyweds described earlier, the actual amount of money being raised by the district – in this example, $75 million – doesn't change. The only thing that changes is the tax rate. The actual amount paid by a property owner is going to depend on the rate of increase in his or her property's assessed valuation.

Lessons Learned

The lesson of these two examples is how important underlying assessed valuation projections are in estimating the long-term cost of a bond – and how difficult it is for voters and school district officials to figure out the true cost in advance. In the first example, assuming no increase in assessed valuations, it would be accurate to say that the average cost to a taxpayer would be $60 per year per $100,000 of AV. In the second example, it would be equally accurate to tell voters that the average cost would be $48 per year per $100,000 of AV. Yet, in both cases, the dollar amount of the bond – $42.3 million – and the total amount of interest paid by taxpayers are exactly the same.

Both of the earlier examples assume financings that are structured using level debt service, which is the most conservative approach. However, level debt service structure is only occasionally used for K–14 GO bond financings because, even though level debt service may be the absolute best deal for taxpayers, many districts (but certainly not all) are eager to quickly raise as much funding as possible, in order to complete the projects promised to the voters as early as possible.

For this reason, the ascending debt service structure is much more common. Under this structure, annual debt service payments rise from year to year in order to take advantage of assumed (i.e., expected, but not guaranteed) increases in assessed valuations. (See Figure 2.)

As shown in Table 2, this type of structure will result in greater upfront funding for projects. By allowing the debt service to rise by only 2 percent per year, the bond issue can be increased by more than $9 million to $51.6 million from the $42.3 million in Table 1.

The Term of the Bond

An amortization term for the bonds must be chosen before a tax rate projection can be made. Typically, this term will be between 20 and 30 years. Although a shorter term will reduce total borrowing costs, it will also reduce the amount of funding that can be obtained, or require a higher tax rate.

TABLE 2 ASCENDING DEBT SERVICE		
Principal	$51.6m	54%
Interest	$44.5m	46%
Total	$96.1m	100%

ASSUMPTIONS Assessed Valuation: $5 billion | AV Growth Rate: 2% per year | Tax Rate: $60 per $100,000 of AV | Amortization: 25 years | Interest Rate: 5%

Conversely, a longer term provides greater leverage for a potentially larger bond issue that, of course, comes with higher overall borrowing costs.

Although an amortization period of 20 to 30 years is generally used when financing new construction or the remodeling of an existing building, a term this long should be avoided when the assets being financed have a shorter useful life.

This is a common problem when financing equipment, especially technology. Although you can find many financial advisors, underwriters and bond lawyers who have developed a number of legal rationalizations as to why it's okay to amortize such technology tools as an iPad (which has a useful life of, perhaps, three years) over 10 to 20 years, there is simply no getting around the financial irresponsibility of such an action. Common sense requires that a district's financing plan take into account the useful life of the assets being financed.

To address this issue, we've developed and patented Ed-Tech Bonds, which match district borrowing efforts to the useful life of technology tools, providing an ongoing source of funding for technology at an enormous saving in interest payments. (See Chapter 3's discussion of Ed-Tech Bonds.)

Projected Interest Rates

For all the fuss that financial advisors and investment bankers make over interest rates, they are actually one of the least important factors in a tax rate projection. First of all, trying to predict interest rates for bond sales that will occur years into the future is complete folly. It makes much more sense to simply use conservative assumptions based on current and historical rates.

But even then, the impact of rising (or falling) interest rates on tax rate projections does not cause as much movement in tax rates as you might imagine. Let's look at the effect higher interest rates have on tax rates based on our last bond scenario, presented earlier in Table 2. Recall that this scenario assumed a $51.6 million bond with a 25-year amortization, an assessed valuation of $5 billion, 2 percent growth, ascending debt service, and an interest rate of 5 percent. Under these assumptions, the average tax rate was estimated at $60 per $100,000 of assessed valuation.

The effect of changing interest rate assumptions is shown in Table 3. Note that the effect of increasing the assumed interest rate to 6.0 percent from 5.0 percent – a significant jump – is to reduce the bond to $46.3 million from $51.6 million. In addition, the deal's debt ratio jumps to 2.07:1 from 1.86:1 – a negative, no doubt, but not a game-changer.

While it's wise to base interest rate assumptions on conservative projections of future market conditions, getting those assumptions wrong is not the end of the world. Interest rates generally play a much less important role in the final tax rate estimate than, say, AV projections and the bond's amortization period (although this could change quickly if we were to return to a period of extraordinarily high interest rates, e.g., the double-digit rates of the 1970s).

Multiple Bond Sales

Except for bond elections in which the bond amount is relatively small (say, $5 million or less), most bond authorizations are divided into two or more separate financings (or series), which are brought to market as a district's projects become ready for funding. From a financial perspective, since every sale of bonds brings with it new advisory fees, legal costs, rating agency invoices and so on, multiple bond sales would appear to make little sense. There are, however, three primary reasons bond authorizations are generally sold in series.

PUBLIC POLICY
The first reason has to do with public policy.

A number of years ago I was working with a Los Angeles County district

TABLE 3			
IMPACT ON TAX RATES OF CHANGING INTEREST RATE ASSUMPTIONS			
Interest Rate	4.00%	5.00%	6.00%
Principal	$57.7m	$51.6m	$46.3m
Interest	$38.4m	$44.5m	$49.8m
Total	$96.1m	$96.1m	$96.1m
Debt Ratio	1.67:1	1.86:1	2.07:1
Projected Avg. Tax Rate per $100,00 AV	$60.00	$60.00	$60.00

ASSUMPTIONS Assessed Valuation: $5 billion | AV Growth Rate: 2% per year Amortization: 25 years

Debt Service Type: Ascending

that had just won a $100 million bond election. It had about $20 million of projects ready for construction, and the board was getting ready to pass a resolution authorizing the sale of the first series of bonds.

One of the board members considered himself something of an expert on financial matters and proceeded to propose his own plan for selling the bonds.

"I say we sell all $100 million and invest the money for the next three years," he announced to the board. "Just think of how much interest we can earn on a pot that big."

And he was right. At that time, short-term interest rates were relatively decent, and the district could have easily picked up an extra $10 million or more by just sitting on the money for three years or more.

But from a public policy point of view, the idea was terrible. What was really being proposed – although I was never able to convince the board member of this – was a transfer of funds out of the taxpayer's pocket and into the district's. Even though the district would now have $100 million sitting in an investment account, it was the taxpayers who would be footing the bill through their annual property tax payments. Luckily, the rest of the board opposed the idea and the district ended up borrowing only as much as it needed for its immediate projects.

IRS RESTRICTIONS

The second reason bond authorizations are generally sold in series is the IRS.

The board member just discussed was certainly not the first person to come up with the idea of selling millions of dollars of tax-exempt bonds at one interest rate, investing them in taxable securities at a higher rate, and pocketing the difference (a process known in the bond industry as *arbitrage*). Unsurprisingly, the Internal Revenue Service does not look kindly on local and state governments issuing tax-exempt bonds to generate investment earnings.

In response to schemes like these, there are numerous Treasury Department regulations designed to thwart what Treasury views as "abusive" uses of tax-exempt bonds. Front and center is a regulation commonly referred to as the *three-year rule*. Although there are a handful of exceptions to this regulation, in general the IRS requires the issuer of a tax-exempt bond to have a *reasonable* expectation of spending 85 percent of the funds within three years of the closing date of the financing.

IMPACT ON TAX RATES

The third reason bond authorizations are generally sold in multiple series is that doing so allows the borrowings to more closely track the projects that are being funded and, therefore, allows the tax rate to be distributed over a much longer timeframe.

Table 4 compares the difference between issuing a bond authorization as a single series vs. selling it in three series. For the single series, the same assumptions used in the example above apply: $5 billion in assessed valuation with a 2 percent growth rate, ascending debt service with an interest rate of 5 percent, and a maximum tax rate of $60 per $100,000 of assessed valuation. For the multiple series, the only change is that the authorization is structured into three separate financings issued in years one, four, and seven.

Note that the amortization period *for each series of bonds* remains 25 years. However, by breaking the total financing into three series and spacing each series apart by three years, the total period the bonds remain outstanding has increased to 31 years from 25. More importantly, the size of the bond has grown to $68.1 million from $51.6 million, a 32 percent increase, *even though the estimated average annual tax rate remains at $60.00.*

TABLE 4 **IMPACT OF MULTIPLE SERIES OF BONDS ON BOND SIZING**		
	Single Series of Bonds	Multiple Series of Bonds
Years Sold	1	1, 4, & 7
Amortization per Series	25 years	25 years
Total Years for Repayment	25 years	31 years
Principal	$51.6m	$68.1m
Interest	$44.5m	$59.1m
Total Debt Service	$96.1m	$127.2m
Debt Ratio	1.86:1	1.87:1
Projected Avg. Tax Rate per $100,00 AV	$60.00	$60.00

ASSUMPTIONS Assessed Valuation: $5 billion | AV Growth Rate: 2% per year

Interest Rate: 5% | Debt Service Type: Ascending

ASSESSED VALUATION GROWTH PROJECTIONS

Without a doubt, the single biggest variable in the development of a tax rate projection – and the most complex to nail down – is the underlying assessed valuation growth projections. I'll get into a more thorough analysis of what should go into the development of these AV projections in a later chapter. For now, I'll just cover some of the mechanics and review what a huge impact these AV assumptions can have on a proposed bond's estimated tax rates.

THE IMPACT OF PROP. 13

To understand the underlying assumptions that go into preparing assessed valuation projections – as well as the underlying problems and pitfalls – we need to return to the mechanics of Prop. 13.

Recall that under Prop. 13, tax on secured property (essentially, all buildings and land except exempt property, such as churches) is limited to 1 percent of the property's assessed value. The assessed valuation for such a property was originally set to equal its market price at the time Prop. 13 was enacted in 1978. After that, the property's AV cannot increase by more than 2 percent per year until ownership transfers. (This does not include transfers of real property into or out of a Revocable Living Trust, between spouses, from a parent to a child, or from a child to a parent.)

Once the property is sold, its assessed valuation is recalibrated to the sale price. While this system is great for homeowners (at least for homeowners who have lived in their houses for many years), it has led to a number of unintended consequences. The most obvious is the different taxes paid by neighbors living in similar houses. Families that have been around for years pay far less real estate tax than newcomers because their homes' assessments have never caught up to market reality.

While many consider Prop. 13's artificial suppression of assessed valuations unfair, on an operational level it can actually be something of a benefit in older, more established districts. When homes change hands after decades of ownership, and those homes are evaluated at true market value on county assessment rolls, a district's AV can skyrocket. Even during housing slumps, a handful of sales of long-inhabited homes will keep a district's AV rate growing above Prop. 13's maximum of 2 percent.

Districts with large areas of newer development don't get this bump. While Prop. 13 restricts AV increases to 2 percent annually, **it says nothing about decreases**. Here the market speaks clearly, and periods of declining property values hurt school districts that have experienced rapid, recent development.

THE POWER OF ASSESSED VALUATION PROJECTIONS

To understand the impact of assessed valuation projections, let's go back to our most recent example, which looked at the effect of multiple series on a bond's sizing – the amount of principal available for district projects. (See Table 4.) In that example, we saw that we could increase the bond authorization to $68.1 million from $51.6 million simply by spreading the issuance of the bonds out for an additional six years, assuming a 2 percent annual increase in assessed valuation.

Using the multiple series example from above, Table 5 illustrates the powerful impact of assessed valuation projections. If we assume a 2 percent AV growth rate, the proposed bond would need to be limited to $68.1 million. Upping the AV growth assumption to 4 percent pushes the size of the bond to $89.3 million, a 31 percent increase. And raising the AV growth assumption to 6 percent per year increases the potential size of the bond to $120.1 million, a 76 percent increase. Note, however, in each of these radically different bond sizes, the tax rate projection being disclosed to voters **remains at $60 per $100,000 of assessed valuation**.

This extraordinary increase in bond size has been accomplished solely by manipulating the underlying assessed valuation assumptions, without the use of high-interest financing products such as CABs. And if the underlying assumptions actually come to pass – if, for example, the district's AV does indeed grow by 6 percent annually for the next 30 years or so – then you would look back at such a financing and call it a pretty good deal.

But what if AVs don't grow as much as projected? Then the $60 tax rate projection will need to be tossed out the window and tomorrow's taxpayers will be hit with a tax bill that far exceeds what was advertised.

Moral of the story: The best way to protect tomorrow's taxpayers is to make a realistic, conservative AV growth projection today.

THE IMPACT OF 2013 LEGISLATION ON TAX RATE PROJECTIONS

Revelations in the press regarding interest-heavy CAB financings put in place by many K–14 districts around the state led to an enormous amount of breast beating by editorial writers, elected officials and taxpayers. "Outrageous, despicable, predatory, semi-criminal" – and these were some of the politer opinions.

Shortly following this hue and cry were the predictable demands for new state legislation to prevent future CAB abuses. Now don't get me wrong. I think legislation was needed, and I strongly supported the CAB-regulatory bill (originally proposed by Dan McAllister, treasurer-tax collector of San Diego County) that came out of the Legislature. But I still had to laugh.

I can't tell you how many times I've heard people complaining about Sacramento. "They need to leave us alone," they wail. "The state needs to stay out of our lives and let us handle our own problems." But the moment something like Poway hits the papers, suddenly everybody is demanding a new law.

TABLE 5 IMPACT OF VARIOUS AV ASSUMPTIONS ON BOND SIZING			
Annual AV Growth Projections	2.00%	4.00%	6.00%
Years Sold	1, 4, & 7	1, 4, & 7	1, 4, & 7
Amortization per Series	25 years	25 years	25 years
Total Years for Repayment	31 years	31 years	31 years
Principal	$68.1m	$89.3m	$120.1m
Interest	$59.1m	$88.6m	$134.3m
Total Debt Service	$127.2m	$177.9m	$254.4m
Debt Ratio (=Debt Service/Principal)	1.87:1	1.99:1	2.12:1
Projected Avg. Tax Rate per $100,00 AV	$60.00	$60.00	$60.00

ASSUMPTIONS Assessed Valuation: $5 billion | Interest Rate: 5% | Debt Service Type: Ascending

In response to news articles regarding the high cost of many K–14 GO CAB financings, then-Assemblyman Ben Hueso and then-Assemblywoman Joan Buchanan introduced Assembly Bill 182 on January 25, 2013, which was widely praised by newspaper editorial boards across the state. In fact, despite howls of protest from many in the school finance industry, the changes proposed under AB 182 were, from my point of view, relatively tame and long overdue.

The key components of the bill were pretty commonsensical:

- The ratio of total debt service to principal for each bond issued (not the combined series of all bonds issued under an authorization) would be limited to 4-to-1. That's hardly hard-nosed.

- The term of K–14 GO bonds would be limited to 25 years from the current 40-year maximum. A little severe, but not that hard to live with.

- CABs with maturities of more than 10 years would be required to allow for *optional redemption*, something I've long recommended to our clients. (There's a discussion of bond redemption in Chapter 10).

Given the statewide umbrage over the more outrageous CAB deals and what I thought was the reasonableness of the proposed provisions of AB 182, I predicted easy passage. Boy, was I wrong. The first insight into how big a firestorm these proposed changes would set off came early, when I and a handful of other "industry leaders" – financial advisors, underwriters and legal counsel – were invited to the state Capitol for a sit-down with then-state Treasurer Bill Lockyer and Assemblywoman Buchanan to discuss the bill.

The meeting got off to a good start. The treasurer, widely thought of as a man with – how shall I say? – mercurial opinions, swept into the conference room overlooking the Capitol. He had a wide, avuncular smile and slowly worked his way around the room, shaking hands.

"Okay, let's get down to business," he said after making introductions. He settled into a chair at the head of the table. "We're here," he nodded toward the assemblywoman, "to hear what you have to say about the bill. No holds barred. We think this bill is long overdue, but how can we make it better?" He looked around the room slowly, smiling like a poker player with a winning hand.

The manager of one of the state's leading school bond underwriting houses quickly raised his hand. "With all due respect, Mr. Treasurer," he said, "Why pick on school districts? They're not the only ones …"

"Hold on a minute," the treasurer interrupted. "Nobody's picking on anybody. But these 40-year deals have got to stop."

"But just last year, the state issued a 100-year bond. Nobody complained about that."

(Remarkably, this is true. In February 2012, the Regents of the University of California issued an $860 million bond due in 2112, one hundred years from the date of issuance. The bonds pay 4.858 percent interest.)

There was a collective holding of breath in the room. The treasurer's face went from a healthy tan to red to purple in about two seconds. It was like watching Mr. Rogers morph into the Incredible Hulk.

"I'm not going to sit here ..." he exploded, "... and listen to these chicken-shit excuses. These deals are going to be stopped with you or without you."

This exchange pretty much summed up the next six months of trench warfare over AB 182. Both sides – state and local politicians on one side and investment bankers and school districts on the other – predicted the end of Western civilization if their version of the bill wasn't passed. But, like a lot of what happens in Sacramento (and other state houses), the outcome was neither as good nor as bad as both sides wanted or feared.

AB 182, which became effective January 1, 2014, nips around the edges of the K–14 bond law. By limiting CABs to a repayment term of no more than 25 years and holding firm with the 4-to-1 debt-service-to-principal ratio for each bond (rather than the combined series of bonds), AB 182 limits out-of-control CAB deals. There will be a little bit more disclosure required of issuers (districts), and the whole process is going to take a little longer.

But, oddly, what AB 182 didn't do was address the problem of financial advisors and investment bankers using over-the-top assessed valuation growth projections to slip under the Prop. 39 projected tax rate restrictions. While the 4-to-1 ratio will certainly help slow things down, without a cap on assessed valuation growth rates, we'll continue to see some pretty ugly deals in the future.

As Ron Bennett, CEO of California School Services, once explained to me, "Legislators tend to react first with their hearts and then with their brains." AB 182 was definitely an emotional – from the heart – reaction to the problems plaguing the K–14 bond business. Hopefully, we will see cleanup legislation in the next few years that circles back and deals with some of the issues left on the table the first time around.

Also keep in mind that AB 182 only dealt with the CAB problem *going forward* and did nothing – despite the vehement breast beating of many state elected officials – about the more than 200 non-callable K–14 CAB deals with debt ratios above 4-to-1 that were issued in the decade prior to AB 182. For more about one solution to this problem, see *Special Topic #9: CAB Restructuring Bonds – Confronting the Messy Closet.*

Chapter
THREE

....

BEYOND THE BASICS

....

"Victory has 100 fathers and defeat is an orphan."

~ John F. Kennedy

The last few years have seen a number of innovations in how California K–14 bonds are issued, and I'm proud to say that my firm has been at the forefront of many of these developments. While these new types of bonds certainly won't replace your traditional 25- to 30-year bond structures, they are worth taking a side trip to see how powerful they can be in the right circumstances.

Three new products stand out and I'll take them in the order they were developed: GO Bond Reauthorizations, Ed-Tech Bonds, and GO Flex-Bonds.

GO REAUTHORIZATION BONDS

A few years ago, I was invited to attend a board meeting by a midsized district in the heart of the Central Valley. The district had passed a $37 million GO bond in the November 2006 election, just as the good times were beginning to roll. In the five years before the election, the district's assessed valuation had grown by more than 35 percent, and it grew another 15 percent between 2006 and 2008.

Then all hell broke loose. With the meltdown in the real estate market, assessed valuations slid backward almost to where they had been six years earlier. Fortunately, the district had issued only about half of its authorized bonds. But it had new school construction projects underway and was counting on selling the remaining bonds in order to finish the projects. Worse still, the bonds that had been issued were CABs with pretty rich assumptions regarding future AV growth stretching far into the future. They were already over their tax rate limit with no relief in sight.

We ran a number of scenarios, looking for a solution that would allow the district to issue its remaining authorized bonds, but each scenario came up dry.

"I don't see any set of circumstances that would allow you to issue your remaining bonds until years into the future," I told the school board as they stared glumly at my presentation. "Your best bet," I went on, "would be to park the $18 million of authorized but unissued bonds on the shelf and ask voters to pass a new $18 million bond."

The board members began to give each other the kind of sideways look you see when your crazy uncle starts handing out free investment advice at the Thanksgiving dinner table.

"You want us to ask the voters for another 18 million dollars?" one of them finally said.

"Correct," I answered.

"But," another interrupted, "why do that? They already approved 18 million dollars."

"I know they approved it," I answered. "But because of your tax rate limit, you can't issue those bonds. You're not going to get your hands on those funds for years into the future. Better to forget about those bonds for now and ask voters for a new 18 million dollars."

"But we already have 18 million," said another board member.

It was at this point that the light bulb began flickering on. How, I asked myself, were we expecting voters to understand that even though they *had* $18 million of bonds, they couldn't spend it, when even their own board couldn't grasp the concept.

On the drive home, I began to mull over the meeting. Why not, I wondered, go to voters and ask them to "reauthorize" the bonds that couldn't be sold? That way, we wouldn't be creating any new debt, just replacing the old. However, under Prop 39, the tax rate limit is ***per election***. This way, the previously authorized $18 million in bonds could be reauthorized and sold immediately without having to resort to long-term CABs or waiting 20 to 30 years.

Since that ride home, we've passed nearly $1 billion of GO Reauthorization Bonds, allowing districts across the state that were up against their tax rate limit – due to falling assessed valuations or a lack of projected growth – to continue with their school construction/improvement programs.

Unlike ***tax rate extension elections*** (described more fully in Chapter 5), GO Reauthorization Bond elections do not increase the amount of bonds already approved by voters.

In a GO Reauthorization Bond election (run under Prop. 39), a district asks voters to reauthorize all or a portion of bonds that have been previously approved but have yet to be sold. On a mechanical level, voters are being asked to approve a new bond measure that will replace the old authorized but unissued bonds. The district pledges in the ballot resolution that if the new measure passes it will go through the process, as outlined in the California Education Code, of *decertifying* with its county an equal dollar amount of the old bonds. In this way, no additional debt is created.

If the reauthorization fails (the threshold for victory remains 55 percent), nothing is affected. The old bonds are not decertified and the district, in order to sell more of those previously authorized bonds, would need either to jump over the outstanding bonds' tax rate by selling CABs or wait until assessed valuations climbed high enough to sell the additional bonds.

But if voters say "yes" to the reauthorization, it's a new ballgame. As I said, under Prop. 39, the tax rate limit (e.g., $60 per $100,000 of assessed valuation) is per election. In other words, once the bonds are reauthorized by the voters, the district can sell the reauthorized bonds as current interest bonds. And the financial impact of this decision – the overall savings to taxpayers – is enormous. Let's look at one example.

In November 2006, Jefferson Union High School District in San Mateo County passed a $136.9 million GO bond. Over the next six years, the district issued $95 million worth of bonds with an assumed long-term annual growth rate in assessed valuation of 5 percent. However, between 2008–2009 and 2010–2011, the district's assessed valuations actually fell by nearly 3 percent, pushing the tax rate on the outstanding $95 million of bonds up to the $30 per $100,000 legal limit, making it impossible to issue the remaining $41.9 million without resorting to high-interest CABs.

When the district's board of education heard that the interest costs on a $41.9 million CAB could end up being as high as $282.5 million (more than six times the principal), it decided to place a bond reauthorization measure – Measure E – on the November 2012 ballot. The board figured it had little to lose. If the reauthorization measure failed, it would be in exactly the same spot as it was before placing the item on the ballot. But if the measure passed, not only would the board be saving taxpayers millions of dollars, it would also keep the school reconstruction program on schedule.

In other words, there's not a whole lot to lose – either for districts or for taxpayers – with a GO Reauthorization Bond election. I think this is what most people find so compelling about the program. That's because even though the reauthorization is technically a new bond election, in fact, it operates more like a referendum. As I explained to a group of angry taxpayers one night who had invited me to address their organization, a reauthorization election does not change the total amount of bonds approved by voters. It merely changes when the bonds can be issued. A "yes" vote allows the district to issue the bonds immediately; a "no" vote means they'll have to wait until assessed valuations rise enough to allow the bonds to be sold and meet the Prop. 39 tax rate restrictions. But sooner or later, the amount of bonds already approved by voters in the original election will be sold.

In the case of Jefferson HSD, the voters agreed to the reauthorization, passing Measure E with a 73.5 percent "yes" vote. Before the district could issue any of the reauthorized bonds, it needed to decertify an equal amount of the old bonds with the county. It could then issue new bonds as current interest bonds rather than CABs at a projected interest cost of $41.9 million, saving taxpayers more than $240 million.

ED-TECH BONDS

Ed-Tech Bonds provide California K–14 districts with an ongoing source of funding for educational technology (e.g., tablet computers, e-readers, etc.), financed with short-term bonds designed to match the useful life of the technology. If put together correctly, Ed-Tech Bonds can be approved by voters with a single ballot measure, yet provide technology funding for decades into the future. Better still, because they do not rely on the deep leveraging of future tax receipts, the borrowing costs are slashed to about as close to nothing as you can get.

The story of how the Ed-Tech Bond structure was developed isn't one of those "ah-ha" moments you hear about that people get while running 10 miles through the redwood forest or watching bubbles float to the top of a glass of beer. It came to me as I pulled into the parking lot of a Basque restaurant in Bakersfield. And I was in a rotten, sour mood.

I'd just finished a long day of meetings with various districts in and around the Los Angeles basin. My last meeting of the day was with the superintendent of a midsized district in Los Angeles County, and the conversation kept me grumbling to myself as I drove two hours over the Grapevine on Interstate 5 toward Bakersfield. The superintendent had told me he planned to buy every student in the district an iPad – at more than $400 each, an investment of about $10 MILLION.

"And how are you paying for them?" I asked.

"We're going to be using a *technology endowment bond*," he said. From the smile on his face, it was clear the real cost of the endowment bond concept hadn't been explained to him.

Endowment Bonds

We had already done a complete analysis of the "endowment bond" concept and found it to be overly complex at best and potentially risky at worst. At their core, technology endowment bonds are structured to essentially allow for an end run around federal tax laws that require tax-exempt bond proceeds to be spent within three years.

By avoiding this restriction, technology endowment bond proceeds can be spent over a much longer time period, allowing a district to replace outmoded technology over, say, a decade. Hence, the so-called "endowment." But no matter how much the proponents tried to dress it up, it still came down to asking taxpayers to assume long-term debt to fund educational technology that had a shelf life only slightly longer than junk food. To my mind, while the technology endowment bond was strong on marketing appeal, it had two significant weaknesses. First, regardless of the name, taxpayers were still being saddled with 15+ years of bond payments to buy equipment that would become obsolete long before the bond was paid off. Second, because the proceeds could be withdrawn by the district over a decade, technology endowment bonds obligated county treasurers to invest bond proceeds in other tax-exempt securities (in some cases in order to be exempt from the IRS's three-year spending requirement), and then monitor and actively manage those investments. These investments are counted on to produce a significant amount of future technology funding. While certainly possible, it's unwise to risk a district's technology plan and future educational outcomes on unpredictable financial markets.

The Wool Growers

All this ran through my brain as I pulled into the parking lot of the Wool Growers restaurant in Bakersfield to meet Dennis Scott (no relation), an old client and colleague who'd been CBO of the Kern High School District for two decades before retiring. He was the perfect guy to bounce an idea off of.

"Dennis, I've been thinking," I said, over a glass of Scotch at the bar while we waited for our table. "Why not fund school technology with a bond that matches the useful life of the equipment?"

"You mean a three-year bond?"

"Exactly," I said. "And when the first bond is paid off, you issue another three-year series for the next round of technology funding."

"Is there a market for three-year bonds?"

"There's a market for anything if it's structured right."

"And the voters would only need to go to the polls once…," he mused. I could see crinkles forming around his eyes as he stared into his drink.

"That's right," I jumped in. "One vote authorizes enough bonds to fund a tech program for years into the future. But you'd only issue a small portion of the bonds every three years."

Dennis had been a great district CBO, and he understood school politics inside and out. I could see him working through the various financial and political permutations in his head.

After a few moments, he looked up with a grin. "I think that would work," he said. "I think that would work just fine."

Within two weeks, our team had built the financial models and was running simulations to see how the product would perform in the real world. We met with legal counsel to make sure we hadn't missed anything regarding state law or federal tax restrictions. Within 30 days we'd filed for a patent, introduced the concept to our Board of Advisors, and started giving trusted clients a first look.

A Re-Engineering of the Traditional Bond Structure

Ed-Tech Bonds work by re-engineering the traditional bond structure. The core of any conventional bond is leverage. A GO bond allows a district to borrow – or leverage – against a future stream of tax revenues.

Let's use the example we created earlier to see how the Ed-Tech program works. In our earlier example (see Table 3), we imagined a district with $5 billion in assessed valuation and an annual AV growth rate of 2 percent. Applying a $60 per $100,000 tax rate to this district's AV over 25 years would generate $96.1 million in tax revenue. As we saw in Table 3, long-term leveraged borrowing can be costly. At a 4 percent annual interest rate over the life of a typical GO bond, $38.4 million of that $96.1 million gets paid out as interest, leaving only $57.7 million to use for district projects.

But when funding technology purchases, there's no reason to amortize bonds over the traditional 25 to 30 years (or even the 10 to 20 years proposed by endowment bond advocates). It just makes sound business sense to match the useful life of the asset (in this case, approximately three years) to the life of the loan.

Nor do you need all the money for the technology project up front, as you would when constructing or repairing a school building. Rather, you want an ongoing source of *replenishable* funds, available in smaller increments to replace technology as it becomes obsolete or starts to malfunction with whatever new technology is then available and needed.

With an Ed-Tech Bond election, a district asks voters – on a single ballot – to approve a certain amount of general obligation bonding authority that would fund the district's ongoing technology needs for anywhere from 15 to 30 years into the future. When the bonds are approved by voters (known as *authorized but unissued bonds*), there's no legal limitation as to when they must actually be sold. So, rather than sell the entire authorization as soon as possible, the Ed-Tech Bond structure sells only a portion of the bonds every three years or so until the authorization is depleted over two to three decades.

Replenishability

Providing *replenishability* of funding for ongoing technology needs with just one bond election is one of the greatest strengths of the Ed-Tech product. As I tell districts, there's no way of knowing what technology will be in, say, 15 years, but with a successful Ed-Tech Bond election, the district knows that funding will be on hand to pay for it. (See *Special Topic #2*.)

And here's where it gets really good: By removing the need to leverage the tax revenues over long periods to get as much money as possible in the early years, the enormous interest costs of a typical bond issue disappear. Why? First, since bonds are being sold with a three-year maturity instead of a 20- to 30-year life, the interest rate demanded by investors is significantly lower.

But more important than lower interest rates is that most of the leverage of future tax receipts is no longer needed. Using the example from above for the district with $96 million in total tax revenue, in a conventional leveraged long-term GO bond financing – 4 percent annually over 25 years – the district

FIGURE 4: Comparison of Conventional GO Bond to Ed-Tech Bond

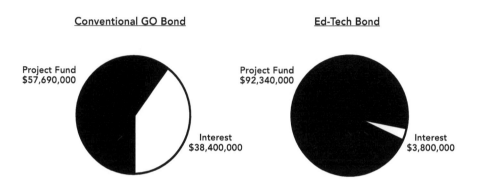

would receive about $57.7 million in project funding, with the remaining $38.4 million of tax revenue being used to pay interest.

But, as shown in Figure 4, by selling eight series of Ed-Tech Bonds over the next 25 years, each with an amortization of three to four years, the amount of tax dollars available to buy educational technology rises to more than $92 million, while the interest costs plummet to $3.8 million.

In other words, whereas in the example above only about 60 cents of every tax dollar go to fund local projects, with the rest needed to pay interest costs, under an Ed-Tech Bond structure, 95 cents of every tax dollar go to fund local projects. And instead of having a debt ratio of 4-to-1, or even 2-to-1 – common for a standard home mortgage – the Ed-Tech Bond debt ratio is just 1.05-to-1.

....

Special Topic #2
WOULD YOU FINANCE A FAX MACHINE WITH A 25-YEAR LOAN?

In 1988, my CFO came to me with a radical request. "I think we should buy a fax machine," he said.

Now this was a very conservative and levelheaded fellow, and certainly not one to throw money away. So, I was slightly surprised.

"Really?" I asked. "You think we'd use it?"

"It might come in handy," he said, so we bought one. It was about the size of the San Francisco phone book. We plugged in the fax machine, and for the next few weeks, a little bell would go off once or twice a day and we'd all come running into the back room to watch a Chinese restaurant menu curl out from a roll of thermal paper.

That was over 30 years ago – the same amount of time as the repayment of many K–14 general obligation bonds. A 25- or 30-year term for bonds that build or renovate schools makes sense. But look at the changes in technology since we bought our fax machine. If we'd financed the fax machine with a GO bond, we'd still be paying today for something we tossed into the recycling bin 27 years ago.

....

GO FLEX-BONDS

Given the enthusiastic acceptance of Ed-Tech Bonds, it didn't take long for clients to begin asking if they could use the Ed-Tech model for facility funding too. At first, I was skeptical about using short-term bonds to finance the construction or rehabilitation of educational facilities that had a useful life of 20 to 30 years. First, one of the main reasons bonds are amortized over several decades is to enable future tax receipts to be leveraged in order to raise enough money to fund large capital projects.

In addition, from a public policy point of view, it makes sense to spread the cost of a facility that will be used by multiple generations over a number of years so that everybody pays his or her fair share.

Finally, many K–14 districts simply don't have the assessed valuation tax base needed to allow them to repay a loan for the construction of a new school in the three- to five-year timeframe used in the Ed-Tech Bond model.

But as we began to dig deeper, we realized that the "spread the costs" paradigm might not always make the most sense for K–14 facilities. In fact, the conventional method of constructing a bond program – issuing bonds in multiple series, each amortized over 25 to 30 years and layered on top of one another – relies, in many cases, on assumptions regarding the future that, as history has shown, may not always turn out to be true.

For example, we often assume that a district's projected facilities improvement funding schedule is firmly set in stone. I can't tell you how many times we've designed a bond program around the funding schedule laid out in the district's master plan, only to watch it go up in smoke as delay after delay kicks in.

As a longtime CBO for a San Diego school district explained to me, "The problem is that the guys on the facility side always think projects are going to get done faster than is really possible."

Part of this has to do with all-too-common construction delays. But for most districts, there's also a "burn rate" for pushing projects through the system. At a certain point, the internal organization can handle only so many projects at once.

"The fact is," the CBO added, "just about any project you can think of is going to take longer than planned. That's just the nature of the beast. And on top of that, if you try to rush a project, you'll end up wasting a ton of money."

In other words, districts often borrow too much too soon and could get by with much smaller bites of the apple, allowing for significantly shorter amortization periods.

Second, there's a widespread belief that's been drummed into all of our heads by political consultants and pollsters that voters have a *tax tolerance* regarding a bond measure. This mantra has become so embedded in the polling data that even I have trouble not falling into the trap of talking about the dollar amount that voters are willing to spend.

Even though I can't prove it, my 20-plus years of working on school bond campaigns makes me doubt that this number can be predicted with much accuracy. No doubt some voters are keenly aware of the cost of school bond programs and vote up or down depending on the cost. But other voters – even though they certainly care about the cost – care *more* about other issues: good schools, technology, safety, property values, the amount of interest being paid. Here's an example.

I was running an election for a small elementary school district in middle of LA County. The polling results were overwhelmingly positive. But the responses to the tax rate question were in the tank. In fact, there wasn't one tax rate we tested that was supported by the voters. In other words, they loved the idea of having great schools, but they didn't want to pay for them.

"This is terrible news," the superintendent said as I briefed her over the phone. "What are we going to do? I'm walking into a board meeting tomorrow night and need a recommendation about the size of the bond."

"Look," I said, "You've got great support for everything except the tax rate. So, in a way, it doesn't make any difference. Right?"

"How's that?"

"Well, if the voter survey shows that no tax rate works with voters, then we might as well just ignore the data and go for the dollar amount that the district truly needs. In other words, you're not going to win because of the tax rate you pick. Your only chance is to make your case on why your children need better schools and forget about the tax rate."

"I guess," she said, but she didn't sound too convinced. However, there weren't a lot of other alternatives, so that's what we did. Four months later, the bond passed by 77 percent.

Finally, having a limitation on an *estimated* tax rate without any restrictions or oversight as to the underlying assumptions is an open invitation to game the system. And, boy, has it ever been gamed. I remember sitting through a presentation by another financial advisor who was trying to justify to a school board why his estimated assessed valuation growth rate of 9 percent *per year* over the next 40 years (which, by the way, pencils out to a nearly *3000 percent* increase in AV) made sense. My recollection is that it had something to do with the cost of a toothbrush in 1969, but by then I'd stopped listening since it was obvious he'd backed into the assumption in order to produce the result he was looking for.

Even though it's painful to have to listen to this kind of pseudo-econometric mumbo-jumbo, it belies a larger problem that school boards too often lose sight of. By structuring a GO bond program around overly aggressive assessed valuation assumptions, K–14 districts bind the hands of future boards for years into the future. By taking a slower and more measured approach over a number of years, it becomes harder to play fast and loose with the AV assumptions.

GO Flex-Bonds address these problems by turning the conventional bond model on its head. Instead of issuing a series of long-term bonds that are layered on top of one another, GO Flex-Bonds are structured as a sequential series of short-term (four- to six-year) bonds. They work especially well in a district that has a series of ongoing rehabilitation projects and a reasonably strong assessed valuation base.

The plus side of the program is that GO Flex-Bonds can provide a district with a continuous source of funding and save taxpayers millions of dollars. The downside is that a district has to be patient in its borrowing schedule. Even for the most conservative of districts, that's not as easy as it sounds – as the following story shows.

Not too long ago, we had an interview with a midsized district in Orange County, California. Given Orange County's reputation for staunch conservatism (more than 34 percent of the registered voters are Republicans compared to less than 23 percent for the rest of the state), we thought the GO Flex-Bond program would be a natural fit.

"This pie chart," I said to the board members seated on the interview panel, "represents the estimated principal and interest payments for a *conventional* bond." The chart showed a blue pie slice of $300 million of principal – the amount they were looking for in an upcoming election – and a red slice of about $220 million in interest. The numbers were based on

FIGURE 5: Conventional GO Bond

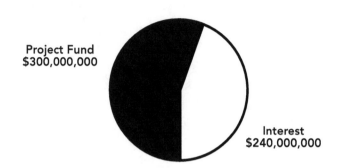

Project Fund
$300,000,000

Interest
$240,000,000

their master facility plan and assumed a $40 tax rate, an increase in AV of 3 percent per year, and a 25-year bond term at current interest rates. (See Figure 5.)

"The second chart," I said, bringing up the next slide, "shows how this bond financing would work under our GO Flex-Bond program. Note that we're talking about the same amount of principal – $300 million. The same tax rate. The same AV assumptions. But look at the interest costs."

As shown in Figure 6, interest costs under our GO Flex-Bond program plummet, shrinking from $220 million to about $19 million – *a savings to taxpayers of more than $220 million.*

I've been to a fair number of board meetings in my time and it's a rare day when a group of elected officials are struck silent. But besides the whir of the projector fan, there wasn't a sound to be heard as each board member silently stared up at the screen, trying to comprehend how this could be possible.

Finally, the chair cleared his throat and said, "Uh … are you going to tell us how this works?"

I took them through how GO Flex-Bonds are structured, explaining that it would require the district to pursue a more disciplined borrowing plan with a series of smaller financings spread out over a longer period of time.

FIGURE 6: GO Flex-Bond

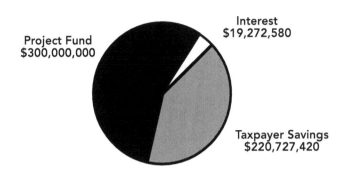

Project Fund
$300,000,000

Interest
$19,272,580

Taxpayer Savings
$220,727,420

Even in this overwhelmingly Republican district, it didn't take long for the pushback to begin.

"But if we go with this plan," one of the Board members protested, "we'd need to delay some of our projects. True?"

"Yes," I replied. "Anywhere from five to ten years."

"But our schools are in desperate need of repairs right now," he argued, shaking his head. "How can we ask people to wait even longer?"

"And wouldn't this mean that the entire burden would fall on today's taxpayers?" asked another. "Is that really fair?"

And there you have it, I thought to myself. At the core of the GO Flex-Bond model is a policy decision, not a financial decision. Being able to save taxpayers millions of dollars in interest costs makes enormous fiscal sense. But the trade-off – delaying projects and shifting tax payments onto current taxpayers rather than spreading them out over the useful life of the project being financed – is one that not every district is going to be willing or able to make.

TEACHER-STAFF HOUSING GO BONDS

It didn't take Dan Burns long to figure out that he had a problem on his hands. As the newly appointed superintendent of Jefferson Union High School District in Daly City, California, he got an upfront and personal view into one of the biggest challenges facing many of the district's teachers and staff members before he even started the job.

"I'd been living in the same house in Salinas (a small city located an hour south of San Jose, California, and Silicon Valley) for most of my adult life," Dan said. "A few weeks before I was supposed to start at the district, my wife and I drove up on a Sunday to take a look at houses in San Mateo County. I was like – Whoa! If I can't afford to live here, how's a young teacher supposed to make it?"

The answer wasn't good. Because of rapidly escalating housing prices and rental rates, Dan quickly realized that buying a house or renting an apartment anywhere near Daly City was next to impossible for a new district employee.

"Finding great teachers and staff members is always a challenge," he said. "But this was a whole different ballgame." Because of the high cost of housing, Jefferson Union HSD now found itself competing with neighboring districts and tech companies for top talent while losing candidates to districts in other parts of the state where rents could be up to half that in the San Francisco Bay Area.

Dan wasn't the only one who was worried about Jefferson Union's housing prices. The Jefferson Union HSD Board of Trustees had been gritting its teeth over this problem long before Dan arrived. They were convinced they had to find a way to provide staff members with affordable rental housing if they were going to remain competitive in attracting top talent. "We knew *what* needed to be done," said Kalimah Salahuddin, a member of the district's Board of Trustees. "The hard part was figuring out *how*."

Unfortunately, there were not a lot of places to turn to for advice. Although two teacher-staff housing projects existed in the state,[2] they had been developed nearly two decades prior when land was plentiful and

....

2 Santa Clara Unified School District and San Mateo County Community College District

construction prices were a fraction of today's cost. And while there were a number of other districts in the San Francisco Bay Area struggling to develop below-market teacher-staff housing, few were making any progress due to financial and political hurdles ranging from the high cost of construction – to lack of an adequate building site – to union objections to NIMBYs – to the simple lack of a viable plan.

THE TRAIL BLAZERS

Looking back to the day of Dan's house-hunting drive, it's amazing that less than four years later Jefferson Union HSD would be breaking ground to construct over 100 units of below-market teacher-staff housing.

But what's really jaw-dropping is how, starting essentially from scratch, the district blazed a new trail by designing one of the most innovative and creative teacher-staff housing programs in California, if not in the country, and creating a template which other districts can now follow to develop their own projects. Their success led to national recognition in the media, review by legislatures in other states, and the award of the *The Bond Buyer's* 2018 Small Issuer Deal of the Year.[3]

But all of this success and the accolades came later.

In the beginning, it was far from clear whether the proposed project had any chance of succeeding. A few months after Dan was hired, I was sitting in his office, together with his chief business official (CBO), walking them through spreadsheets of various financing alternatives for the proposed project. The concept at the time was for the district to build apartments on a long-ago shuttered high school property and to finance the construction

....

3 To make sure credit is given where credit is due, Superintendent Terry DeLoria - Dan's successor at Jefferson Union HSD - did an extraordinary job in overseeing the passage of the district's bond and moving the project towards completion. She was aided by her exceptional Chief Business Official, Tina Van Raaphorst. In addition, the work done by all the Board of Trustees members was critical, especially the tireless efforts by Andrew Lie and Kalimah Salahuddin.

FIGURE 7: Teacher-Staff Housing Cash Flow

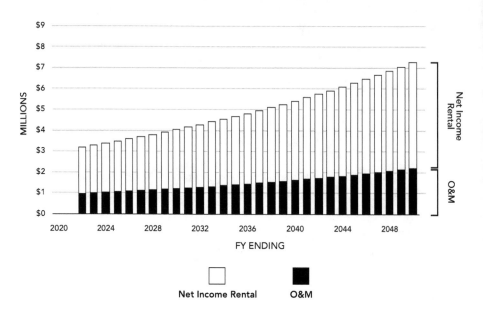

with Certificates of Participation (COPs). The COPs would, in turn, be repaid by rental income generated by the apartments, similar to how both the Santa Clara USD and San Mateo County CCD teacher-staff housing projects were financed.

There was only one problem. The numbers didn't work.

As shown in Figure 7, the projected net rental income available to repay the COPs after the payment of operations and maintenance ("O&M") was impressive, ranging from $2.1 million in the project's first year to over $4.5 million in the last year. (This assumed a 100-unit mix of one-bedroom, two-bedroom, and three-bedroom units with rents set at 70% of the current market and increasing by 3% per year. O&M was estimated at 30% of gross rental income based on historical information available from other teacher-staff housing projects.)

But even though the available net revenues were substantial, they still weren't enough to repay the COPs that needed to be issued to build the 100 housing units. In fact, our analysis showed that if the District were to

FIGURE 8: Teacher-Staff Housing Cash Flow with COPs Repayment

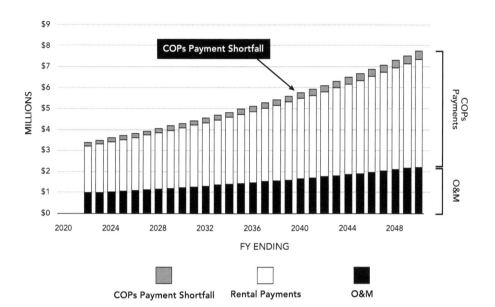

go down the COPs road, it would need to pay an average of $200,000 per year from its general fund for close to three decades to make the financing doable. (See Figure 8.)

The underlying problem was fairly simple. When the first phase of the Santa Clara USD staff housing project was built in 2002, the average cost per unit was around $150,000. Since that time, the cost of construction had skyrocketed and was now estimated to be anywhere from two to two-and-a-half times that cost.[4] While rents had also risen, the increase simply wasn't enough to cover both the operation and maintenance of the units, and the repayment of the COPs.

Over the next few weeks, I continued to push the numbers around with little success. The more I stared at the numbers, the clearer it became. The

....

4 Keep in mind that as a public agency, the district is required to pay "prevailing wage" on its construction projects.

only way Jefferson Union's project was going to get built in the current environment was to fund the project with a general obligation bond.

As shown in Figure 8, the issue of having sufficient rent to repay both operations and maintenance and the loan to finance the project's construction goes away with GO bonds. The debt no longer needs to be repaid with rental revenues because it's now the obligation of local property taxpayers. In fact, the GO bond structure is actually a revenue *generator* for the district. The excess rental income after the payment of O&M goes directly to the district's general fund, increasing revenue that can then be used to enhance the educational mission of the district.[5]

It was immediately clear that using general obligation bonds to build teacher-staff housing was an incredible idea that would not only turn the Jefferson Union HSD project into a reality but provide the district with a stream of new revenue for decades into the future.

By using GO bonds to fund the construction of teacher-staff housing, the problem of making the numbers work disappeared. But now there was a new problem. It had never been done before.

Although there had already been two successful California school district teacher-staff housing projects, they had both been financed with COPs. However, as explained to me by the district's legal counsel, while the California Education Code gives school districts wide latitude in the types of projects that can be funded with COPs, GO bonds are bound by much tighter legal constraints, including the requirement that bond proceeds be spent on *school district facilities*.

Fortunately, two new laws had been passed in 2016 and 2017 that established clear authority for school districts to develop programs that would make housing available to their teachers and staff.

The **Teacher Housing Act of 2016** (Health and Safety Code 53570 et seq.) creates a policy supporting housing for teachers and school district employees, and states that its purpose is to facilitate the development of affordable housing for teachers and staff of a school district. By declaring that

....

5 Alternatively, with the GO bond in place, the rental revenues can be used to secure supplemental COPs in order to reduce the amount of GO bonds needed to be issued. This is, in fact, the structure that was ultimately used by Jefferson Union HSD.

affordable housing for staff and employees is within the educational purposes of a school district, these housing projects become eligible for expenditure of general obligation bond proceeds if approved by the voters. The Act also allows a school district to restrict occupancy to district employees so long as the project is built on land owned by the school district. The previous law required that homes or apartments be open to anyone who meets the low-income requirement if they used state and federal low-income housing funds or tax credits.

This was followed in 2017 by **Teacher Housing Assembly Bill No. 1157**, which clarified that financing proceeds expended for capital outlay purposes could be used for school district employee housing. (This legislation also exempted school districts from the required district advisory [*"7–11"*] committee hearing when surplus land or facilities will be used for teacher and school district employee housing.) Taken together, these two Acts clearly establish that district-owned teacher-staff housing is a school district facility and that providing affordable housing for district employees serves a legitimate educational purpose.

A DISTRICT PROBLEM OR A COMMUNITY PROBLEM?

At the same time that legal counsel and my firm were beginning to get comfortable with the idea of using GO bonds to fund teacher-staff housing, the Jefferson Union HSD's Board of Trustees was also beginning to rethink the problem.

"Starting out," said Board President Andy Lie, "I think we all viewed the lack of affordable teacher-staff housing as the district's problem. But the more we discussed it, the more we began to realize that this wasn't just *our* issue, this was our *community's* issue."

The GO bond option, in the school board's eyes, could provide them with a *community solution* to the teacher-staff housing challenge. "Suddenly, we could see a path to success," said Lie. After spending time vetting the GO bond option numbers, legal foundation, and political ramifications, the board directed my firm to conduct random telephone surveys of high-propensity voters to determine the likelihood of support for a teacher-staff housing GO bond.

The results were overwhelmingly positive, with voter support hovering around 68%. However, the survey was designed with the assumption that the bond measure would be placed on the upcoming November 2018 gubernatorial ballot. But after seeing the strong level of support in the survey, the Board made a gutsy call and decided to speed the process by placing the measure on the June 2018 gubernatorial *primary* instead of waiting until November 2018.

"We knew that the lower voter turnout for the primary would hurt us," said Board Vice-President Kalimah Salahuddin, "but, we figured the possibility of jump-starting the project by five months was worth it."

I think we all underestimated just how miserably low the June 2018 voter turnout would turn out to be. While 75% of the registered voters in San Mateo County cast ballots in November 2018, in the June gubernatorial election the turnout was an anemic 44%.

Nevertheless, the bet paid off – barely. After an agonizing month of following the release of daily vote count totals by the county's election office, Measure J was approved with a 55.8% "yes" vote. It became the first voter-approved teacher-staff housing general obligation bond in the country.

WHY BUILD TEACHER-STAFF HOUSING?

The high cost of housing has overrun the San Francisco Bay Area and Silicon Valley. This is why much of the effort to provide affordable teacher-staff housing is located within these regions. But, in reality, the ability of school district employees to find adequate, affordable teacher-staff housing that doesn't break the bank is a problem in many parts of the state – a shortage that's not going away in the foreseeable future.

Nevertheless, given all of the challenges facing school districts today, many are justifiably reluctant to take on the enormous task of providing housing for their employees. As one school board member recently put it, "Look, this is a great idea. But we have millions of dollars of facility improvements that need to be funded first."

He has a point, of course. But in my experience, the districts that are actively pursuing teacher-staff housing projects are not doing so solely out of altruism but, rather, for a variety of reasons that will improve their ability to fulfill their educational mission for decades to come. Here are a few of the major reasons:

MAINTAINING A COMPETITIVE ADVANTAGE

Districts located in areas of the state with excessively high housing costs report that many qualified applicants simply will not consider employment in a district with a high cost of living. Other applicants may accept a position but end up declining the job after struggling to find affordable housing.

RETAINING CURRENT EMPLOYEES

As part of their analysis of the impact of housing costs on staff, Jefferson Union HSD undertook an online survey of its employees. Approximately half of the employees responded. Of these, **35% reported they were considering leaving the District due to the high cost of housing.**

In addition to frequent employee turnover making it difficult for faculty and staff to develop collaborative relationships with their colleagues, their students, and the community, there is a financial cost as well. In a report by the Learning Policy Institute,[6] the annual cost of teacher turnover in Jefferson Union HSD ranged from $440,000 to $840,000 per teacher.

LACK OF AVAILABLE RENTALS

There's no doubt that the high-cost communities along the coast stretching from Northern California down to the Mexican border have the toughest challenge. But in other parts of the state, including the Central Valley, resort areas, and remote rural districts, the issue is not so much affordability as much as it is the lack of supply of rental housing at any price. As the superintendent of a midsized district in the Central Valley said to me, "We're not talking about just a few teachers having to commute. Even I can't find a decent place to rent in this community."

....

6 "What's the Cost of Teacher Turnover?", September 2017

Like the high cost of housing, this lack of rental housing in rural areas creates a huge financial headache for school districts. A new teacher hired in one of these districts often has few housing options beyond renting in a larger city or town nearby, requiring a long, grueling commute. So, it surprises no one when a teacher jumps at the chance to take an open position closer to his or her residence, even when the smaller district had spent thousands of dollars in staff training.

ADVANTAGES IN THE FILLING SPECIALIZED TEACHING/ COUNSELOR POSITIONS

I recently met with a district in Southern California and walked them through the numbers of how a teacher-staff housing bond might play out for them. At the end of the presentation, the superintendent looked over at his chief business official and asked, "What'd you think?" She replied that she thought there was plenty of affordable rental housing in or surrounding the District and wasn't sure if the program would work for them. I nodded and moved on to the next topic.

A few days later, I was in my office when the superintendent called. "Listen, I ran your idea by the head of our human resources department. He thinks we'd be crazy not to try this." He went on to list all the different positions they were struggling to fill. "There's no doubt in his mind that if we could sweeten the pot for certain applicants with below-market-rate housing, we'd be their first choice." The district is now moving forward with their own teacher-housing project.

GETTING STARTED: A FIVE-STEP PLAN

The ability to develop a successful teacher-staff housing project involves hundreds, possibly thousands, of decisions. It requires a board that is unified around the need to address their district's housing problem, a superintendent who is willing to invest the political resources necessary to achieve success, and a very sharp chief business official who is able to keep the project on track.

But from a management point of view, there are five essential steps in the process that need to be tackled:

1. MEASURE DEMAND

While there may be a fair amount of anecdotal evidence that teachers and staff members are having difficulty finding housing they can afford, the actual demand for the project needs to be measured. The fastest and cheapest method of assessing this demand is through a survey of staff members. Although there are a number of methods by which this can be accomplished, we've found that the simplest and cheapest method is to send teachers and staff a link to an online survey. The survey doesn't need to be long and involved, but it should get a sense of the level of interest in the project and the type of units the staff members would prefer (e.g., one bedroom, two bedrooms).

A side benefit of conducting a staff survey is that a district's administration can obtain a quick view of the overall morale of its staff and a sense of the number of employees who may be considering leaving the district in the near future. For example, we recently ran a staff survey to assess the potential demand for teacher-staff housing in a moderate-sized district in Monterey County. In addition, respondents were asked how long they anticipated working for the district. Nearly 75% of the survey respondents[7] answered that they planned on remaining with the district for five years or longer. Of the remaining 25%, most said that they either weren't sure of their plans or were planning on retiring.

2. IDENTIFY A SITE

While most district CBOs will have a good sense of available property owned by the district, a deeper dive may be needed to answer this question. Generally, this involves hiring a firm that specializes in real estate planning or development to answer a number of questions, including the practicality

....

7 Nearly 36% of the district's employees completed the three-minute online survey.

of any potential sites, the number of units that could fit on the site, and zoning status. They will also red-flag any potential issues that need deeper investigation, such as environmental or geological concerns.

For a handful of districts, finding a site on which to build teacher-staff housing is a no-brainer. With declining enrollment, a former school site is usually a perfect match. In other cases, a district may have acquired a potential school site, assuming future growth, that was never developed. Recent state legislation, Teacher Housing Assembly Bill No. 1157, has helped to fast-track the conversion of vacant school property into teacher-staff housing by making the reuse of such property exempt from the requirement of holding 7-11 committee hearings.[8]

However, for some districts without surplus property, creative solutions must be developed. Examples include:

Reconfigurations: Many schools and administration center buildings were constructed years ago when land was plentiful. By reconfiguring a more efficient use of the facility (or relocating to a commercial area), new space often can be created. For example, one district in Southern California has a multi-acre administration center in the middle of a residential neighborhood. The site is filled with sprawling one-story buildings with a bus yard tucked in the rear. By turning the administrative center into a two-story building and relocating the bus yard to an unused site at the edge of town, they will be able to create over five acres for teacher-staff housing.

Land Swaps: In some districts, a little creativity is required. While the district might have an available site, the area isn't suited for residential development. However, by reaching out to other local governments (e.g., a city or the county office of education), occasionally a deal can be struck. For example, one district in the Central Valley is swapping a parcel they own in the central business area for one owned by the city in a more appropriate area.

....

8 A state requirement, 7-11 advisory committees consist of no less than seven members and no more than eleven members. The committee's purpose is to advise a school board in developing policies for the disposition of unused school buildings or land.

Joint Projects: Even though cities and counties currently do not have the legal ability to use general obligation bond funds to build workforce housing, they can still participate in other ways. For example, south of San Jose, a small school district and the city are in discussions to jointly develop a project. The city will contribute the land and the district will use its voter-approved general obligation bonds to construct the below-market rental housing. The project will be jointly managed by the city and the district, and the units will be available to employees of both entities.

Purchase of Existing Rental Housing: Often during the initial discussions regarding the need for teacher-staff housing, someone will float the idea of purchasing an existing apartment building rather than constructing new units. On the surface, this sounds appealing. Development and construction of new housing units is a complex and time-consuming process. In addition, the purchase price of an existing building is likely to be lower than new construction, given the prevailing wage requirements under which school districts operate.

However, even if existing apartment buildings or houses could be found, acquiring them for teacher-staff housing doesn't help solve the community's housing problem. In fact, by gobbling up existing units so that they are no longer available to the general public, it makes the problem worse. And, not to be overlooked, an existing building will more than likely come with tenants. The idea of a school district serving these current renters with eviction notices so they can move teachers into the units probably isn't a great strategy for winning public support.

3. MEASURE VOTER SUPPORT

As described in Chapter 5, undertaking a statistically valid random survey of voters is critical in judging the potential for a bond's success. This is especially true if your district's GO bond measure is going to include a teacher-staff housing component. In addition to determining the overall level of support, a survey of voters can also give guidance regarding messaging (e.g., teacher-staff housing vs. workforce housing) and wording of the measure (e.g., affordable housing vs. below-market housing).

4. DEVELOP *PRO FORMA* CASH FLOWS

Teacher-staff housing is a rapidly evolving field with new financing ideas, structures, and proposals popping up faster than a prefab building. However, the vast majority of proposed projects rely on securing the financing with either the project's rental revenues or voter-approved bonds, or a combination of the two.

Regardless of the financing method, they all need the same thing to get started: the development of a pro forma cash flow. This cash flow needs to include information, estimates and assumptions covering the following items:

- **The number of units:** The final number to be built is likely to move around quite a bit. Starting off with a number that is based on the results of the teacher-staff survey makes sense.

- **Unit mix:** When people first think about teacher-staff housing, they often envision a project that's a step or two above a college dorm. In fact, in order to be viable, the project needs to include a mix of one-bedroom, two-bedroom and three-bedroom apartments. The staff survey will guide the mix of units.

- **Market rates:** The current market rate for comparable rentals can be found on a number of websites.

- **Rental Rates:** Teacher-staff housing programs are structured to offer below-market rental rates. How much below-market is up to the district.

- **Annual increases:** An estimate of the annual rent increase.

- **Occupancy Rates:** While the expectation is that demand will remain high for below-market teacher-staff housing, it is prudent to build into the cashflows the possibility of some units being vacant now and then.

- **Operating and Maintenance Costs (O&M):** The O&M for a teacher-staff housing project might be higher than that of a typical rental building. The district will need to hire an outside firm with specific and specialized skills to manage and maintain the property. For example, assuming there is an income restriction on how much a family can make and still be a tenant, the property manager will need to acquire and review confidential information, such as tax returns. For planning purposes, assume approximately 30% of rental revenues will be needed for O&M.

- **Construction Costs:** The average construction cost per unit. Keep in mind that as a public works project, any contract for its construction would fall under prevailing wage requirements.

5. SEEK VOTER SUPPORT

There is plenty of discussion on future pages about strategies to use (and avoid) in placing a GO bond on the ballot. But for teacher-staff housing, there is one additional wrinkle that deserves discussion.

Jefferson Union HSD's bond election in June 2018 is believed to be the first teacher-staff housing GO bond in the nation. But what made the measure doubly interesting was that it was crafted to give voters a clear choice as to whether or not they wanted to raise their taxes to support the building of below-market housing for local educators. To that end, the ballot measure that was placed before voters was solely to fund the construction of below-market teacher-staff housing.

It was a bold move and one that put the issue up front and center for local voters.

But there is a different path that's also available to school districts looking to fund teacher-staff housing with general obligation bonds. In developing a bond measure to put on the ballot, there is no requirement that teacher-staff housing projects be run separately. These projects can just as easily be combined with any number of other classroom and campus improvement and construction projects funded by the same bond measure.

So, which method is better? It depends on how much emphasis you want to place on the issue of housing. For Jefferson Union HSD, it was very important. They wanted to ensure that both their citizens and their employees knew that they were committed to providing below-market housing.

But other districts have decided they're better off keeping the expectations low, and there have been a handful of districts across the state that included the ability to use bond funds for workforce housing in the measure's project list without any mention in the 75-word ballot language.

In the end, both methods work. But before a district decides to use GO bonds to fund teacher-staff housing, it needs to candidly assess how the issue will play in their community.

ONGOING ISSUES

Finally, while passing a teacher-staff housing bond on the ballot involves a great deal of preparation, and designing and constructing the project is intense, be prepared to deal with a whole host of complex post-construction challenges connected to the implementation of a teacher-staff housing program. These include:

- Who gets to live in the units?

- What income restrictions, if any, should be applied?

- How long can an employee remain a tenant?

- What happens if the employee is terminated? Or retires?

- What happens to the employee's spouse/significant other if the employee dies?

- Will there be income restrictions on the total family income of tenant families?

- What about non-related significant others? Does their income apply to this limit?

- Can the units be rented to non-district public sector employees?

- Luckily, districts such as Jefferson Union HSD and the other teacher-staff housing programs around the state have already worked through many of these issues and can provide your district with a roadmap to help you decide what's best for your community.

Chapter
FOUR

....

ASSEMBLING THE TEAM

....

"Politics ain't bean-bag ..."

~ Finley Peter Dunne

Taking a K–14 GO bond from conception to implementation requires a winning team effort. This chapter explains the various "positions" on a district's GO bond team and suggests criteria for selecting the best candidate for each.

THE FINANCIAL ADVISOR

When I formed DS&C in 1987, only one other independent financial advisory firm in California specialized in school district finance. Today, there are more than 15 such firms.

What accounts for this growth? Some of it, of course, is due to the overall growth of the California K–14 market. But much of this increase, I believe, stems from the realization on the part of district officials that school finance is arcane, complex and, if mishandled, extraordinarily expensive.

As one school board member put it to a colleague who was questioning whether the district really needed to hire a financial advisor, "Look, I'm a pretty damn good oral surgeon. But that doesn't make me an expert in bond finance!"

So, what, exactly, does a good financial advisor provide clients? At a minimum, you should expect your financial advisor to provide you with the following information:

- When a sale of bonds is appropriate

- If the proposed structure makes financial sense

- If the underlying interest and growth assumptions are realistic

- If the *optional call feature* is suitable

- If the bonds should be sold through a competitive sale or a negotiated sale (*These sales methods are described more fully in the next chapter.*)

- If the pricing and fees are fair

Most important of all, a financial advisor should be independent, experienced, and willing to give a client recommendations that may not be in the advisor's own best interests.

This brings up the obvious question of how to determine whether your financial advisor is able and willing to give you this kind of advice. This is a murky area. And beauty, as they say, is in the eye of the beholder. I'll occasionally run into a district business official who will extol the brilliance of his or her financial advisor, even though I know that their next-door neighbor can't say enough bad things about that particular firm.

So, what should you do when trying to select an advisor for your district? *Special Topic #3* (on p.70) reviews the various methods for choosing a financial advisor. Here are a few extra steps to take before you sign up with anyone.

Make Sure Experience Claims Stack Up

A retired client who was serving as interim CBO at one of the state's largest school districts called me up shortly after taking the job. He asked what I knew about a particular firm that was pitching the district for work on an upcoming financing. This firm claimed to have hundreds of deals under its belt, he told me. This statement was technically true – except that none of the deals were for California K–14 districts.

Pumping up the résumé with work done at another firm is also a common practice. Luckily, checking out a firm's credentials is a snap in California. The California State Treasurer's website (www.treasurer. ca.gov/ cdiac/debt.asp) provides a complete database of every state and local financing done in California since 1985; this database can be downloaded into an online spreadsheet.

Call Additional References

Why would anyone send you the name of a client who would give a bad reference? Call a few of the districts on the list you've developed from the state treasurer's website – not the list the FA gave you, and not just the districts in your own county. We all prefer to talk only to people we know. But get out of your comfort zone and call some districts in other parts of the state. Ask them about their experience with the firm. Did the firm present well to the board? Did they try to push you into products you didn't fully understand? Try to sell you services you didn't need? Did they suddenly start bringing in other firms to be part of the team without consulting with you?

And, remember, no one is liked by everyone. With enough digging, you're sure to find a district that was unhappy with the service of a particular advisor. The question you need to answer is whether this is an isolated incident or a pattern of poor performance.

Watch Out for Joint Presentations

An independent financial advisor is supposed to be independent. Unfortunately, far too many financial advisors think nothing of linking up with an investment bank to joint-pitch a district for business. Unless you are already working with one of these two firms (and trust it) and the purpose of the meeting is to discuss a specific issue or concern, this should be an immediate red flag. Remember, the financial advisor is supposed to be your representative, not the underwriter's business partner.

....

Special Topic #3
HOW TO CHOOSE (AND HOW LONG TO KEEP) A FINANCIAL ADVISOR

Like the porridge in "Goldilocks and the Three Bears," school districts tend to either be too hot or too cold when going through the process of selecting a financial advisor.

Way Too Hot

Some districts take the "more is better" approach to hiring a financial advisor. Rather than doing a little homework and trying to identify two or three that might be a good fit for their district, they'll have their purchasing department send out a request for proposal (RFP) to any firm that appears to have a pulse. I cringe when I see these multi-page RFPs filled with legal gobbledygook like, *Provide the signature and full title of the senior officer with authority to sign the proposal submitted hereto on a separate page.*

Too often, a committee consisting of people without any financial experience is assigned to review the proposals. Their job is to grade the responses, assigning points to various subject areas such as (I'm not kidding) *completed the proposal* and *provided references.* If what you're looking for is rock-bottom lowest cost of services, this may be your best method. But as a way of identifying the advisor that's the best fit for your district, I don't see how it gets you there.

Way Too Cold

Districts that have never placed a bond on the ballot, especially small districts, too often err on the other side of the spectrum and hire the first financial advisor who walks through the door. Why a district administrator or board wouldn't take the time to at least talk to one or two other firms before signing a six-figure contract is hard to imagine, but it happens all the time.

One caveat: if a financial advisory firm has a proprietary program and asks that it not be shared with competitors, you need to respect that request. That doesn't mean you shouldn't take the time to meet the competitors, but giving them someone else's idea is unprofessional and unethical.

This Porridge Is Just Right

The relationship between a client and a financial advisor will be most productive if it's grounded in personal and professional respect. To put it another way, in addition to reviewing an advisor's references and rankings and hearing about the deals he or she did with your neighbors, you need to decide if you can trust the advisor's judgment. And you have to judge whether there's that intangible fit between the advisor and the district.

What's the best way to do this if you're starting from scratch? Put together a group of people within your organization who understand finance, politics or both (e.g., the chief business official, the superintendent, a board member, a retired CBO). Bring in two to four advisory firms that you believe – based on your own research – to be at the top of the game and a potential fit for your district.

Be prepared to spend at least an hour with each one, and make sure you have enough time to probe and not just hear the canned pitch. What do they know about your district? What's an example of a recent failure, and what did they learn? How do they suggest you handle hostile voters? Most critical of all, ask yourself if you feel that this candidate will put the district's interests ahead of their own, if necessary?

This leads to the question of how long, after you've hired a financial advisor, you should keep him or her around. Lately, I've been hearing more and more people claim districts should change their financial advisors every few years, the same way they rotate audit firms.

This analogy is bunk. No disrespect to auditors, but their role is to make sure a district has adequately and correctly managed its money, and auditors do this same task every year. Auditing is a job that cries out for having a fresh set of eyes at regular intervals.

A better analogy is to think of your financial advisor the way you think of your doctor. If you're happy with your doctor, you wouldn't replace her or him every couple of years just to provide a fresh look at your health. One of your doctor's greatest strengths is the deep knowledge he or she has developed about you over the years. The time to look around for a new doctor is when you believe your doctor isn't paying sufficient attention, not treating you properly or unfairly overcharging. In my view, the same criteria apply to a district's choice – and retention – of a financial advisor.

Certainly, keep your eyes open, make sure your financial advisor is doing a good job, and be ready to replace him or her if necessary. But at the same time, recognize the value of having a financial advisor with a long-term understanding and deep experience of your district's needs.

....

BOND COUNSEL

The role of bond counsel is to prepare and review the legal documentation required to place an item on the ballot. If the bond measure passes, bond counsel is responsible for drafting the resolution and other documents needed to bring the financing into the market. Also, a bond counsel needs to provide a legal opinion assuring investors that the bonds have been legally issued and, if tax-exempt, that the interest payments on the bonds are exempt from federal and state income taxes.

In addition, bond counsel will often review the structure of the proposed bond authorization and advise the district on a variety of legal issues, ranging from the federal tax requirements regarding the spending of bond proceeds to the drafting of a "do and don't list" memo regarding district activities during a bond campaign.

So, how best to hire bond counsel? Even though it has the potential for a conflict of interest – and I've seen plenty of cases where the district's bond counsel seemed more devoted to protecting the relationship with the financial advisor or investment banker than representing the district's legal interests – I think relying on the recommendation of your FA or investment banker works best. The work of bond counsel is highly specialized, difficult to learn and highly nuanced. The financial professionals rely heavily on the lawyers to draft documents correctly and keep everybody's nose clean. It would be a self-destructive financial advisor or investment banker who'd recommend an incompetent bond lawyer.

Yet, remarkably, I've seen that happen, too. So, even though I think you should rely on the recommendation of your financial professional, take the time to do your own due diligence and background check – especially if this is your first financing or if a firm you've never heard of has been recommended. Ask for a list of the law firm's past transactions and make sure the firm – and the lawyer who is being recommended – has the experience needed to get the job done.

It's a major plus, in my experience, if a firm has a dedicated tax attorney on its permanent staff, as opposed to needing to go outside and retain one just for this transaction. Not having an in-house counsel tends to slow down the process – which is already challenging enough – and I've found that retained outside lawyers tend to be unreasonably cautious and conservative, raising time-wasting objections to what is often common and accepted practice.

When it comes to bond counsel fees, most firms will work for a flat fee (contingent on the sale of the bonds) that covers the entire process, rather than bill by the hour. It might be tempting to try and lower the fees by hiring a firm on an hourly basis, but you then risk being reluctant to call with questions and might end up not asking about an issue that later turns out to be crucial.

Finally, be careful that firms don't make their presentations to the district with senior lawyers and then assign a junior lawyer to do your work. Delegating much of the legal grunt work to new associates makes sense. But you need to know up front who exactly is going to be senior counsel, and to demand as well that he or she be available and hands-on in moving the deal forward.

THE INVESTMENT BANKER AND THE UNDERWRITER

Within the muni market, we are all guilty of using the terms investment banker and underwriter interchangeably. In fact, even though these people work for the same firm, their roles in a K–14 GO bond are strikingly different.

THE ANIMALS AND THE PRETTY BOYS

An investment banker is the person a client will work with when doing a negotiated financing. In these transactions, the banker is responsible for the same types of activities as a financial advisor. The investment banker also negotiates with his or her underwriting desk in the setting of interest rates.

The underwriter's job is to set the interest rates of a new GO bond and purchase those bonds from the district for resale to investors. This can be done by working directly with the district in a negotiated sale or acquiring the bonds through a competitive bid.

Not surprisingly, there's often a fair amount of tension between investment bankers and the underwriters, even though they work for the same firm. The investment bankers are trying to convince their school district clients that they've gotten them a great deal, while the underwriters are trying to move product and not get caught with a bucket-load of bonds they can't sell.

Some firms do better than others in keeping peace between these two groups. In others, it can be open warfare. When I worked on Wall Street, the guys on the sales and underwriting desk would regularly call the investment bankers "the pretty boys," while the bankers would refer to guys on the desk as "the animals."

As a financial advisor, I naturally believe a K–14 district is generally better off hiring an investment banker after the bond election, regardless of whether the bonds are being sold through negotiated or competitive sale. While an investment banker can certainly offer insights into the overall structuring of the proposed bond deals, there's really not a lot for a banker to do before the election takes place.

Having said this, I realize that many disagree, including a number of highly competent district CBOs and every public finance investment banker on earth. They believe investment bankers bring valuable skills to the pre-election process and feel it's important to have the entire team assembled before Election Day.

Clearly, there is disagreement over this issue. But you need to be aware of one irrefutable fact before making a decision on this subject. In adding an underwriter to your team before Election Day, *you are effectively closing the door to selling any of your future bond issues through competitive sale*. This topic is discussed in greater detail in Chapter 5: Preparing for the Ballot.

Nevertheless, if this is the direction you decide to take, then you should go through the same selection process I described above for financial advisors. Make sure the banker has had significant experience in the K–14 market. Call more than just the references you're handed. Find some deals they worked on that they don't list as references, and call folks involved with those deals.

Explore the underwriter's relationship with financial advisors: ask how they structure their teamwork with financial advisors and request examples of past deals where the relationship worked well and worked poorly.

Dodd-Frank

The *Dodd-Frank Wall Street Reform and Consumer Protection Act* (commonly known as Dodd-Frank) was signed into law by President Obama on July 21, 2010. The muni market occupied only a tiny corner of this staggeringly long (2,300 pages) bill designed to promote financial stability by improving transparency and accountability in the nation's financial systems. Nevertheless, the impacts of Dodd-Frank on the municipal finance market have slowly begun to seep into the system, causing a scramble among underwriters and financial advisors as they recalibrate their decades-old business models to meet these new requirements.

From my vantage point as a financial advisor to California K–14 districts, the single biggest impact of Dodd-Frank is its attempt to better define the roles of the various players in the muni market – especially financial advisors and underwriters. Let's start with financial advisors (referred to in the legislation as municipal advisors). Here's how Dodd-Frank defines their role:

"*A municipal advisor ... **shall be deemed to have a fiduciary duty** to any municipal entity for whom such municipal advisor acts as a municipal advisor, and no municipal advisor may engage in any act, practice, or course of business which is not consistent with a municipal advisor's fiduciary duty or that is in contravention of any rule of the Board.*" (Emphasis added.)

In addition, Dodd-Frank attempts to close one of the municipal industry's most gaping loopholes. Most people are shocked to learn that, unlike almost every other segment of the nation's financial industry, financial advisors were, until recently, totally unregulated. To put this in perspective, in most states, it was tougher to become a hair stylist than a financial advisor. Up until Dodd-Frank, anyone – and I mean anyone – could put the words *financial advisor* on a business card.

This is slowly – ever so slowly – changing. Financial advisory firms must now register with the Securities and Exchange Commission (SEC) and the Municipal Securities Rulemaking Board (MSRB). In addition, all financial advisors are now required to take a licensing exam, similar to the exams required for stockbrokers and underwriters.

The Underwriters

I started a financial advisory firm specializing in California K–14 districts in 1987. The early years were definitely an uphill climb. It was challenging to convince school districts or community college districts they needed a financial advisor. A large part of that challenge was trying to explain the difference between a financial advisor and an underwriter. I'd sit down with a district and tell officials that having a financial advisor on their side of the table would help ensure the financial advice they were receiving from their investment bank was truly in their best interests.

"But we're already working with Banker X at Bank Y. He already gives us our financial advice."

"I know," I would patiently explain. "I know Mr. X, too. He's a great professional. But as honest as he may be, you should still have an independent advisor looking over his shoulder to make sure you're getting the best deal possible."

"But wouldn't that mean I'd be paying twice for the same work?"

That was also the argument that some (but, to be fair, not all) investment bankers would make to keep us out of the room. "Why pay twice," they'd repeat to their clients, "if you don't need them?"

This barrier evaporated when the MSRB, reacting to Dodd-Frank's directive to provide greater protection to municipal issuers, put some additional teeth in what is known in the muni industry as Rule G-17, an MSRB regulation that governs the conduct of municipal securities underwriters. For starters, the MSRB prohibited underwriters from discouraging issuers from using a financial advisor in a negotiated sale of bonds. Here are the specific instructions the MSRB put out in an interpretive notice concerning the application of the various sections of Rule G-17:

"An underwriter may not discourage an issuer from using a municipal advisor or otherwise **imply that the hiring of a municipal advisor would be redundant because the underwriter can provide the same services that a municipal advisor would**." (Emphasis added.)

In addition, Rule G-17 requires underwriters to make a number of disclosures to their clients regarding their role. Of the many disclosures required by the MSRB, two in particular caught everyone's attention:

1. "The underwriter's primary role is to purchase securities with a view to distribution in an arm's-length commercial transaction with the issuer and *it has financial and other interests that differ from those of the issuer.*" (Emphasis added.)

2. "*Unlike a municipal advisor*, the underwriter does not have a fiduciary duty to the issuer ... and is, therefore, not required by federal law to act in the best interests of the issuer." (Emphasis added.)

The Takeaway

From the outside looking in, I can imagine these changes seem both obscure and meager. Financial advisors are now to be required to take a licensing exam and are reminded that they are to represent the fiduciary interests of their muni clients. Underwriters need to disclose that, as financial institutions, their other financial interests may very well differ from the interests of their municipal clients. Not exactly earth-shattering disruptions.

But in the sometimes too-cozy world of municipal finance, these seemingly innocuous regulations have made and continue to make a big stir. Take underwriters, for example. Prior to G-17, an investment banker could call up any school district he or she wanted and suggest a meeting to discuss various financing alternatives. That world has changed. As one banker explained to me, "It's one thing if I'm calling up someone I've already worked with. But try getting an appointment with someone you don't know when you have to first explain why they need to sign a disclosure form stating they understand that I might have a conflict of interest."

And while taking a test may not sound like a big deal, remember that, until now, this was an unregulated industry. A number of people, whose financial skills don't go much further than balancing their checkbooks, are now required to take one hell of an exam, covering a vast amount of detail about a very arcane financial market. And when it's over, how many will still be standing is anybody's guess.

But the big question, of course, is whether all the tougher regulations and required disclosures will make any difference. The jury, as they say, is still out. Remember that one of the key components of Dodd-Frank regarding the role of financial advisors is that they have a fiduciary responsibility to their clients. And yet, I can come up with example after example – recommending refundings of questionable savings, steering business to favored underwriters, failing to recommend certain financing solutions because they've been developed by a competitor – where K–14 financial advisors have failed that test.

Nor did it take too long for some of the less scrupulous underwriters to start gaming the G-17 disclosure requirements, slapping a statement onto the front of their presentations that they weren't giving any specific advice, just general information. And then at the end of the meeting, suggesting that they email the district a copy of their contract.

So – *caveat emptor!*

Different Incentives

Finally, it's also worth noting that financial incentives for underwriters and financial advisors are quite different, which may influence where their ultimate loyalty lies. Financial advisors are paid on a per-deal basis. Although the fee may rise or fall somewhat depending on the size of the deal, generally speaking, the size of the deal is not of central importance to a financial advisor. A financial advisor's sole focus should be on the welfare of the school district client.

The underwriter's compensation, on the other hand, is based on a percentage of the value of the bonds sold, so the bigger and faster the bond issue, the larger and faster the compensation. Financial advisors have a legally mandated fiduciary duty to the school district, but underwriters do not. Their primary concern is the success of their own organization.

Nothing wrong with that. Business is business. But it's something school boards need to keep in mind as they review the various alternatives being proposed by their underwriter.

....

Special Topic #4
PAY-TO-PLAY

Whenever I hear someone start in on the subject of pay-to-play in school bond campaigns, I'm reminded of Justice Potter Stewart's 1964 Supreme Court decision on pornography, in which he wrote that although he wasn't able to define it, "I know it when I see it."

Pay-to-play presents the same tough-to-define challenge. Although many claim the problem is rampant, few can agree on what it is exactly or identify specific examples. Instead, like Justice Stewart, they rely on the I-know-it-when-I-see-it argument, throwing the pay-to-play blanket over all bond campaign contributions made by bond professionals, regardless of the facts.

First things first. Hiring a vendor because of an agreed-upon campaign contribution is illegal. Period. It's also a felony under California law (Ed. Code § 7054) to use school district resources in support of a school bond measure. This includes vendors making bond campaign contributions that are recouped by laundering them through their later invoices.

Does this mean it doesn't happen? Of course not. And there have been a handful of toe-curling examples that have been exposed over the past few years. But in my 30-plus years of work in the field of municipal finance, I've had only one occasion when I felt I was being hit up for a legally questionable campaign contribution – and that was in Nevada.

So, if there are already laws on the books against pay-to-play, and its occurrences appear rare, why do so many state and county officials, federal financial agencies, and editorialists continue to call for new laws to ban bond professionals from contributing to K–14 bond campaigns?

There is, I'm afraid, no single, simple reason. I suspect that some see a legislative crackdown as a backdoor maneuver to shut down all negotiated K–14 district GO bond deals in favor of competitive bids. Those financial advisors and Wall Street underwriters who have long refused to make such contributions may think they'll get more business if their competitors are legally required to do the same. And, frankly, I think the controversy has all the juicy story elements (money, politics, investment banks, etc.) that are catnip to some news media outlets.

Those considerations aside, there are two major problems with calls for a wholesale ban on K–14 bond campaign contributions. The first is the U.S. Constitution. Federal courts have held that governments cannot limit contributions to ballot measure campaigns unless there is a compelling governmental interest, and that prevention of corruption or the appearance of corruption of elected officials is the "only legitimate and compelling government interest thus far identified for restricting campaign finances." (*Blount v. SEC* (1995) 61 F.3d 938, 944; *Buckley*, supra, 424 U.S. at 26.) Furthermore, the U.S. Supreme Court found that "the risk of corruption perceived in cases involving candidate elections simply is not present in a popular vote on a public issue…" (*Citizens Against Rent Control*, supra, 454 U.S. at 298.)

The second problem is, where do you stop? If you're going to ban contributions from bond professionals who do business with K–14 districts, what about the architects, or the contractors, or the teachers union or, for that matter, the supplier of hot dogs for Friday night's football game?

Not that I think these concerns are going to stop advocates from calling for additional pay-to-play restrictions. But to a certain extent, proposed pay-to-play legislation is becoming a solution in search of a problem. The SEC is actively dissuading underwriters from managing bond campaigns. The MSRB is considering extending contribution limits to bond campaigns.

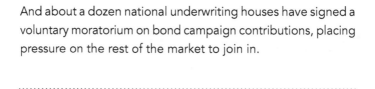

And about a dozen national underwriting houses have signed a voluntary moratorium on bond campaign contributions, placing pressure on the rest of the market to join in.

THE ELECTION CONSULTANT

By law, California K–14 districts may not spend public funds to advocate the passage of a bond issue. But before a board votes to place an item on the ballot, a district can hire a consultant to help prepare the measure.

Fewer and fewer districts are willing to risk placing an item before the voters without using a consultant to assist with this pre-election process. Placing an item on the ballot is costly both to the district's general fund (the costs of running an election are covered below) and in people-hours. Election consultants help make those investments worthwhile.

(I should note that a handful of financial advisory firms, including mine, also provide election consulting services. The topic of using your financial advisor as a campaign advisor is covered in Chapter 7.)

A good election consultant will help determine if a bond package is ready to go to the voters. Consultants can help craft the Project List, assess the impact of local political issues on the timing of a potential bond election, help interpret the poll results, and spend time with district stakeholders and critics, making sure questions are answered and concerns addressed.

Make sure there's clarity regarding any potential conflicts between your district's goals and the financial incentives of the election consultant. This is rare, but I have seen it cause problems now and then. If, for example, the district pays the election consultant a monthly retainer, it may not be in the consultant's best interest to get the district on the ballot as soon as possible.

On the other hand, if the election consultant is charging a minimal fee to the district because the consultant knows he or she will later be hired – and paid by outside contributors – to run the campaign, the consultant may want to push the district onto the ballot earlier than necessary.

Let me offer two examples:

1. **An Abundance of Caution?** In early 2012, all signs pointed to the November election as being highly advantageous for school bonds. Turnout in presidential elections is generally high, and the Obama campaign looked determined to keep it that way by bringing out as many liberal-minded supporters as possible. Even though a statewide tax measure to help fund schools was likely to be on the ballot, all our polling showed widespread support for local bond measures, even among voters who were against the statewide tax increase.

   It was a textbook case: an excellent time to get on the ballot. Nevertheless, a number of election consultants around the state were cautioning their clients – clients who were paying them monthly retainers to help prepare for the ballot – to avoid the November 2012 ballot, claiming the statewide tax measure would hurt their chances of passage.

   Maybe these reluctant consultants had their reasons. But given that the November 2012 ballot turned out to be very good timing for K–14 bond elections – as all historical precedents said it would be – it's fair to question these consultants' motivations or their political skills.

2. **Throwing Caution to the Wind?** At the end of 2011, a Bay Area district – and client of DS&C – was trying to decide whether it should wait for the November 2012 presidential ballot or jump into the June 2012 presidential primary. The district asked its political consultant to present his election-date recommendation at the board's next meeting.

   It seemed like a no-brainer to me. The district was overwhelmingly Democratic, and I could see no compelling reason not to wait five months for an expected heavy November pro-bond turnout and avoid what was looking to be a low pro-bond turnout in the June primary.

   Still, I had one nagging concern as we all walked into the board meeting to hear the consultant's recommendation. Just a few weeks prior, this same consultant had called me, asking if I had any campaigns he might work on. His June calendar, he said, was completely empty.

Too late, I realized I should have gone to the superintendent about my concerns prior to the board meeting. I'll never know if the consultant really thought June was the best election date or he was simply looking to fill in his calendar. Whatever the case, he made a passionate recommendation for June 2012, and the district board accepted his advice without a single question. Truth be told, he ran a great campaign for the district but, in the end, the low voter turnout killed them.

THE POLLSTER

I'm always stunned when a district objects to running a random poll of voters to determine the extent of community support in a bond election. Given the time, energy and cost needed to place a bond on the ballot, why wouldn't you want to know in advance how voters are feeling?

On the other hand, I'm also often stunned by the amount districts are willing to spend on a poll. Sure, I say to myself, it would be nice to know how people feel about the district and the proposed bond, but do we really need a 100-page report filled with glossy pie charts and crosstabs?

As I explain to clients, you run a poll for one of two reasons. In some districts, you can be pretty sure, based on past elections, voter registration, neighboring district elections, etc., that voters will support the bond measure and the proposed projects. You run a poll to confirm these beliefs and give the board the comfort (and the backbone) to move forward with an election.

In other districts, however, you run a poll because you honestly don't have a clue how the voters feel about the district or the potential for success in a bond election. These tend to be large, highly diverse districts in which the local public schools are far from the center of everyone's universe. In addition, they are typically districts where there is no shortage of people eager to tell you they know how voters really feel and that there is no way in hell a bond could ever pass in their community.

A few years ago, I delivered survey results to a large Central Valley district. Even though this was one of the most conservative parts of the state, the poll results were overwhelmingly supportive. But one board member wasn't buying it. Throughout my presentation, this member, every inch the retired successful farmer, fixed me with a hard-eyed stare. I had barely finished when he leaned forward and flipped on his microphone.

"Are you telling me," he asked incredulously, "that over 70 percent of the voters in our district would support this bond? That seems impossible. I don't know a single person who'd vote for this thing."

I took a deep breath and replied, "According to the survey, that's exactly what I'm telling you." I had a feeling I knew what was coming next, and assumed he was either going to rant that he didn't believe in polls or rip into how I obviously didn't understand the politics of his community.

Instead, after a few moments of silence, his face broke into a wide grin and he leaned back in his chair, shaking his head in disbelief. "Well," he laughed, "I guess that just goes to show that my grandkids are right. I am totally out of touch with reality."

Four months later, voters passed the district's bond measure by 72 percent.

Chapter
FIVE

....

PREPARING FOR THE BALLOT

....

"Oh dear! Oh dear! I shall be too late!"

~ The White Rabbit, speaking to himself, in
Alice in Wonderland

HOW MUCH TIME IS REQUIRED TO GET READY FOR A GO BOND ELECTION?

The most common question I'm asked by a district considering a general obligation bond election is, "Do we have enough time to get everything done?"

Assuming the question isn't being asked a few weeks before the county filing deadline, the answer is almost always yes. Most of the financial professionals and bond lawyers in the California K–14 market have placed scores of bond issues on the ballot and know what needs to be done.

There's no doubt a district's potential for success in a bond election improves greatly when there is adequate time to assemble a team, develop a full and comprehensive Project List, carefully consider various tax-rate scenarios and analyze voter attitudes. Obviously, this is going to take more than a few weeks. But, still, most districts (assuming they're not completely dysfunctional) should be able to pull together the required pieces of a bond election in three to six months.

Human nature being what it is, giving yourself too much time to prepare for a bond election can be just as big a problem as too little. Paralysis by analysis is the most common problem that sets in when a district tries to game an election date or nail down every possible twist and turn. Successful bond elections require both enthusiasm and momentum, and having too much time saps energy.

COMPETITIVE OR NEGOTIATED SALE?

I know it might seem premature to be worrying about the method by which you sell your bonds to investors. However, many districts, without knowing they're doing it, err by committing themselves to a certain type of sales method at this point in the process.

Municipal bonds are almost always sold to the public with the help of an underwriter. Underwriting firms can be either large, well-known investment or commercial banks or small boutiques that few people have heard of. Either way, the role is the same. Underwriters buy, or underwrite, an issuer's bonds, setting the interest rates for each maturity in the process, then turn right around and sell the bonds to investors. If they've done their job well, they'll make a profit on the spread, or difference, between the price at which they've purchased bonds and what they sell them for.

Just how an underwriter is selected is the source of long-running argument. First, an overview of the two methods by which underwriters are selected.

Competitive Sale

In a competitive sale, the details of the financing, including its structure, term, prepayment features, rating, etc., are managed by the financial advisor. A legal notice is published inviting underwriters to submit an underwriting bid on a certain date at a certain time. The winner is chosen based on the lowest cost of interest (factoring in any underwriting fees).

Negotiated Sale

In a negotiated sale, the underwriter is selected in advance and manages the bond sale, or, if there is also a financial advisor on board, assists with the structuring of the financing, which can be done either with or without a financial advisor. On the day of the sale, interest rates are set based on the underwriter's assessment of the current market.

The Never-Ending Debate

The debate over which method of sale is best is, at times, quite contentious. On one side are those (including the Governmental Finance Officers Association, as well as many California county treasurers) who believe the competitive bid process provides an open and transparent forum for selling school district bonds and guarantees the lowest cost of interest for the district.

Underwriting firms, on the other hand, counter that by being hired in advance of the sale, they can pre-market the bonds and answer investors' questions regarding the security and the issuer. This, they argue, results in more favorable rates than can be obtained in a competitive sale.

As with many disputes, the truth lies somewhere in the middle. For a general obligation bond issued by a well-known, highly rated district, it is hard to argue (although some certainly will) for any method other than a competitive sale. But in certain situations – a complicated structure, a district with a poor financial track record, a distressed local economy – a negotiated sale can make more sense.

As premature as it may seem, you really should have some sense of the method of sale that will work best for your district before you begin to assemble your team. To put it simply, the moment you hire an underwriter to help you place your bond on the ballot, you have effectively committed your district to a negotiated sale and preempted the possibility of offering the bonds through a competitive bid. There's nothing wrong with doing this if you know what you are signing up for.

My comments may make it sound as if financial advisors, as a group, would naturally lean toward competitive sales, especially since, all other things being equal, the competitive sale method appears to have strong arguments – both political and financial – in its favor. But, oddly enough, that's not the case.

According to the California State Treasurer's Office, of the 27 financial advisory firms that worked on K–14 GO bonds between July 1, 2008, and June 30, 2012, 15 didn't bring a single competitively bid financing to market during this four-year period. How could it be that more than half the state's K–14 financial advisory firms didn't work on even one competitively bid deal four years running?

Frankly, there is no legitimate justification. The sad truth is that many of these firms either lack the technical know-how to run a competitive sale and/or have longstanding relationships with various underwriters and are worried about losing future business referrals. Of course, these financial advisors will deny this is the case, which is why I encourage districts to do a little research on their own.

I remember being in a final interview in front of the board of a Central Valley district, competing for its business against one of the 15 firms cited above. Although it's unusual for competitors to be interviewed at the same time, this board had decided it wanted to have both finalists in the room so it could ask them both a few questions.

One board member immediately raised the question of a competitive versus negotiated sale. "I'm confused," she said. "How do we decide whether to sell the bonds through a competitive or negotiated sale? Is that your decision or ours?"

My competitor jumped to the microphone with a long and erudite answer about the pros and cons of these two methods. "Naturally," he said, "our final recommendation will be based on current market conditions. But, in the end," he assured her, "the decision will be yours. I guarantee it."

The board member turned to me and raised an eyebrow. "Mr. Scott?"

I am not often left speechless, but this was one of those times. Earlier in the day, anticipating this exact question, I'd logged onto the state treasurer's database to check how many competitive sales this competing firm had actually worked on in the past 10 to 15 years. The answer: zero.

"Mr. Scott?" the board member repeated. "Anything to add?"

I wish I could say I pulled the treasurer's data from my briefcase and hurled it across the room with a Perry Mason flourish. But, alas, I didn't.

By this point in the interview I was pretty sure we were going to be hired (in fact, we were) and decided to let my competitor's flagrant prevarication pass with a shrug.

The point remains, however: When a prospective financial advisor assures you his or her firm is a strong believer in competitive sales, ask how many competitive vs. negotiated sales they've run in the past. And then make sure you check their answer against the state treasurer's database.

BUILDING A PROJECT LIST

Some districts get twisted up in knots over the development of the Project List, and I've seen more than one district decide it was going to delay getting on the ballot because it felt its Project List wasn't in good enough shape.

Even though the Project List is certainly a key piece of any bond campaign, its development doesn't need to be an all-consuming event that completely bogs down the organization. In fact, before the passage of Prop. 39, bond elections didn't even require a Project List. Under the pre-Prop. 39 two-thirds election laws, districts were – and still are – free to develop their Project Lists after the election, so long as the projects are broadly described in the official 75-word ballot language.

Prop. 39 changed all this by requiring districts seeking approval under the 55 percent rule to provide voters "a list of the specific school facilities projects to be funded ..." for school bond elections.

When Prop. 39's Project List requirement was first published, I remember a collective head scratch among finance professionals, since the new law was silent as to exactly how this Project List was to be shared with voters. It was obvious it couldn't be put into the 75-word ballot language. But could we simply include it in the district's resolution? Or publish it in the local paper?

The solution – putting the Project List into a document called the Full Ballot Text and then publishing that document in the sample ballot – was adapted from the way information for state referendum propositions is provided to voters. In California propositions, the 75-word ballot language is essentially a summary of the proposed changes that are to be made to existing law. These 75-word summaries don't explain the mechanics of how propositions will be implemented. In 75 words, all that can be communicated is an overview of the proposed changes. If voters want the details, they turn to the full text of the measure printed in the sample ballot.

It took a few iterations to work the kinks out of this approach. The first few Full Ballot Texts for Prop. 39 bond elections often ran 20 pages or more, providing an extraordinary level of detail about each proposed project. But, as the years passed, these lists have evolved and today provide a relatively specific overview of the scope of the projects rather than a detailed line-by-line analysis.

For example, for funds to be used to rehabilitate schools throughout the district, you may want to list each school's name and then simply bullet-point the projects to be completed at each one. Voters can thus get a quick view of what projects are planned at their neighborhood school. For larger projects, such as a new high school, be sure to include enough detail so voters will know precisely what the project entails.

Build It and They Will Come (But It Better Be on the List)

Here's the most important rule to remember in putting together a Project List: *You don't have to complete every project that appears on the Project List. But unless a project is on the list, you can't spend money from the bond to fund it.*

For example, let's take a district with 10 elementary schools. In the Full Ballot Text, the district lists the "repair and remodeling of restrooms" at each of these schools as well as a number of other projects. Is the district obligated to actually make these repairs at all 10 schools?

No. Typically, it would prioritize, starting with the most critical and continuing until the money runs out. The construction of various projects can often be spread over five to 10 years or more, and there are no guarantees what the cost of a project might be so far in the future.

But what happens in the opposite situation; that is, when a district fails to list everything it would like to do? Say the district listed only five of its 10 elementary schools for restroom repairs, but then construction costs came in much lower than expected. Could it then use the funds to work on the restrooms at the other five schools?

Unfortunately, it couldn't. Unless the project is on the Project List, it cannot be funded with bond proceeds. I say unfortunately, because many districts try to get around this potential problem by placing more projects on the Project List than can possibly be funded from the amount of bonds being authorized.

This overstatement often leads to complaints that voters are being misled by rosy promises as to the number of projects a bond's passage will enable. Despite the complaints, a smart district will list everything it would like to do within reason, and err on the side of listing too much.

A REAL-LIFE (AND VERY COSTLY) HORROR STORY

Constraining the potential scope of the proposed projects can result in horror stories. Some years ago, a district in Northern California passed a bond issue to "repair and rehabilitate school facilities to meet current health, safety and instructional standards." There's no doubt this language accurately described exactly what everybody thought needed to be done, and I'm sure it would have seemed like legal overkill to add the words "construct and acquire" to the ballot language.

The measure won overwhelmingly, and the architects and engineers began a more in-depth analysis of the condition of one of the district's high schools. They soon realized the building was in much worse shape than they'd thought, and that the cost of repairs would far exceed original estimates. The district quickly switched gears and began demolishing the entire building with the intent of building a new one from scratch.

Not so fast, said the opponents, who filed a lawsuit against the district, claiming that the ballot language (and the Project List) made no mention of new construction. Work on the project screeched to a halt. The district ended up spending tens of thousands of dollars on legal fees in a failed bid to fight the opponents. In the end, the district had to spend even more money to hold a new election to "amend" the original Project List language to allow for new school construction.

The moral of the story: Throwing every conceivable project and every conceivable permutation of a project into the Project List gives voters less clarity into how bond funds will be spent. However, making the Project List as inclusive as possible not only complies with the letter and spirit of Prop. 39, but also is the only way a district can maintain flexibility as its needs evolve over time.

But Don't I Need a Comprehensive Facility Master Plan?

I was talking with a superintendent recently about the district's plans for getting on the ballot the following year. "Before we even consider taking this public," the superintendent said, "We'll need to update our Comprehensive Facility Master Plan. Right?"

Like so many parts of the GO bond preparation puzzle, the answer is "yes" and "no". A Comprehensive Facility Master Plan has nothing to do with a single election, and it needn't be shared with voters. It's a strategic document listing everything a district plans to do over a 10- or 15-year period.

There certainly is no legal requirement that such a plan be in place before going to the voters. And the cost of hiring consultants and architects with general fund dollars to produce a full-blown Comprehensive Facility Master Plan that offers a detailed cost breakdown of all conceivable future projects is beyond the financial reach of many districts.

On the other hand, voters have a right to expect that, when a district is asking them to raise their own taxes, there's a good overall plan for how the money will be spent – and the deeper and more strategic the planning, the better. It needn't be flashy or have pictures. It doesn't need to get down to the level of costing out doorknobs. But for internal planning and external communications reasons, a Comprehensive Facility Master Plan should map out a long-term vision of what a district needs to build and repair to keep pace with its students' needs.

WHAT CAN BE FUNDED?

Under either 55 percent or two-thirds voter-approval, bond proceeds can be used for land acquisition; the rehabilitation, improvement, and remodeling of existing facilities, including but not limited to classrooms, administration buildings, maintenance buildings, and athletics facilities; and the construction of new facilities.

In addition, while most districts use GO bond funds to directly purchase the school facilities or pay for the improvements, Prop. 39 specifically allows bond funds to be used to lease real property, giving districts the option of acquiring facilities through a lease-purchase arrangement.

Outstanding Debts

While not expressly mentioned in the law, GO bonds can also be used to pay off or "refund" existing school district or community college district debt, such as COPs.[9] This is done by "buying" the underlying asset that was financed by the COPs. For example, imagine a school district that had sold COPs in order to finance the construction of a new school building prior to passing a GO bond.

Under a typical COPs structure, a third-party entity such as a "school facilities financing corporation" would serve as the "owner" of the building. This organization might be newly created (in fact, its board and administration are often the same as the district's), or it might already be in existence, set up to assist districts with financings like these. The district wouldn't own the new building but, rather, would lease the building from the facilities corporation for a rental payment equal to the debt service on the COPs.

....

9 COPs are a type of debt financing used by K–14 districts to provide upfront funding for capital projects with repayment made over a multiyear period. The structure involves setting up a lease between the district (as lessee) and a passive lessor, such as a non-profit financing corporation. The lease is then securitized and sold to investors. Although the structure is very similar to a GO bond with annual principal and semiannual interest payments, the financing is the sole obligation of the issuing district and not the district's taxpayers. For this reason, COPs can be issued without voter approval.

These payments would typically be made out of the district's general fund.

So, when a district wants to pay off its COPs with new GO bond proceeds, it essentially "buys" the facility from the financing corporation with those proceeds, paying off the COPs debt.

Refunding COPs with GO bonds may sound too slick by half, but as long as voters understand the concept, this use of bond funds is beneficial because it reduces districts' general fund borrowing costs. Unfortunately, this can be a tricky political issue and often voters will simply see the move as a backdoor attempt to shift a district's costs onto the backs of voters.

My advice to districts thinking of using this method is to be open and candid about it with voters, making sure they understand why the COPs were issued in the first place, as well as the positive impact the refunding will have on the district's ability to provide students with a quality education.

Equipment

Up until the passage of Prop. 39 in 2001, GO bonds could be used only to fund the "acquisition or improvement of real property." This inability to fund furniture and equipment under two-thirds elections caused districts (and their lawyers) tremendous headaches. A district would pass a two-thirds bond to fund the construction of a new school or classrooms but would have to come up with some other source of funding to pay for desks, tables, curtains, etc.

This restriction led to quite a few legal backflips and headstands, as the bankers, financial advisors and lawyers tried to unravel what could and couldn't be funded as an improvement to real property. For example, while a desk would clearly not qualify, what about a blackboard if it were attached to the wall of a classroom?

Prop. 39 gave districts the ability to fund "the furnishing and equipping" of school facilities with bond proceeds, thereby addressing a huge problem with school facility funding. Curiously, equipment can now be funded by bonds passed by 55 percent of the voters under Prop. 39, but not by bonds passed under the older two-thirds legislation.

What About Salaries?

On the surface, the answer to this question seems pretty clear. Section 3 of Prop. 39 specifically states that the proceeds of a general obligation bond shall not be used for "teacher and administrator salaries." But not all salaries are created equal.

According to a 2004 opinion by the California Attorney General, school districts may use Prop. 39 bond proceeds to pay the salaries of district employees for administrative oversight work on construction projects authorized by voter-approved bonds, because these costs are an integral part of the construction process and would not be generated but for the existence of the project.

This issue has also been litigated. In *San Lorenzo Valley Community Advocates v. San Lorenzo USD* (2006) 139 Cal. App. 4th 1356, a local citizens group challenged the use of GO bond proceeds to pay administrative costs associated with the bond project. In this case, an assistant superintendent at the district was given construction management responsibility. She carefully documented her time, and the district was reimbursed for 15 percent of her salary out of bond proceeds, representing the time she dedicated to the supervision of bond-funded construction spending.

Citing the 2004 California Attorney General's opinion, the appellate court found that under Prop. 39, costs that are incidentally but directly related to the bond project may be paid from bond proceeds, including administrative costs.

Obligation to Charter Schools

Prop. 39 requires school districts to share their facilities fairly among all public school students, including those in charter schools. Early on, this requirement led to concerns that districts would have problems accomplishing their goals because they needed to split bond money with charter schools. Experience has shown, though, that districts and charter schools can get along quite well, and that district money need not be materially diverted.

Under the law, districts must provide charter schools with facilities sufficient to accommodate all the charter schools' in-district students in conditions reasonably equivalent to those in which the students would be accommodated if they were attending other in-district public schools. The district must also make reasonable efforts to provide those facilities near where the charter schools wish to locate. In return for providing facilities, the district may charge the charter schools a pro-rata share of the facilities' costs.

As long as districts meet these requirements, they're under no obligation to give charter schools pro-rata portions of their bond proceeds outright. Districts should meet with their facilities crews and legal counsel to make sure they are meeting these Prop. 39 requirements.

PRELIMINARY TAX RATE PROJECTIONS

The process of developing a Project List – bringing together the timing and costs of projects the bond issue will finance – yields good information that can be used to build a preliminary tax rate projection. Though there's major temptation to spend a lot of time and energy refining numbers at this stage, I suggest saving some of that time and energy for later, and accepting that this first tax rate estimate is going to be rough and subject to change. (The same applies to developing a drawdown schedule for issuing the bonds and getting the money. There are always changes, so best-guesstimates are fine at this stage.)

Using estimates for timing and the cost of the projects covered by the bond, the financial advisor or investment banker can begin to develop the tax rate projection for a proposed general obligation bond election. It's a good idea to allow all participants in the bond measure process – the financial advisor and/or investment banker, legal counsel, district administrators and district board members – to carefully consider, analyze and review the underlying analyses that go into calculating the tax rate projection. Unfortunately, this broad collaboration remains more the exception than the rule, but working together now can save major headaches down the road.

District officials need to be wary, because too often the financial professionals fail to fully explain the many decisions and variables that go into their tax rate projections. Instead, they present the analyses as straightforward mathematical calculations when, in fact, projecting tax rates is in many ways more art than science, requiring the juggling of numerous financial and political variables – most of which will undoubtedly change over time – along with federal tax law restrictions, state constitutional provisions and California Education and Government Code sections.

Among the quantitative variables at play in developing these tax rate estimates are:

- The dollar cost of the various projects and when the funds will be needed

- The term of the bond (the number of years over which repayment will be spread)

- Projected interest rates

- If there are to be multiple bond sales under one voter authorization, the timing of the sales

- Assessed valuation growth projections

Some of these variables, and their impacts, are fairly simple. For example, holding all other factors constant, the impact of doubling the size of the bond will double the tax rate. But the impact of other variables is not so clear. This is especially the case with the underlying assessed valuation assumptions, an area that deserves a more in-depth look.

Assessed Valuation Growth: Crucial to Developing Projections

Underlying assessed valuation (AV) growth assumptions are the big enchilada in the development of tax rate projections. Although all the elements cited above affect this calculation, none have the impact of AV growth.

Considering the crucial importance of AV growth, it's astonishing how little review goes into the development of these numbers. Ideally, the financial professionals putting together these projections should review a long list of data points in developing this model, including:

- long-term and recent assessed valuation trends;

- the mix of property classes such as commercial and industrial;

- the amount of property taxes deriving from mineral rights;

- the amount of past AV growth that resulted from major residential developments and the potential for future development;

- the condition of the current housing market;

- the overall economic condition of the region.

Too often, however, the FA or investment banker will simply take the average percentage change in AV over the past five or 10 years and slap that number into the model for the next four decades. Or, in a handful of egregious situations, the advisors will work backward and manipulate the assumptions – no matter how fanciful – to arrive at the number that will provide them with the biggest payoff.

THE $14 MILLION STARTER HOME

Not long ago we were asked by a Bay Area school district to review a GO bond election financing plan that was being proposed by another financial advisory firm. The firm was urging the district to place a new bond on the ballot in an amount well over $500 million, even though the district's previous election, held eight years earlier, had been for only $175 million.

"It's not that we don't trust the other firm," the superintendent assured me. "And Lord knows we could use the money. But the amount just seems high compared to what other financial firms have showed us."

That was an understatement. A quick review of the numbers revealed the main ingredient in this financial advisor's secret sauce was a baked-in assessed valuation increase of 9 percent *every year for the next 40 years.*

After we'd unraveled the numbers, I sat down with the superintendent, the CBO and two board members to explain how this firm could come up with the $500 million number. I'm not sure what reaction I was expecting when I shared this information with them, but it certainly wasn't the one I received. After explaining the fanciful 9 percent annual growth rate assumption, everyone around the table just stared back at me with a kind of *"and your point is?"* stare.

"Look," I said, changing gears, "let's back up. The average assessed valuation for a single-family home in this district is currently about $475,000." I then quickly ran them through the district's AV potential: Even though the district was an affluent suburban enclave, its tax base consisted almost solely of single-family homes. There was no significant industrial base, only a small retail center, and virtually no available land left for development. In other words, any assessed valuation growth would have to come almost exclusively from an increase in the value of its current residential units.

"So, if assessed valuation were to grow at 3 percent per year for the next 40 years," I explained, "your average single family home would be assessed at about $1.5 million by 2050. Anybody want to guess what that number would be if we raised the assumed growth rate to 9 percent per year?"

The board president scribbled a few numbers on a pad of paper. "Maybe $4.5 million," he said, looking up. Not a bad guess if it were simple multiplication. But as Einstein said in another context, the greatest invention of mankind is compound interest.

"At 9 percent annual growth, by 2050 the average assessed valuation for a single-family home would be somewhere around $14 million," I said. Was such a number possible? Yes. Likely? Hard to imagine.

The district apparently felt the same way, since the $500 million bond proposal quickly died a silent death. But there are plenty of other examples of bond elections around the state that are based on similarly aggressive assessed valuation assumptions. The question is why. Assuming financial advisors and investment bankers are smart enough to run the kind of reality check we did in this Bay Area district, why would they use such aggressive assumptions in the first place?

The unfortunate answer is that it's in almost everyone's best interest to increase the size of the bond. The schools need the money to build projects.

TABLE 6				
IMPACT OF VARIOUS AV ASSUMPTIONS ON BOND SIZING				
Annual AV Growth Projections	2.00%	4.00%	6.00%	9.00%
Years Sold	1, 4, & 7	1, 4, & 7	1, 4, & 7	1, 4, & 7
Amortization per Series	25 years	25 years	25 years	25 years
Total Years for Repayment	31 years	31 years	31 years	31 years
Principal	$68.1m	$89.3m	$120.1m	$195.2m
Interest	$59.1m	$88.6m	$134.3m	$253.6m
Total Debt Service	$127.2m	$177.9m	$254.4m	$448.8m
Debt Ratio (=Debt Service/Principal)	1.87:1	1.99:1	2.12:1	2.30:1
Projected Avg. Tax Rate per $100,00 AV	$60.00	$60.00	$60.00	$60.00

ASSUMPTIONS Assessed Valuation: $5 billion | Interest Rate: 5% | Debt Service Type: Ascending

Investment bankers and bond counsel get paid on a percentage basis. Financial advisors typically charge higher fees for larger transactions. And pushing AV assumptions is the fastest way to ramp up the size of a deal to fatten everyone's payday.

How fast? Real fast.

Remember our previous example (see Table 5) of the district with $5 billion in assessed valuation and the effect of various assessed valuation growth rates (2 percent, 4 percent and 6 percent) on the size of the bond. If you assumed 2 percent annual AV growth, the bond would be sized $68.1 million. Table 6 shows the impact of changing the AV annual growth assumption to 9 percent. The result? The bond could now be sized at $195.2 million, nearly triple the amount using a 2 percent growth rate.

The scary part of all of this is that from the outside looking in (for example, a voter reading the sample ballot), there is absolutely no way to tell what underlying AV assumptions are being used and how realistic they are.

Think of it this way. Imagine there were two nearly identical districts in the same community – District A serves the west side of town, District B serves the east. Their assessed valuation is the same. Their underlying

FIGURE 9: Tax Rate Example - AV Growth at 6%

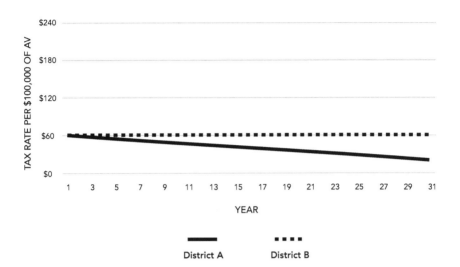

economy and housing stock are exactly alike. District A and District B both put bond measures on the same ballot. But District A's advisor assumes 2 percent annual growth, while District B's advisor assumes 6 percent. District A asks the voters for a $68 million bond and tells voters the tax rate will be $60 per $100,000 of assessed valuation. District B asks the voters for a $120 million bond and also tells the voters the tax rate will be $60 per $100,000 of assessed valuation.

If voters from the two districts got together and compared all the information provided to them in the sample ballot, would they be able to see how District B could get twice as much as District A but somehow pay the same tax rate? No – it would be impossible to figure out. There would be no difference in the ballot language. The Full Ballot Text would be silent on the issue. And, except for a recent change in the law that requires the total cost of a bond to be disclosed (*See* "The Tax Rate Statement" in Chapter 6), the tax rate statements would be exactly alike, and the independent legal counsel's opinion would read the same.

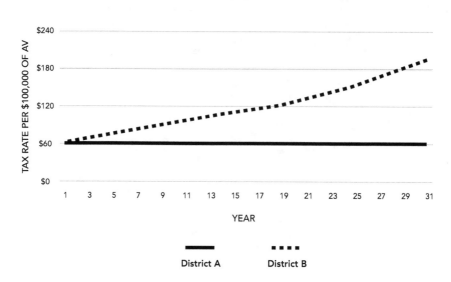

FIGURE 10: Tax Rate Example - AV Growth at 2%

Only future developments would reveal which of these two districts was using the wrong tax rate projection. If District B had it right and assessed valuation grew at 6 percent per year, then its taxpayers would keep paying a $60 tax rate over the life of the bond, while District A's tax rate would fall to about $20 per $100,000 of AV. (See Figure 9.)

But if District A had it right and assessed valuation only grew by 2 percent, the impact on District B's voters would be severe. As shown in Figure 10, if AV grows by 2 percent annually, District A's taxpayers would keep paying a $60 tax rate, but the rate for District B's taxpayers would balloon to nearly $200 per $100,000 of AV.

Given all this uncertainty, a district sorting through tax rate estimates must ask its outside financial experts some hard questions: What's the rational projected rate of AV growth? What would assessed valuation be in 25 years under these assumptions? What would the tax rate be if these growth rates are not achieved?

And be sure to get it in writing. We have an absolute policy that all tax rate assumptions be documented and reviewed, and then we ask clients to sign a statement saying they've reviewed the assumptions and agree with them. If a district's financial advisor or investment banker doesn't require this, the district should insist on written statements so it has documentation of these critical numbers.

....

Special Topic #5
A TALE OF TWO DISTRICTS

To see how much impact changes in assessed valuation can have on a bond program, let's look at two districts:

Albany Unified School District serves the small, affluent town of Albany in Alameda County, covering about five square miles just north of Berkeley. The population is stable, growing from 16,327 in 1990 to 18,539 in 2010 – an increase of 13.5 percent in 20 years.

San Jacinto Unified School District lies just north of Hemet, in Riverside County, halfway between the cities of Riverside and Palm Springs. It serves the city of San Jacinto, covering about 26 square miles. Unlike Albany, the population of San Jacinto underwent explosive growth at the turn of the 21st century, climbing from 23,779 residents in 2000 to 44,199 in 2010, an increase of more than 85 percent in just 10 years.

Figure 11 compares assessed valuation growth for the two districts over the past 20 years. From 1992 to 2004, the AVs of these two districts were almost exactly the same. Albany's grew from $654 million to $1.26 billion, an average annual increase of 5.64 percent. San Jacinto's grew from $862 million to $1.25 billion, an average annual increase of 3.42 percent.

Then, all hell broke loose in San Jacinto. With its surge in population (and plenty of cheap money from a go-go economic bubble) came frenzied new housing construction and increased assessed valuations. In the four years from 2005 to 2008, AV in San Jacinto climbed to nearly $3.4 billion – *an increase of more than 130 percent.*

Then came the crash of 2008. In the following four years, almost all of San Jacinto's run-up in AV evaporated. By 2012, San Jacinto and Albany were just about tied again.

In November 2006, San Jacinto USD voters passed a $150 million GO bond. However, only $42 million of the bond had been issued as of the end of 2012. Because of the district's AV free-fall, the tax rate on the $42 million outstanding portion of the bond is approximately $100 per $100,000 of assessed valuation, $40 over the legal $60 cap. The potential for the district to access the remaining $108 million of authorized but unissued bonds in any reasonable timeframe (in the absence of a GO Reauthorization Bond, described in Chapter 3) is highly unlikely.

FIGURE 11: Comparison of Assessed Valuation for Albany USD to San Jacinto USD

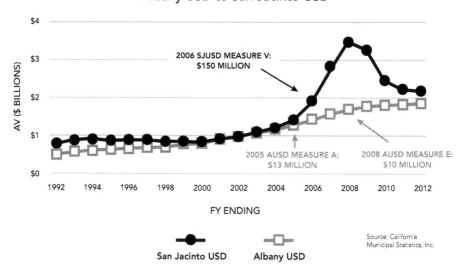

Lessons Learned

Given all the above, how best to develop assessed valuation projections when building a tax rate analysis? Here are a few things to keep in mind as you review the proposed projections:

1. **No Tree Grows to the Sky.** Beware of straight-line projections that take an average of the past, say, five years, and run them out for the next 30. It's a cliché but true: past performance is no guarantee of future performance.

2. **In the End, Real Estate Is Just Another Investment**. No matter how frothy real estate in a district may be at any given time, in the long term it doesn't make sense that one investment class will consistently out-perform others year after year. Unless you think the national economy is going to grow at 9 percent per year for the next 20 years, it's unlikely that real estate prices will. Real estate tends to move in seven-year bubble cycles, and the market has only a three-year memory.

3. **Prop. 13 Can Be Your Friend (or Your Enemy)**. As the city of Albany found, the way Prop. 13 masks the true assessed valuation of older homes provides a slow, steady and, in most cases, reliable stream of AV increases. Even if people don't move or die, their older homes will usually increase in value each year at Prop. 13's 2 percent annual maximum. If those older homes change hands and can therefore be assessed at true market value, AV will climb higher, faster. But for districts like San Jacinto, without an established, older housing base, Prop. 13 can whipsaw total AV numbers in a falling economy due to the lack of a cushion. Newer, speculative housing developments, such as those in San Jacinto, can fall sharply in value in rough times, pushing a district's AV picture into the red zone.

4. **Beware of Solving Backward**. If the financial advisor or investment banker is jacking up the estimated assessed valuation growth rate in order to produce a particular bond size, maybe it's time to find a new advisor.

5. **Kick the Tires**. Ask questions. Challenge the assumptions. Demand to see reasonable stress tests. Don't be afraid of asking questions that start, "*What if*..."

SIZING THE BOND AUTHORIZATION

By analyzing the cost of the various projects, the timing of the funding for the projects, AV growth rates and other variables, the financial advisor or investment banker can begin the process of determining the size of the bond authorization to be placed on the ballot. This is one of the most important decisions in the preparation of a bond measure. Unlike the Project List, which can be expanded or contracted as the needs of the district shift, the dollar amount listed in the ballot cannot be changed after it's approved by voters (although, as described later, that hasn't stopped some finance professionals from trying).

Think Line of Credit

It's important to keep in mind, however, that the passage of the bond authorization, in and of itself, does not result in any taxes being levied on taxpayers. Think of a voter-approved bond as a line of credit. While the district has voter approval to draw down on the line, until funds are actually borrowed, there is nothing to repay.

Take, for example, a school district that passes a $100 million GO bond. If it issues $20 million of that authorization, the county controller would place a tax rate on the next property tax bill sufficient to pay the upcoming debt service payment, but only for the $20 million that was borrowed.

Once the $20 million is issued, the remaining "line of credit" is reduced to $80 million. Again, these remaining funds – again, known as *authorized but unissued bonds* – do not cost anybody anything. The authorization just sits there until the district decides to issue its next series of bonds. This is where the line of credit analogy ends. Typically, with a line of credit, once you pay back the principal, you can re-borrow the funds again. But with a GO bond, you only get to borrow the funds once.

How long can the unissued funds sit there? Theoretically, forever. Although I've heard some legal theories that the validity of an unused authorization could be challenged after sitting unused for a certain number of years, there's no statutory expiration date on authorized but unissued bonds, and it would appear that the legal authority to issue the bonds never goes away until, of course, the bonds are finally issued.

An illustrative story: In the late 1990s, a large school district in San Diego County passed a bond issue of nearly $100 million. This was the first bond issue passed by voters that anyone in the district could remember, and they were justifiably jubilant.

We were getting ready to sell the first series of bonds when I received a call from someone in county treasurer's office. "Did you want to add in that last $25,000?" he asked.

Wondering what I'd missed in the documents, I asked, "What $25,000?" "Back in '64, the district passed a $2 million bond," he explained, "and there's still $25,000 that's never been issued."

Figuring it would cost at least $30,000 in time and legal fees to figure out just what these funds could be used for, we declined the treasurer's offer and, for all I know, the $25,000 is still sitting on the books, unissued.

The Statutory Debt Limit

The last step to be taken in sizing a bond issue is to check how the authorization will affect a district's statutory debt limit. This is one of the most misunderstood aspects of a bond issue and is commonly brandished by opponents in their arguments against a bond measure.

TABLE 7
EXAMPLE OF STATUTORY DEBT LIMIT CALCULATIONS
$5 BILLION ASSESSED VALUATION

	Year 1	Year 2	Year 3
Assessed Valuation	$5.0b	$5.2b	$4.7b
Debt Limit @ 2.50%	$125.0m	$130.0m	$117.5m
Outstanding Debt	$20.0m	$19.5m	$18.8m
Available Debt Capacity	$105.0m	$110.5m	$98.7m
Total New Debt Issued	$0	$110.0m	$110.0m
Net Debt Limit	$105.0m	$0.5m	-$11.3m

The statutory debt limit rarely impedes a district from issuing its bonds, for reasons described below. Still, the California Education Code instructs districts to comply with the debt limit or, if unable to comply, to seek a waiver from the provision before issuing their bonds.

The most important fact to keep in mind about the debt limit is that it only applies to *outstanding* general obligation bonds – not authorized bonds. For unified school districts and community college districts, the amount of outstanding debt may not exceed 2.5 percent of the district's assessed valuation. For elementary and high school districts, it's 1.25 percent.

Let's go back to our example of the unified school district with total assessed valuation of $5 billion. Let's imagine that this district had already had one successful bond election 10 years ago for $25 million, and all the bonds have been issued. Taxpayers have been making regular payments on the bonds and, as of today, only $20 million of the original $25 million is outstanding.

Using the 2.5 percent limitation, the district's gross statutory debt limit in the first year would be $125 million. Subtracting the district's outstanding debt ($20 million) from the statutory debt limit gives us an available net debt limit of $105 million. (See Table 7.)

Let's say the district runs another successful bond election for $275 million in Year One. Since its debt limit is only $105 million, is it now in violation of the debt limit? No, because, as noted above, the debt limit applies only to outstanding, not authorized, debt. Since none of the new bonds have been sold, they do not apply against the debt limit. (Receiving authorization for an amount of bonds in excess of a district's debt capacity happens more often than you might think. Many districts seek bonding authority far in excess of their debt capacity to "bank" that authority for future years when anticipated AV growth increases their debt limit.)

In Year Two, the district's assessed valuation grows by 4 percent, to $5.2 billion. In addition, another $500,000 of the prior bond's principal is repaid, raising the district's available debt capacity to $110.5 million. In that year, the district issues $110 million of bonds, going right up to the edge of its statutory bonding capacity.

But what happens in the following year (Year Three) when the district's assessed valuation falls, lowering the available debt capacity to $98.7 million? The answer is, even though the district's previous issuance of $110 million will now push it over the debt limit by $11.3 million, there isn't any impact. The debt limit calculation only matters when the district is teeing up to sell bonds. Once they're sold, a district's falling AV has no repercussions.

And even when a district is over its debt capacity, it can still sell bonds by seeking a waiver of its debt limit from the California State Board of Education. Because the statutory debt limit is a statutory restriction (as opposed to a constitutional requirement, such as Prop. 39), the debt limit can be waived upon application to the state. Although there are signs that the State Board is becoming more restrictive on granting waivers, to date it has shown itself generally willing to grant waivers as long as a district can make a compelling argument.

At this point it makes sense to ask: What's the use of having a debt limit if it's not really a hard-and-fast limit? Answer: The ability of a K–14 district to apply for a waiver from the debt limit is really no different from the flexible rules that apply to other statutes and civil code sections.

If, for example, the owner of a vacant corner lot wants to build a neighborhood café in an area zoned residential, she can apply for a waiver (or variance) from the residential zoning regulation. A city could grant that waiver if it were in the best interests of the neighborhood and the city. This is similar to a district requesting a waiver from the debt limit. In the end, the State Board of Education has the authority to decide whether such a waiver is in the best interests of the state.

Summing up, there are two points to keep in mind regarding the debt limit. First, it's applied only to bonds that are outstanding (i.e., already issued), rather than those that have been approved by voters. Second, the calculation of the debt limit is a moving target and will change every year (up or down), depending on what happens to assessed valuations and debt repayment.

TOUCHING BASE WITH THE VOTERS

You've now assembled the key internal components needed to place a GO bond on the ballot. Your financing team is in place. You've developed a working Project List with estimated costs. Your financial advisor or investment banker has developed the underlying assumptions needed to determine the bond's size and required tax rates.

Now it's time to go external – to reach out strategically to different voting groups in the district to assess their level of potential support or opposition. Taking your public's temperature is critical for planning, but it must be done subtly, making as few waves as possible.

At this point in the process the board has probably taken no overt or official actions regarding putting a bond on the ballot, so asking voters questions about their potential support or opposition would be strategically premature. You'd risk losing control of your story. As you begin testing the waters of local public opinion, avoid specifics. Say nothing yet about the contemplated size of the bond, election dates, tax rate, etc. First, there are no hard-and-fast specifics yet. More importantly, when a voter hears about a potential new bond issue, his or her first thought isn't specifics, it's, "Oh, no! Another tax!"

A Pizza a Month?

That's why the message in these first discussions must center on the needs of the district, not the dollars, and certainly not the mechanics. You must be ready to explain, clearly and simply, how proposed improvement projects will fill a *compelling community need* for which no other source of funding exists.

Second, don't focus on how little it's going to cost voters. I cringe when I hear a school district official tell a group of citizens, "The bond will cost less than a pizza a month." Comparing bond-payment taxes to the price of a pizza or a trip to Starbucks has its place in giving voters a relative sense of the cost of the bond. But just because something's cheap doesn't mean it's worth paying for. People need to hear how the bond will be good for them and their community. After all, without knowing the benefits, maybe they'd prefer the pizza.

Third, unless you're speaking to a parents' group, don't talk about how great this will be for the kids. In most districts, fewer than half the voters – and in some districts, many fewer – have kids in schools now or have ever had kids in local schools. While they may care about what's good for the children, what they really want to know is how improving the schools – and raising their taxes – is going to benefit them as citizens and property owners.

Finally, don't be overly concerned about opposition. There are plenty of die-hard tax opponents who are eager to let you know that "nobody" supports the bond and/or they're going to fight you to the death. Fine. Just remember, your role at this point is not to be an advocate but simply to make sure people have the facts, and to listen to what they say once they've heard the facts.

In addition to reaching out to various segments of your voter population, you must give special attention to three distinct groups: (1) the Citizens' Oversight Committee (assuming one has been formed for a previous Prop. 39 election), (2) major commercial stakeholders and big-ticket taxpayers in the community, and (3) the district's board of education.

Reaching Out to the Citizens' Oversight Committee

I remember when I first read the Prop. 39 language requiring a *Citizens' Oversight Committee* (COC), muttering to myself, "This is going to be a disaster." Wrong again.

In most districts, COCs are often a new bond issue's biggest boosters. They know first-hand – from previous experience – the facility needs of the district, know the projects that remain uncompleted due to lack of funds, and have learned how complex the world of school facility construction and management really is. (There's a fuller discussion about populating and working with COCs in Chapter 9.)

If a district has had a previous Prop. 39 bond election and the COC remains in place, a briefing of its members should be one of the district's first stops in building support for the new bond. I've seen many cases where the COC, after hearing the case for a new bond, becomes one of its strongest advocates and actively supports the measure. Of course, this assumes there is a good working relationship with the COC – which requires districts to keep COCs well supplied not only with information but also with context.

Reaching Out to Major Stakeholders

Standard School District is a small elementary district in Kern County. Its boundaries stretch about 10 miles to the north of Bakersfield into some of the prime oil-producing areas of the Central Valley. There's a reason the Standard School District has that name. Approximately 65 percent of all the assessed property in the district is owned by Chevron – the former Standard Oil.

So, when district officials start thinking about putting a general obligation bond on the ballot, one of the first stops is a sit-down with Chevron to talk about what the district is hoping to do, why the projects make sense, and what it's going to cost.

Granted, there aren't a lot of districts in the state where a single owner accounts for more than half the district's assessed valuation. But it's not uncommon for a small group of local businesses, farmers, ranchers or high-wealth single-family homeowners to own property that will be disproportionately affected by an *ad valorem* tax.

In some of the more affluent areas, assessed valuations of $1 million for a single-family home are not uncommon. For a bond measure with a $60 per $100,000 tax rate, this translates to an annual tax of $600 per year – not an inconsequential amount, but probably not enough to rile up people with million-dollar houses.

But what if in one of these communities there were also a mega-mansion or two on the property tax roll for, let's say, $25 million. The bond tax on this property would be $15,000 – per year. For 25 to 35 years.

You could, of course, argue that a person who lives in a $25 million home can afford to pay $15,000 a year in additional property tax. But that's not the point. The point is whether he or she is willing to pay it for 25 or more years, because if not, someone that wealthy probably has enough money to make your bond campaign pretty miserable.

This gets us back to Standard SD. The example of a district being savvy enough to identify and reach out to its major property owner is one that other districts should follow as they prepare to put a measure on the ballot.

Start by having your financial advisor or investment banker compile a list of the top 20 taxpayers in the district. The list will include not only the name of the taxpayer but also the total amount of assessed valuation and what percentage of the district's total AV each property owner's holdings represents. Some of these taxpayers may be major corporations and difficult to reach out to. But a number will be local businesses and residents. (Some of the names might not be easily recognizable. Properties may be held in trusts and under a corporate name for tax purposes. Ask around – the board is usually a good source of information – to see if anyone knows who the owners are.)

Try to schedule a sit-down with as many of the top taxpayers as possible. Explain the district's needs and plans. Make sure you have an example of what the proposed tax rate might be, because I'll guarantee you'll be asked. Above all, let these prominent people know that no decisions have been made but, as important members of the community, they deserve the courtesy of hearing what the district is considering.

Reaching Out to the District Board of Education

You would think that support from the board of education to place a bond measure on the ballot to improve a district's schools would be a slam-dunk. Think again. For whatever reason – the economy, publicity surrounding some poorly structured bond deals in other districts or a simple aversion to taxes – board members have become touchier and touchier over the past few years about calling a bond election.

In addition, some board members seem to think that by voting to place a bond measure on the ballot, they are actually voting to raise their constituents' taxes. And even when you (gently) point out to these board members that they're not actually raising taxes but giving voters the chance to decide if they want to *raise their own taxes*, these board members can still have a hard time agreeing to vote in favor of the measure.

Boards of education are not single units, but groups of five (or seven) politicians, each with personal perspectives, strengths, weaknesses and agendas. Think through who, exactly, each board member is, how that member will likely react to a proposed bond measure, and how best to frame a conversation with that member.

The following list is certainly not all-inclusive, but it includes the most common board-member typologies, along with some suggestions on the best way to broach the subject of a bond measure with each one:

- **Leader of the Pack.** On most boards, there's one person everyone looks to for advice when financial issues arise. Make sure his or her questions are fully answered before bringing the idea to the full board.

- **Slow but Steady.** These board members tend to have a strong understanding of their district and the community, but need to deliberate long and hard before making a move. The best approach is to bring them the idea in a study session where they can ask as many questions as they want without worrying about the next item on the agenda.

- **The Quick Decider**. Just the facts, please. What will the money be used for? How much will it cost taxpayers? How soon can the resolution be placed on the agenda? After getting his or her questions answered, this person is eager to stop talking and start moving.

- **The Hidden Opponents**. "It's not that I'm against the bond," this board type will assure you. "I just don't think this is the right time." Sometimes they'll have a legitimate point. But more often than not, they just want to derail the process. I've tried everything with this kind of board member – financial reports, news articles, voter polls – but have found nothing that works.

- **The Straight-up No**. No games and no drama. These people tell you right up front they are going to vote "no". Maybe they don't like taxes. Maybe they have dreams of higher office and don't want the vote on their record. It doesn't matter. You won't change their mind. In many ways, these are the easiest members to deal with. They deserve your respect and they deserve to be heard.

RUNNING A VOTER SURVEY

Given all the time, people-power, and expense involved in placing a GO bond on the ballot, it's a no-brainer to undertake a random survey of voters to measure the level of community support for a bond measure. In addition, a survey can provide a wealth of information about district voters, their attitudes about the district, how they obtain information about the district, and how they feel about major district policy issues.

Dealing with Pushback

Still, many districts are leery of conducting a poll, and it's not uncommon to get pushback on the recommendation to survey voters. Much of this reluctance comes from a misunderstanding of the purpose of the voter survey. Though district officials and board members may be eager to educate voters about why a bond is needed, that's not the purpose of this first poll. Its purpose is to gauge people's attitudes about the proposed bond based on what they *already know* (even if they don't know anything). Then, properly administered, the survey seeks to measure any shifts in their attitudes as they hear information on what bond funds will be used for, how much it will cost taxpayers, etc.

Another concern I often hear is that a poll will "stir things up" by telling people about the district's plan to put a bond measure on the ballot before the district has decided what to do. Given that only about 300 to 400 voters are typically interviewed, this is hardly a signal flare shot into the sky (although, of course, this is not the case in small districts). And besides, if there is so much opposition to a new bond that just conducting a survey can cause a ruckus, better to find out earlier than later.

Finally, there's the "I don't believe in polls" argument and its corollary, "I don't know anyone who would answer the phone to talk to a pollster." There's some basis for this argument. Clearly, the reliability of polling data gathered for school bond elections has deteriorated over the years, as people are less and less willing to answer the phone and talk to a stranger. In a Pew Center study of voter behavior, the percentage of households that can be contacted and are willing to be interviewed for a survey of voters plunged to 9 percent in 2012 from 36 percent in 1997.

Still, despite the challenges, survey research remains the best and most cost-effective tool for taking the pulse of a community. While a survey needs to be augmented by reaching out to neighborhood and political organizations, unless you're dead certain of your community's overwhelming support, the idea of flying blind into an election without the benefit of survey research simply makes no sense.

Choosing a Pollster

Districts have a wide range of options in selecting a pollster. On one end of the spectrum are the professional pollsters. These are firms trained in the art of conducting survey research and its mathematical underpinnings. The survey professionals know how to draft questions in a way that drills down to obtain the essential information and know how to interpret the data. Their work is exemplary.

The downside is that they're expensive. Often very expensive.

At the other end of the spectrum are financial advisory firms and investment banks that, like my firm, offer survey research as part of a bundle of other consulting services. These firms will typically charge a much lower fee than the mainstream pollsters. Some will even defer the fee, making it contingent on the district running and winning its bond election.

It would be hard to argue that the quality of the polling produced by financial advisory firms and investment banks is equal to that of the professional pollsters. In many ways, you can think of it as the difference between flying first class and coach. In first class, you get more individual attention and a bigger seat. (Or, in this case, a thicker report.) On the other hand, tickets are more affordable in coach and you arrive at the same time.

In deciding which type of pollster would work best for your district, consider – especially in less complicated or fractious districts – if the extra level of service is worth the extra money. Also consider the potential political damage of spending thousands of dollars of general fund revenue on pollsters when the district is about to ask voters to raise their taxes.

Complicated and contentious districts with swirling undercurrents, various factions and complex politics might be better off with a firm that specializes in measuring the nuances of voter opinion. It might also be worth hiring a completely independent firm that cannot be criticized for having an interest in the results of the poll.

Speaking of such a criticism, some argue there's a conflict in having the voter survey undertaken by the same financial advisory firm that stands to benefit if the bond is put on the ballot. The implication is these firms somehow "cook" the numbers to their benefit. Why a firm would do this is left unanswered – mainly because it makes no sense. After all, firms like mine that provide clients with survey research on a contingent fee have nothing to gain (and much to lose) in recommending that a district go forward with a campaign when polling data points in the opposite direction.

....

Special Topic #6
A QUICK AND DIRTY GUIDE TO POLLING

The pioneering pollster George Gallup is reported to have said that sampling public opinion is like sampling soup. Just one spoonful can reflect the taste of the entire pot so long as the pot is well stirred.

The concept that a small random selection from a larger pool will reflect the characteristics of that larger pool is the underlying essence of survey research. Here's a quick example: Imagine we take an enormous barrel and fill it with 10,000 white marbles and 90,000 black marbles. Let's also imagine that the marbles are well stirred, like Mr. Gallup's soup.

Now, close your eyes, reach in and pull out 100 marbles. The theory is you don't have to count all of the marbles to figure out how many are white and how many are black. By sampling (i.e., selecting a representative part of the data), the probability is that about 90 of the selected marbles will be black and 10 will be white.

Notice I used the word "about." This is what the statisticians refer to as the *margin of error* as in, "The *margin of error* in the sample is plus or minus 4 percent." The larger the sample size, the lower the margin of error. By selecting only 100 marbles, our margin of error would be around 10 percent (plus or minus). But if we increase our sample size to 600 marbles, the margin of error will fall to 4 percent.

Margin of error, by the way, refers only to the mathematical probability of the sample size. It doesn't account for errors that may be baked into the survey by poorly phrased questions, mistakenly surveying voters who have little likelihood of actually voting, or other missteps.

Properly conducted polls can provide a remarkably accurate insight into voter attitudes *at the time the poll is conducted.* The problem is, people often want to treat a poll as a *predictor* of future behavior rather than a snapshot of current voter attitudes.

If nothing changes between the date of the poll and Election Day – and assuming the poll was conducted correctly – then the results of the survey should mirror the election returns. But the likelihood of nothing changing in those ensuing months is close to zero. Opposition to the bond might surface. A scandal could erupt in the district. Aliens might land on the high school football field. It's always something.

Therefore, you need to treat the results of a poll with a grain or two of salt. A poll's greatest value is not to predict ultimate success or failure but, rather, to gain insight into how voters feel about the district, the proposed bond projects, the tax rate, and the overall concept of passing a bond to improve the community's schools.

Getting Ready for the Voter Survey

A number of years ago, we were working with an elementary district north of Los Angeles whose schools were unbelievably overcrowded. Instead of shutting down for the summer, this district had to keep its doors open year-round. Every quarter, one-fourth of the students would be on "summer break" (even though it might be the middle of February) while the other 75 percent attended classes. The district had also implemented "double-track" scheduling with every desk assigned to two students. When one student was at lunch, the other used the desk. When that student came back from lunch, the one at the desk went to P.E., and so on.

The situation was intolerable. Parents were beside themselves. Teachers were up in arms. Community leaders were demanding a solution.

We ran a survey to assess voter support for a bond to build a new school, and the results were overwhelmingly positive, except for one odd response. The district thought one of the strongest "yes" arguments would be that by building a new school, the district could go off a "year-round" schedule and return to the traditional school year. But, to everyone's surprise, voter support of this argument was lukewarm.

This was especially puzzling since the district had heard nothing but complaints from parents about the disruption this year-round schedule inflicted on families trying to plan vacations, arrange for child care in the middle of the year, etc.

BEWARE OF EDUCATION SPEAK

After taking a deeper look into the data, the light bulb went on. Voters who were parents understood what was meant by "year-round" schools and strongly supported the bond measure. But close to half of the voters were non-parents, and they didn't respond well to this argument at all. After a little digging, we realized that when they heard the statement about going off a year-round schedule, they thought it meant students' schedules would be reduced and they'd be spending less time in school.

We'd screwed up by letting school district jargon slip into the questionnaire, which taught a great lesson about how different sub-groups of voters can hear the same question differently, depending on their point of view. This is why a well-constructed survey will often come at the same question from a couple of different directions, and also why you have to maintain a certain level of skepticism in reviewing survey results.

While you can never completely eliminate the possibility of misunderstandings like these, districts can drastically reduce missteps by careful planning and review of the survey questionnaire. In general, the run-up to conducting a voter survey involves the following steps:

1. Draft a list of proposed questions and circulate them to district officials – the superintendent, the board president, the chief business official, etc. – for comments, discussion and approval. The smaller this group, the better, in order not to get bogged down in long arguments over questions' wording.

2. The pollster contracts with a call center to handle voter interviews. These companies specialize in telephone interviews and have a large centralized staff that knows how to get people on the phone and keep them talking.

3. The call center does a mock run-through of the poll to measure the time it takes. The more questions, the longer the poll. The longer the poll, the more it costs. Also, if a survey runs too long (over 10 minutes is the rule of thumb), interviewees may lose patience and end the call.

4. Assemble a list of potential interviewees from voter files, and determine a target number of interviews. (The method of selecting potential interviewees is described below.)

5. When the final survey draft has been approved and the list of phone numbers determined, the calls begin. A good call center will make sure the interviews reflect the community's demographics. For example, they may find a significantly higher proportion of women agreeing to be interviewed than men, and will adjust who gets called in order to reflect the true nature of the community.

Who Gets Called, and Why

School board members and administrators tend to think of parents as their constituents. This makes a certain amount of sense in that it's often parents who have worked on their campaigns, parents who show up for board meetings or call board members with concerns or complaints, and parents who buttonhole board members at the supermarket or football games.

But, as mentioned earlier, in most California school districts, half or more of the registered voters either don't have children or grandchildren currently attending local public schools or they never did – and they don't plan to.

Given these numbers, understanding the concerns and opinions of non-parents is critical to putting together a winning strategy. Yet, with few exceptions, non-parents know very little about what the local schools are doing (except what they hear from friends and family or read in the local press – assuming there is one).

Likewise, school district officials don't know much about how non-parents feel about their community's schools. A voter survey is one of the few tools available that provides insight into non-parents' attitudes and opinions. This, in turn, provides strategic guidance on what issues will be critical to non-parents during the bond campaign.

Including non-parents in the voter survey makes obvious sense. Less obvious is figuring out just who exactly – parent and non-parent alike – gets included on the list of possible interviewees. This process, known as a voter screen, seeks to identify only those voters who are likely to vote in the election, and this is a lot murkier and more difficult than it might appear on the surface.

The obvious first step is to eliminate anyone who has shown no prior evidence of actually voting. This is a much larger number than you might suspect. One of the districts profiled earlier, Albany USD, is a stable, relatively well-educated community just north of the UC Berkeley campus. And yet, in the 2012 presidential election, voter turnout in Albany USD was only 78.5 percent. In other words, even in one of the biggest, most publicized elections in recent history, more than 20 percent of Albany USD registered voters failed to cast a ballot.

Dropping non-voting voters from the potential interview list is an easy call. But what about voters who turn out in some elections but not all of them? That becomes more of an artful judgment call than a science.

Let's take the Bellflower Unified School District as an example. Located just north of Long Beach in Los Angeles County, Bellflower USD has about 39,000 registered voters. As shown in Table 8, the number of registered voters who vote swings wildly from election to election. In the 2012 presidential election, 65 percent of Bellflower USD's voters went to the polls. But just a year earlier, only 7 percent turned out for a local school board election.

Looking at the Bellflower data, it's clear you need to adjust the screen of whom to include in the list of potential interviewees based on which election date is being considered. If a district were considering putting a bond measure on the same ballot as a presidential election, we'd specify a very wide screen

	TABLE 8		
	BELLFLOWER USD VOTER TURNOUT		
Total Registered Voters (as of January 2013): 39,253			
Election Date	Election Type	Voter Turnout	Percent*
Nov. '08	Presidential	23,820	61%
May '09	Special	5,845	15%
June '10	Gubernatorial Primary	7,129	18%
Nov. '10	Gubernatorial	17,711	45%
Nov. '11	Local School Board	2,917	7%
June '12	Presidential Primary	6,896	18%
Nov. '12	Presidential	25,218	64%

*Percentage based on January 2013 voter registration

that might include anyone who had voted in one of the last three major elections (plus newly registered voters). On the other hand, if the election were being planned for an off-cycle board election date (the one with the 7 percent turnout), the screen might include only people who voted in at least two out of three of the last major elections plus the last local board election.

The Survey: Design and Questions

The most common technique for school bond surveys is a "pre/post" poll. In this type of poll, once the interviewer gets the voter on the line, the voter is assured that this call is not a sales pitch but an independent survey assessing attitudes toward the local school district or community college district.

Assuming the voter agrees to be surveyed, the interviewer generally starts by asking a handful of "warm-up" questions. An example would be a general question regarding the voter's attitude about the quality of education in his or her community.

After these warm-up questions, and *without any additional information,* the voter is told the district is considering placing a bond issue on the ballot, is read the proposed ballot language and is asked whether he or she would vote "yes" or "no". (This is known as the pre-test question.)

Ideally, the ballot language read over the phone will be as close as possible to language that actually ends up on the ballot. What's being measured is the voter's attitude toward the bond, as if he or she had just stepped into the booth and read the ballot measure for the first time without having any other information. (Frankly, this is how a remarkably large percentage of people actually vote.)

After the ballot question, the voter is given information on a variety of topics (e.g., how the bond funds would be spent, what the cost would be to taxpayers) to see what impact this information has on attitudes toward the proposed bond. For example, a voter might be asked, "*If you knew that bond money would be used to improve athletic facilities at schools throughout the district, would you be more or less likely to vote for the bond?*" After all the bond-related questions have been asked, the interviewer will then ask the voter one more time how she or he would vote on the bond after hearing the additional information. (This is referred to as the post-test question.)

TAX RATE QUESTIONS

Another area of inquiry is voter attitudes regarding the cost of the bond to taxpayers. This is a particularly tricky area to measure, and one about which there is a fair amount of disagreement. Some pollsters, financial advisors and investment bankers believe the tax rate question is the most important piece of information coming out of the poll and recommend slashing the proposed bond amount in an election to keep the tax rate below the tolerance threshold found in the voter survey.

I think this is overreacting, since it not only oversimplifies what the survey data is measuring but also ignores how information about the bond is presented to voters. Let's look at a recent survey from a poll we conducted on behalf of a school district in Northern California. In this poll, 77.3 percent of the respondents said they would support the bond measure after being asked the *pre-test questions* but before hearing any other information. Opposition came in at 15.3 percent and "undecided" came in at 7.5 percent. About halfway through the poll, we asked respondents the following question:

"If you knew that the bond would annually cost district property owners $14 per $100,000 of assessed valuation in property taxes, would it make you **more or less likely** to vote for the bond?" (Emphasis added.) We also asked voters the same question at a $9 tax rate.

NO DIFFERENCE "YES" OR NO DIFFERENCE "NO"?

The results seemed pretty clear. As shown in Table 9-A, at a $14 tax rate, support plummeted from 77.3 percent to 43 percent after hearing the cost, with 26 percent claiming they would be more likely to vote "no", and 23 percent saying it made no difference to them. But when the tax rate dropped to $9, those who said they'd be more likely to vote for the bond jumped to 52 percent.

This is where too many financial advisors mistakenly slam on the brakes and recommend lowering the size of the bond authorization in order to hit the apparently acceptable tax rate. But note that voters were not asked if they were *for or against* the bond based on the $14 tax rate. All they were asked was if they would be *more or less likely* to vote for the measure knowing that it would cost $14 per $100,000 of assessed valuation. And what about the 23 percent who said it made no difference to them? Does that mean no difference and they're still voting "yes" or no difference because they are voting "no"?

By digging into the survey cross tabulations, we can unravel how these "no difference" respondents sort out. These cross-tabs let us analyze the responses from those voters who voiced support for the bond in the pretest question as compared with those who responded that they would vote against the bond. When that is done (see Table 9-B), we see – looking again at the $14 tax rate – that what 18 percent of the voters were really saying was, "I already told you I would vote for the bond and hearing this tax rate doesn't change my mind."

When we add that 18 percent to the 43 percent who reported they would be more likely to vote "yes" after hearing the tax rate, the support level jumps to 61 percent, not an overwhelming mandate, perhaps, but lot better than 43 percent.

TABLE 9-A RESULTS OF 2012 VOTER SURVEY LIKELINESS TO SUPPORT BOND MEASURE		
	$9 per $100,000 of AV	$14 per $100,000 of AV
More Likely to Vote "Yes"	52%	43%
No Difference	22%	23%
More Likely to Vote "No"	19%	26%
Don't Know/Unsure	7%	8%
Total	100%	100%

TABLE 9-B RESULTS OF 2012 VOTER SURVEY LIKELINESS TO SUPPORT BOND MEASURE (EXPANDED)		
	$9 per $100,000 of AV	$14 per $100,000 of AV
More Likely to Vote "Yes"	52%	43%
No Difference – "Yes" Voter	18%	18%
Subtotal	70%	61%
More Likely to Vote "No"	19%	26%
No Difference – "No" Voter	4%	5%
Subtotal	23%	31%
Don't Know/Unsure	7%	8%
Total	100%	100%

Some might argue that 61 percent favorable is still not a wide enough margin to support a recommendation of going forward with the bond. This argument misses the point. The tax rate question should not be treated as the defining up-or-down question in a voter poll. It is only one piece of information – albeit an important one – being given to surveyed voters in an attempt to discover their attitudes regarding a potential bond.

The essence of poll results is derived by measuring the movement between *pre-test* and *post-test* questions. The pre-test question attempts to measure voter attitudes *without information*. Then, during the course of the survey, relevant information – both positive and negative – is provided regarding the proposed bond.

By the end of the survey, voters will have heard what the funds are being used for, what educational programs may or may not be affected, and what the projected cost of the measure will be. They may also hear arguments against the bond and be asked how additional local or state bonds on the same ballot would affect their vote. The question is not about the impact of a single fact (such as a proposed project or a tax rate) but, rather, the cumulative effect of hearing all the information.

Significantly, this analytical framework is consistent with how people actually vote. Many voters mark their ballot after reading only the 75-word ballot language. Others will come to a decision based only on what they hear from friends and family, or what they pick up through the media. Still others will dig into their sample ballot, weigh the arguments, calculate the tax rate's impact on their own tax bill, and carefully read the Project List.

Rather than hanging your go/no-go decision on a single tax-rate threshold question, the best way to obtain a full and complete picture of a potential bond's prospect for success is to measure how different groups of voters (parents vs. non-parents, Democrats vs. Republicans, etc.) react to multiple pieces of additional information.

WHAT'S THE RIGHT TYPE OF ELECTION FOR YOUR DISTRICT?

Since the passage of Prop. 39, all but a handful of K–14 bond elections in California have been run as 55 percent elections. And why not? Having run more than my share of two-thirds elections prior to 2001, I can attest to a huge difference between 55 percent and 66.7 percent.

But while almost all bond elections are now Prop. 39 elections, different forms of Prop. 39 elections have evolved over time that can provide additional advantages in winning voter approval. These alternatives come with additional costs and risks that are often not fully disclosed or appreciated by the financial professionals who suggest them.

School Facility Improvement Districts (SFIDs)

Created by special legislation in 1998, School Facilities Improvement Districts (SFIDs) allow for the formation of a special "financing district" within the boundaries of a school district or community college district. SFIDs were originally created for two-thirds-approval elections, and in 2001 the Legislature added the option of running a 55 percent Prop. 39 election as an SFID.

An SFID is formed solely for the purpose of creating special boundaries for running and administering a general obligation bond election. It has no appointed board, bylaws or special powers. While the creation of an SFID has quite a few twists and turns that must be carefully engineered, once it is up and running its administration is straightforward and simple.

LEISURE VILLAGE

SFIDs are structured in different ways to address specific political and financial challenges within a district. They were originally created to address what I call the "Leisure Village" problem. In this case, a specific section of the district, often a housing development that caters to retirees where there are no children and therefore no need for schools, is carved out of the newly created SFID.

A GO bond election is held within the boundaries of the newly created SFID – which now excludes Leisure Village – and, if passed, the tax for the bond's repayment is assessed only on property within the SFID, sparing residents of Leisure Village.

Note that there must be a realistic and defensible relationship – beyond the desire to win the election – between who is getting the benefit of the bond funds and who bears the cost of the bond's repayment. For example, while it may be politically expedient to exclude a particularly conservative part of the community in order to reduce the number of potential "no" voters, this would be improper, unless the district can prove the area in question would in fact not receive any significant benefits from the improvements being financed.

This "carve out" solution also works with Thompson Act school districts. (A Thompson Act district is an elementary district that opts not to join in the unification of a high school and its feeder elementary districts.) If a bond measure is being put on the ballot to improve the elementary schools in a unified district that includes a Thompson Act elementary school district, this sub-district can be carved out of the larger district.

SFIDs may also be used when there is a large disparity in the amount of taxes being paid by residents within the district due to Mello-Roos bonds (special bonds often used to finance schools in newly developed areas).

For example, the Chula Vista Elementary School District in San Diego County includes an older, developed area on the western side of the district, as well as large, newly developed neighborhoods to the east. Most of the new schools in the eastern portion of the district were financed through the use of Mello-Roos bonds, and these residents pay a hefty annual tax assessment for bond repayment.

When the district decided that the schools in the older, western portion of the district needed improvements, it concluded it would be unfair to ask residents in the eastern portion to bear the additional cost of these improvements. An SFID was formed to include only the older areas on the western side of the district.

Finally, larger school districts and community college districts have used SFIDs to create financing sub-districts that more closely match the underlying communities within their borders. These tend to be communities that have strong internal regional jealousies and have shown a history of unwillingness to support a district-wide bond issue.

WHEN THE PARTS ARE GREATER THAN THE WHOLE

West Hills Community College District, headquartered in Coalinga, is a good example of how to use an SFID properly. The district includes the western half of Fresno County and all of Kings County, and has three separate campuses: one in Coalinga in southwestern Fresno County, a second campus in Lemoore in Kings County, and a third in Firebaugh in northwestern Fresno County. The drive between any two of the three campuses is well over two hours and, besides being administered by one community college district, there's little else the three campus communities have in common.

Although the district was able to pass a $19 million two-thirds district-wide GO in November 1998, its next three Prop. 39 attempts failed to break 55 percent, with one even falling below 50 percent. In reaction to these past losses, we recommended the district divide itself into three SFIDs that roughly corresponded with the natural boundaries of the three campuses.

Separate bond elections were then held in each SFID. As a result, not only did each bond pass (one by almost 75 percent), the total amount of funding authorized by the three elections exceeded the amounts for the previous district-wide elections that had been defeated.

CREATING AN SFID

Helpful as SFIDs might be in solving a district's election problems, their creation can be a long haul. At a minimum, plan on adding at least two to three months to the pre-election schedule in order to get the SFID designed and created.

The first potential roadblock is the county. In order to form an SFID, a district needs permission from the county board of supervisors. In some counties, the board of supervisors will have passed a blanket resolution authorizing the formation of SFIDs. But not all counties have taken this action, and districts need to check early in the process to determine their county's status. (Weary experience shows many county officials don't have a clue if they've passed the blanket SFID resolution or not.)

Next, districts will need to hire an engineering firm that specializes in the drafting of special district maps. This map will provide a geographic description of the SFID along with voter precinct boundaries and tax rate areas. Engagement of this firm is typically handled by the financial advisor or investment banker.

In order to form an SFID, the district will need to schedule a public hearing regarding its formation. Notices announcing the date and subject of the hearing must be posted in three separate public spaces, and two public notices must be published in a local paper of record. The first notice needs to be published at least 14 days prior to the hearing and the second one at least seven days.

Tax Rate Extension Elections

Tax rate extension elections are like nuclear power: if used carefully and under the right conditions, a force for good. But in the wrong hands (in this case, financial advisors and political consultants who put winning ahead of saving taxpayers millions of dollars in extra interest costs), it's a force for evil. Under the right conditions, tax rate extension elections are an orderly and thoughtful way to transition voters from an expiring bond authorization into a new one. But like a science experiment gone horribly wrong, they can spiral out of control by making promises to voters that can rarely be kept.

First, an example where the concept worked: Prior to the passage of Prop. 13, California school districts could seek voter approval for what was known as a lease override tax. If approved, the district could levy a fixed tax rate for a fixed number of years in order to complete specified projects.

In 1976, voters in Atascadero Unified School District (San Luis Obispo County) passed a lease override tax set at $97.50 per $100,000 of assessed valuation that was to remain in place until FY 2010–2011. In November 2010, with time running out, the district went to voters with Measure I-10, a $117 million Prop. 39 bond measure. The main message was simple. If Measure I-10 was approved, a voter's property tax rate would not go up. In fact, it would fall to $60 from the then-current $97.50 per $100,000 of assessed valuation.

The bond measure passed by more than 65 percent, in large part because

TABLE 10 COST OF DELAYING REPAYMENT FOR TAX RATE EXTENSION ELECTION			
Years Repayment Made	1 to 25	11 to 25	Difference
Principal	$100.0m	$100.0m	$0
Interest	$86.4m	$139.7m	$53.3m
Debt Ratio	1.86:1	2.40:1	
Total	$186.4m	$239.7m	$53.3m

ASSUMPTIONS AV Growth Rate: 2% per year I Amortization: 25 years I Interest Rate: 5%

Debt Service Type: Ascending

voters find it far more palatable to extend an existing tax than to pass a new one. The message – "we're not asking for any new taxes, just an extension of the old one" – is compelling.

Which leads to the force-for-evil part of the problem. Because it's easier to pass a tax rate extension bond than one requiring a new tax rate, some political consultants are willing to go through contortions worthy of a circus acrobat in order to get there – even if that means the result will cost taxpayers millions of dollars more in unnecessary interest. In fact, a tax rate extension election was at the core of the Poway USD CAB controversy. (See *Special Topic #1: The Law of Unintended Consequences*.)

Here's how it works: Let's say that unlike Atascadero USD's bonds, a district's outstanding bonds won't be paid off for 10 more years. Table 10 compares the cost to district taxpayers of using current interest bonds (CIBs) to pay off $100 million in bonds over the next 25 years, versus using CABs to delay any repayment for 10 years, then paying off the bonds between years 11 and 25. (In both cases, I used an interest rate of 5 percent, although in reality the CAB rate would be significantly higher.) The result? Even though the district could claim the new bonds would only "extend the current tax rate," the actual impact would be to increase the overall cost to taxpayers by more than $53 million.

GO Reauthorization Bond Elections

I already covered how GO Reauthorization Bonds work in Chapter 3, but in case you missed it, here's a brief recap.

GO Reauthorization Bond elections allow a district to access bonds that have been previously approved by voters but which the district is now unable to issue due to Prop. 39 tax rate limitations. This generally occurs either because the district's assessed valuation took a big tumble or the original AV growth assumptions proved overly optimistic (or both).[10]

With a reauthorization election, voters are asked to approve a new bond measure that will replace the old authorized but unissued bonds that have yet to be sold. The district pledges in the ballot resolution that if the new measure passes it will *decertify* the old bonds. In this way, no additional debt is created.

If the reauthorization fails, no harm – no foul. The old bonds are not decertified and the district is in exactly the same position as before the election.

But if voters say "yes", the reauthorized bonds have their own Prop. 39 tax rate above and beyond the original bonds. This allows the district to sell the bonds immediately as current interest bonds, allowing not only for the facility projects to get back on track but to do so with enormous interest savings.

Two-Thirds Elections

In fact, from 2001 through 2018, California K-12 districts held 111 two-thirds bond elections, of which 56 – slightly more than half – achieved the required two-thirds voter approval.

....

10 Ironically, AB 182, the bill passed in 2014 that decreased the term of CABs from 40 to 25 years, is also a culprit in limiting the amount of bonds that can be issued. Numerous districts with large amounts of authorized but unissued bonds were relying – for better or for worse – on the ability to tap into the long-term CAB market in order to float additional bond series. Some rushed forward with CAB deals before AB 182's January 1, 2015, effective date. The others are now in a holding pattern as they patiently wait for assessed valuations to recover.

Given this daunting won-lost record, why would a district try for a two-thirds election instead of a 55 percent election? Simple: to avoid the tax rate limitation. Under a two-thirds election, there is no limit on the tax rate. This allows districts – especially smaller districts with a limited tax base – to move more quickly on their projects, as well as avoid costly and politically explosive capital appreciation bonds (CABs) in order to stay under the Prop. 39 tax rate limit.

By the way, even though there's no requirement that a Project List be published by districts seeking two-thirds voter approval, printing a Project List in the sample ballot has become so commonplace under Prop. 39 that it is now generally done for two-thirds elections as well.

PICKING THE RIGHT ELECTION DATE

I've heard numerous campaign advisors tell districts they shouldn't try to "game the ballot" – that is, choose the election date that seems the most promising – and that the best time to get on the ballot is simply "when you're ready." In my opinion, this advice is dead wrong. By all means, game the ballot, because choosing the right election date can mean the difference between victory and defeat.

There are, of course, some districts that have such compelling needs that they simply don't have the luxury of waiting for the best election date. And districts that have an expiring tax rate and the chance to dovetail the tax rate for a new bond with the end of the previous tax measure should certainly go for it. But in almost every other situation, the choice of the election date is one of the most critical variables in determining the success of the ballot measure.

Determining the right date for your bond election needs to include both a review of the legal restrictions and a cold-eyed analysis of political reality in your district.

Election Date Legal Requirements

A district can schedule a two-thirds election on just about any Tuesday it chooses. Clearly, such elections can take place on any primary or general election (i.e., presidential, gubernatorial, congressional) date. But two-thirds elections can also be run as special elections so long as the date falls on a Tuesday and isn't a state holiday or too close to a regular election date. (There are a handful of other restrictions too obscure to note. If running a two-thirds election off-cycle is under consideration, you should make sure legal counsel carefully reviews the date.)

The guidelines for Prop. 39 election dates, on the other hand, are much more restrictive, requiring such elections to be held at the same time as a "regularly scheduled local election." That sounds pretty clear except for the fact that the term "regularly scheduled local election" isn't defined in any law or in the California Elections Code.

This oversight led to an extraordinary amount of confusion and discussion right after Prop. 39 was passed. However, it is now generally accepted that Prop. 39 bond elections can only be placed on the following ballots:

- A presidential or gubernatorial primary or general election

- A special statewide election (e.g., a recall of the governor)

- An odd-year district school board election[11]

- An election being held by some other governmental entity that encompasses all of the district wishing to place the Prop. 39 bond on the ballot (for example, a community college trustee election if the trustee represents the entire local school district)

....

11 Note that an off-cycle district board election needs to be district-wide to qualify. Also, it doesn't actually have to occur – often no one will run against an incumbent – it simply has to be *scheduled* to occur.

Strategy for Choosing the Right Date

While there are some districts for which date doesn't seem to matter – Berkeley USD has won 11 straight elections since 1986, never getting less than 70 percent "yes" – for the vast majority of districts, identifying the optimum election date is one of the most important decisions to be made in preparing for the ballot. And depending on the type of election chosen – presidential, gubernatorial, primary or local off-cycle races – there are significant differences in how to prepare, organize and implement a bond campaign.

The first and foremost fact to keep in mind is that all elections are not created equal. The buzz around a presidential election will result in high voter turnout but also a long and crowded ballot, which may be a good or bad thing. At the other end of the spectrum, a local off-cycle school board or city council race will guarantee your bond election will not get lost among scores of other ballot measures. However, voter turnout will probably be anemic, and you might quickly find your bond the center of too much attention.

The biggest single factor in choosing election dates is voter turnout. Figure 12 shows the number of California voters casting ballots in the various

FIGURE 12: Voter Turnout in California

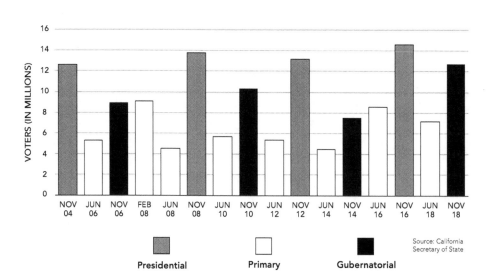

statewide elections since November 2004. Let's focus on just one year – 2008 – to see how significantly voter turnout can shift from election to election.

In 2008, there were three statewide elections. The first was in February. Anticipating highly competitive presidential primaries (Barack Obama was facing off against Hillary Clinton for the Democratic nomination, while John McCain was running against Mitt Romney, Mike Huckabee, and Rudy Giuliani on the Republican side), the Legislature decided to give the California primaries more national importance that year by moving them to February from their traditional June date.

With those big names on the ballot, plus major get-out-the-vote campaigns by both Clinton and Obama, more than nine million voters cast ballots in the primaries, more than had voted in the previous gubernatorial election in November 2006.

Even though the Legislature moved the presidential primaries to February, the regularly scheduled statewide primaries were still held in June. To judge by turnout, these races (for State Senate, Assembly, Superior Court judges, etc.) were a yawner: turnout fell by 50 percent from the February presidential primaries.

Then, in one of the biggest elections held to that date, 13.7 million voters flocked to the polls in the November 2008 presidential election – a threefold increase over the June primary turnout.

Clearly, the type of election causes large variations in voter turnout. Generally speaking, the higher the turnout, the more likely bond elections are to win. That should be sufficient reason to choose high-turnout elections for bond measures.

There are ancillary reasons, too. Districts usually save money in high-turnout elections because county elections departments charge less to place the bond on the ballot. Bond campaigns cost less and require less staff and volunteer effort in high-turnout elections (as explained below). And placing bonds in high-turnout elections avoids the charge from opponents that the district is trying to sneak something past the voters. But the main thing to keep in mind, if I may repeat myself for emphasis, is that bond elections scheduled for high-turnout contests tend to win.

Figure 13 reviews Prop 39 GO Bond Election results from 2004 to 2018. GO bonds on the ballot during what are generally low-turnout primary

FIGURE 13: Percent of Winning Prop 39 K-14 GO Bond Elections by Type of Election

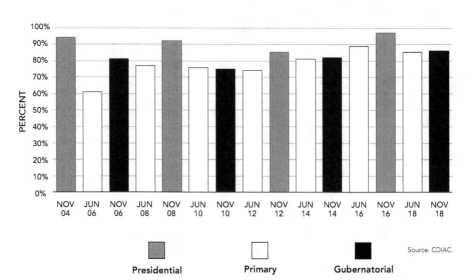

Source: CDIAC

■ Presidential   □ Primary   ■ Gubernatorial

elections (presidential or gubernatorial) had an average success rate of 76 percent. Bonds on the ballot during a gubernatorial general election (with a slightly higher turnout than primaries) were successful 81 percent of the time. The success rate for bonds on the same ballot as presidential general elections was 92 percent.

A CASE OF BAD SUNBURN

Okay, fine. High-turnout elections are good for bond measure success. But why? It all comes down to the casual voter. As a rule of thumb, *the less likely a person is to vote, the more likely that person is to be your supporter.*

Your typical "never-miss-an-election" voter is generally older, more conservative, less likely to have children, and more likely to be a "no" voter. By contrast, the casual voter is likely to be younger, more liberal, to have children in district schools, and vote in support of bond measures. But getting this potential supporter to vote in any election other than a gubernatorial or presidential contest is very tough.

One time we were running a bond measure on a presidential primary ballot for a small elementary district that had a college campus within its boundaries. (This was before the passage of Prop. 39, when the threshold for success was still 66.7 percent.)

We were feeling confident. Polling showed that, even though the election would be tight, the college student voters in the district overwhelmingly supported the bond. We tried everything we could to get these students to the polls, even stationing sorority members at men's dorm elevators to point them toward the polling place. We got close, but couldn't get over the two-thirds hurdle. Sadly, voter turnout in the college precincts didn't break 10 percent.

After hearing the results, one of our campaign professionals and I went out for a late dinner and a few beers. We started talking to the server and found out she was a college student who lived in the district and claimed to be an enthusiastic supporter of the bond.

"So, did you vote today?" I asked.

"Er ..." she sighed and looked at the floor in embarrassment. "I mean, I meant to but ... but ..."

"But what?" I asked, still trying to figure out where we had gone wrong. "You knew today was Election Day, right? There were signs all over campus."

"I know, I know," she answered, "I meant to but ... well, I had a really bad sunburn today and ..."

Turning out the casual voter – the voter who tends to say "yes" to school bonds – isn't the only benefit of scheduling a bond election on a high-turnout ballot. When your bond measure is one of the few items on the ballot and opposition arises, you suddenly become the only fight in town. And the media love a good fight. Try as you might, you will not be able to run, hide or fight back with the facts.

In fights like these, the opposition will control the high ground (*"They have too many administrators! They waste money! They should live within their budget and stop asking for more money! They want to raise your taxes!"*) and it won't take long for bond sponsors to feel like the target in a game of Whack-A-Mole.

HIDING IN PLAIN SIGHT

But in a presidential or gubernatorial election with a crowded ballot, even though it can be daunting to get your message heard above the general din, it's just as tough for the opposition to be heard. While they can jump up and down, send attack emails, and announce neighborhood meetings, with a president or governor to be elected, the room is too full for opponents to get noticed. Should opposition to a bond measure arise, a crowded ballot allows you to hide in plain sight.

Here's an example: During one presidential election, we ran a bond campaign for a Southern California district that had a highly contentious and vocal neighborhood/taxpayers' organization with a long history of battling the district. The leaders of the opposition held town hall meetings against the bond, lectured the school board at meetings, filed an argument against the bond and even put "Vote No" yard signs around town.

Even though it was tempting to fight back, we could see the opposition campaign was getting no media traction. With scores of other national, state and local issues on the ballot, there was simply too much for the media to cover. And without press coverage, there was no way this small group of opponents was going to be able to communicate with the 37,000 voters in the district.

Refusing to be drawn into a conflict, our client stuck to the plan of giving voters calm, factual reasons why the bond was in the best interests of the community. The measure was approved by 63 percent.

Finally, there is the issue of mobilization versus persuasion. If the bond is scheduled for a low-turnout election, the challenge is tougher, and the campaign must focus on mobilization – identifying potential supporters and convincing them to get to the polls, even when they normally wouldn't vote. Get-out-the-vote walks and town rallies can be effective, as well as inspirational and transformational. But they require a huge amount of energy and, far too often, come up short. Getting a casual voter to cast a ballot in a low-turnout election is hard, as the sunburned waitress illustrates.

Campaigns run during high-turnout elections, on the other hand, are about focusing on those most likely to vote rather than trying to increase turnout among people who tend not to vote. It's pretty safe to assume that if a person doesn't vote in presidential elections, that person isn't a voter.

Instead, the tactical focus of a high-turnout campaign is to increase support for the bond among those likely to show up and vote anyway.

ELECTION COSTS

There's one big cost to the district that's often overlooked until the last minute. The cost of placing a bond measure on the ballot must be paid to the county registrar of voters out of the district's general fund. Depending on the number of voters in the district and in which election the measure is placed, the cost can be sizable. If the bond measure is successful, the general fund can be fully reimbursed from bond proceeds. But if it fails, the district eats it.

Election costs include the printing and mailing of the sample ballot and absentee ballots. Some counties also provide voters with return postage for absentee ballots. There's also the printing of the ballot, stipends for poll workers, voting machines, overtime costs, etc.

These total costs are then divided on a pro-rata basis among the various jurisdictions on the ballot. If a GO bond is on the same ballot with congressional races, statewide propositions, city council races, etc., the cost to the district goes way down. But in an off-cycle election such as an off-year school board race, these costs can soar.

California counties have become extraordinarily aggressive (and creative) in calculating election costs. There seems to be little rhyme or reason to how these costs are calculated from county to county. I've seen them range anywhere from $1 to $6 per voter in the same election. Make sure you check early regarding your county's policy in computing these costs.

IS THE SUPPORT OF DISTRICT EMPLOYEES' UNIONS IMPORTANT?

A district begins putting together the building blocks to place a bond on the ballot and reaches out to the district bargaining units for their support. But instead of support, they get an icy silence at best, or, at worst, a direct threat to oppose the bond. It's not as rare as you might think.

This opposition, as shortsighted as it might seem, usually relates to the status of contract negotiations between the unions and the administration. I've been involved in some elections where the unions actually threatened to campaign against the bond unless the board of education agreed to their salary demands.

How critical to a bond measure is union support? Without a doubt, having the active support of teachers in the district is a major plus for any bond campaign, regardless of the community. Even though school districts themselves may not be held in as high esteem as they once were, the word of a teacher is still gospel to many parents.

But words coming from a union – including the teachers' union – are different, and you need to consider how they will be heard in your particular community. In certain highly Democratic blue-collar districts, union opposition is a death sentence. But in more conservative communities, having union support is not needed and may very well work against you. Something to consider.

Chapter
SIX

....

CALLING THE ELECTION

....

"One of the penalties for refusing to participate in politics is that you end up being governed by your inferiors."

~ Plato

It's show time. To place a bond measure on an upcoming ballot, the school board must pass a resolution requesting the county to do so. This action, as simple as it sounds, kicks off a flurry of activities that must be carefully managed and choreographed.

WHEN TO TAKE BOARD ACTION

Under California law, a district must file a resolution requesting the county elections department to place a bond measure on the ballot at least 88 days prior to Election Day. (A number of counties refuse to recognize this section of the Elections Code and set their own deadlines.)

The required date to *file* this resolution is one of the few hard deadlines in planning for a bond election. How many days, weeks or months before this deadline the board should *pass* the resolution calling for the election is harder to nail down. Part of the answer depends on where the district is in the development of the Project List, the voter survey, etc. But, in general, try to give yourself between 30 and 60 days before the filing deadline to take the resolution to the board.

Waiting until the last minute invariably produces a nail biter: the board member you were counting on suddenly has to fly off on a family emergency. A particular project was inadvertently left off the Project List, and the bond size and tax rates need to be changed. The board member who was a strong supporter suddenly wants additional information before agreeing to vote for the measure. And so on.

But taking action too early can also create problems. The more time between the board's action and the election, the more time for opposition to arise and organize. In addition, as odd as it sounds, having more time to put together the campaign in favor of the bond measure can sometimes work against you. A looming deadline gets people moving.

THE BOND RESOLUTION CALLING FOR THE ELECTION

Typically, bond counsel drafts the resolution calling for a bond election with input from the financial professionals. Every once in a while, a district will try drafting this resolution on its own, which is not a smart idea. This important document requires professional guidance.

Although different law firms will knit the resolution together in different ways, five major items need to be covered:

- A request to the county board of supervisors (and the county elections division) to place the bond measure on the ballot for an upcoming election.

- The basic facts surrounding the election, including the dollar amount of bonds to be approved, the date of the election, and whether the measure is being authorized under Prop. 39 or will require a two-thirds vote. If the measure is an SFID or reauthorization election, this also needs to be included.

- If the election is being run under Prop. 39, the resolution needs to include a number of certifications and declarations required under Article XIIIa and subsequent legislation. These items are then expanded on in the Full Ballot Text that is attached to the resolution as an appendix.

- Again, assuming a Prop. 39 election, the Full Ballot Text should incorporate the Project List. (This is required for a Prop. 39 measure but, as noted earlier, is now also customary in two-thirds measures.)

- The 75-word ballot language.

I always encourage clients to let us add a section in the resolution that gives the superintendent or assistant superintendent authority to make changes in the resolution to comply with the county's specific legal requirements. This saves a trip back to the board if a mistake is made or the county elections department suddenly decides to change its filing requirements – which happens more often than you might imagine.

THE FULL BALLOT TEXT

Legally Required Boilerplate

I recently met with a superintendent and her board president to review a draft of the resolution calling for a Prop. 39 bond measure that was on the board's upcoming agenda. After spending quite a bit of time tinkering with the 75-word ballot language, we turned to the Full Ballot Text. This document ran on for four or five pages and included not only the Project List but also a recital of the various provisions of the California Government Code and Education Code under which the bonds could be issued, as well as accountability requirements listed in Prop. 39.

"This just looks like a bunch of boilerplate to me," the board president objected.

He was right, of course. Prop. 39 and subsequent legislation require that a number of accountability requirements be included in any bond measure, and there's no reason for anyone to pay the legal costs of rewriting this verbiage from scratch. Here's a brief list of the boilerplate that needs to appear in the Full Ballot Text:

- a certification that the district has evaluated safety, class size and information technology needs in developing its list of school facilities projects;

- a statement that the school board will establish and appoint members to an independent Citizens' Oversight Committee;

- an agreement to conduct annual, independent performance audits to ensure that the funds have been expended only on the bond projects;

- an agreement to conduct an annual, independent financial audit of the bond funds;

- guidelines as to where the bond funds will be deposited; and

- a statement that the bond funds will not be used to fund teacher and administrator salaries or other operating expenses.

In addition, Education Section 15122.5 requires that if the district plans on using any matching state funds that have been promised – but not yet delivered – a statement must be placed in the sample ballot noting that approval of the bond measure does not guarantee that the proposed projects will receive any funding beyond the bond funds generated by the measure. In other words, a district that expects $10 million from the state can't go to the voters for $10 million and say, "We'll have $20 million if you say yes." The state money, though promised, is not guaranteed. So, all a $10 million bond issue will definitely raise is $10 million, and that's what voters must be told.

The Project List

The Project List is also included in the Full Ballot Text. Its inclusion is required under Prop 39's requirement that voters be given "a list of the specific school facilities projects to be funded."

There are no statutory guidelines or restrictions as to how projects on the Project List are to be presented. Nor is there any requirement that cost estimates for the various projects be included. Although it's done occasionally, unless certain projects are clear and absolute priorities, publishing a sequencing of the projects or a priority ranking of how the projects will be funded can be asking for trouble. (What happens if one of the projects gets delayed? Do all the others have to be put on hold as well?) And although there needs to be a certain level of specificity in the Project List, it needs to remain flexible enough to avoid playing havoc with any future change in priorities.

In general, projects are either presented as being provided district-wide (e.g., "repair and replace deteriorating roofs at schools throughout the district") or on a school-by-school basis (e.g., "build a computer lab at Jefferson Middle School"). These two methods can also be combined, with projects intended for specific schools listed first, and then non-specific projects listed in a separate section (e.g., "acquire land for construction of a new elementary school").

Regardless of how the projects are presented, it is critical to keep in mind that, as mentioned before, **unless a project appears on the list, it cannot be funded with bond monies. This point cannot be overemphasized**. I can tick off district after district that has called up after Election Day – in some cases years afterward – wondering if a certain project can be funded under the ballot language. And when that call comes in, it is the Project List that everyone turns to as the one and only source for a thumbs-up or thumbs-down.

However, even though a project cannot be funded unless it appears on the Project List, just because it appears on the list *doesn't* require that it be funded. For this reason, it is common practice to include more items on the Project List than can be funded by the amount of bonds for which voter approval is being sought.

Although this practice has been criticized as misleading to voters (and care should be taken not to list projects that have no actual chance of being funded), it does make a certain amount of sense. To begin with, it is impossible to know the final cost of all future projects. If the actual cost of a project comes in significantly lower than estimated (which often happened in the years after 2008 during the construction industry slowdown), the unused funds can be reallocated to other priority projects on the list.

In addition, the period in which bond funds are spent can often stretch over many years. During this time, the needs or priorities of a district may change. For this reason, even though a Project List needs to provide voters with as many specifics as possible, it must also be drafted broadly enough to allow for unanticipated changes.

DRAFTING THE 75-WORD BALLOT LANGUAGE

While preparing for a bond campaign, hours upon hours are spent sweating the details. The right team needs to be assembled. The Project List needs to be developed and approved. Decisions need to be made about a host of underlying assumptions about tax rates and assessed valuation, among other things. The underlying financial analysis needs to be checked and rechecked. Legal documents need to be drafted. County filing deadlines and requirements need to be confirmed. And on and on. And yet, important as all this work may be, there is nothing, to my mind, as critical to the overall success of the bond election as the 75-word ballot language that voters see, usually for the first time, when they look at their ballot.

This single sentence, which is approved by the district board as part of its resolution calling for a bond measure to be placed on the ballot, must be drafted in the form of a question, and is restricted to 75 words. It must communicate the essence of a bond measure, give voters an overview of how the funds will be spent and briefly describe what voter protections will be in place, including interest rate limitations, annual audits and review by a citizens' oversight committee. At the same time, it must comply with requirements found in both the Elections Code and Education Code (as well as a recent appellate court ruling, described below).

Ballot language is crucial because it's often the key factor voters use in deciding which box to check – "YES" or "NO". In fact, for many voters the ballot language will be the only information they read about the measure, and they'll read it for the first time as they're about to mark their ballots.

And yet, as critical as these 75 words are to success, too often writing the ballot language gets put off to the last minute. In some cases, drafting is handed off to a junior lawyer. In others, the consultant, whether out of laziness or overwork, simply cuts and pastes language from the last election he or she worked on. The result is dull, lazy ballot language filled with legal gobbledygook, tortured punctuation, and educational jargon.

I've had the privilege of writing ballot texts for many California districts. (So many, in fact, that I jokingly tell people that millions of Californians have read my writing over the years – 75 words at a time.) What I have learned from these efforts is that crafting effective ballot language takes time, patience, and a willingness to listen.

It needs not only to reflect the intentions of the district but also be understandable by the average voter. Draft language should be circulated to a wide cross-section of people – office support staff, older and younger teachers, a senior or two. You're not asking them whether or not they'll vote for the measure but, rather, if they understand what's written. Did they grasp it in one reading, or did they have to go back and start over? Were there words or phrases that didn't make sense?

Most important of all, the ballot language should:

- Be clear, concise, readable and free of ambiguous words and jargon.

- Give voters a general idea of how the funds are to be spent without being disingenuous. If half the funds are to be used for improvement of the high school gym, this project should appear in the ballot language, regardless of how well it did in the polls.

- Be neutral in tone and unbiased.

NO ELECTIONEERING ALLOWED

Over the past decade, there has been a trend to include phrases in the ballot language that extol the many benefits that will result from the passage of the bond. It's not unusual to see the opening words of the ballot language include phrases such as "To prepare veterans for good-paying jobs ..." or "To protect quality education ..." or "To prepare students for college success ..."

As tempting as it may be to pump up the ballot language with lofty promises, districts need to be wary of language that advocates (subtly or not so subtly) passage of the bond measure. A decision by the Sixth District Court of Appeal makes this point. In *McDonough v. Superior Court of Santa Clara* (2012) Cal. App. 4th 1169, the petitioners challenged the wording of a City of San Jose ballot measure (Measure B) that sought to modify the city's public pension system.

If passed, the city would have been allowed to make lower pension and retirement contributions for future employees, thereby making more money available for services. The municipal unions challenged the wording of the ballot measure, claiming its language was biased and advocated passage of the measure.

The ballot language started with the title "Pension Reform" and went on to read in part: "*To protect essential services, including neighborhood police patrols, fire stations, libraries, community centers, streets and parks ...*"

The court required the city to change the title from "Pension Reform" to "Pension Modification" and held that the introductory phrase to protect essential services "belong(s) in the ballot arguments in favor of the measure, not in the ballot question, which must be cast in neutral, unbiased language."

The court went on to note, "Even if the preservation of city services and resources is a compelling reason to vote in favor of Measure B, the advocacy inherent in the introductory language of the ballot question is partisan and prejudicial. Consequently, the ballot question must be amended to conform to the standards of impartiality required by the Elections Code."

AB 195: GAME CHANGER OR MEH?

As California school district financial advisors, underwriters, and bond lawyers wandered back into their offices from the New Year's holiday at the beginning of 2018, a slow-moving sense of shock, disbelief, and dread began to seep through the industry. Among the many emails that had piled up over the holidays were a handful of messages from various school finance law firms and lobbyists cataloguing those bills that had become law as of January 1, 2018. Lurking among these many new laws was one that nobody had ever heard of – AB 195.

The origins of AB 195 stretch back to 2015 when a republican assemblyman from Big Bear, California, named Jay Obernolte authored a bill (AB 809) aimed at ballot measures placed on the ballot through the *voter initiative process.*[12] This bill stipulated that if these ballot measures were to cause a tax increase, the 75-word ballot language for the measure needed to include wording that described the amount, rate, and duration of the tax increase. The bill became law on January 1, 2016.

In 2017, Obernolte introduced AB 195, which applied AB 809's requirements to *all local government ballot measures*, including school and college district general obligations bonds. Because the bill was described by the Senate Committee on Elections and Constitutional Amendments as a technical cleanup of AB 809, it effectively flew under the radar of every education lawyer and lobbyist, and became effective at the beginning of 2018. (By the way, the bill passed both the State Senate and Assembly without a single member voting in opposition.)

To be clear, referring to AB 195 as a *technical cleanup* bill is like calling Steph Curry a guy who occasionally likes to shoot hoops. As far as K-14 general obligations bonds are concerned, AB 195 has had the biggest single

---

12 "Initiatives are placed on the ballot through the collection of signatures of registered voters.

impact since the passage of Prop 39. Specifically, it now requires that the ballot language for all K-14 bond measures include:

- The amount of taxes to be raised annually;

- The rate of the tax to be levied; and

- The duration of the tax to be levied.

While this might appear to be a sound public policy that simply increases the level of a bond measure's transparency, remember that a K-14 bond ballot language is limited to 75 words, and there are already a fair number of required phrases that need to be included. So, the first problem AB 195 created was that, by muscling its way into what was already a very tight piece of real estate without so much as a please or thank you, it required that at least fifteen other words be tossed overboard.

The second problem was that, in order to wedge these newly required words into a 75-word ballot measure and still meet all the other legal requirements, as well as give the voter some idea of how the funds were going to be used, the AB 195 language had to be so dumbed-down that it became essentially useless to a voter trying to honestly understand how much a proposed bond measure might cost him or her.

And then there was a third problem – at least what many believed was going to be a problem. This was the potential impact that the AB 195 language might have on voters. Many industry insiders were quick to jump on the doom-and-gloom bandwagon, predicting that by providing voters information on a measure's tax impact, AB 195 would lead to the Armageddon of California GO bond elections.

A few polling firms began pumping out predictions that the wording would cause a *10% drop* in a bond measure's "yes" vote. This number was picked up by the school district lobbying industry, which (perhaps in atonement for being asleep at the switch when AB 195 was working its way through the legislature) began banging the drum for the immediate repeal of the measure before it could destroy those school bond measures queuing up for the 2018 ballot.

(Oddly, my firm's voter survey research showed just the opposite. We ran a dozen or so school bond voter surveys in 2018 and, in each of them, we used a technique known as a *split-sample*. Half of the voters being interviewed were read ballot language with the new AB 195 language included; the other half were read the older pre-AB 195 language. When we compared voter support between the two versions, there was rarely much difference. In fact, in some cases, support was actually *higher* with the AB 195 ballot language.)

Regardless, it appears that somebody in the State Legislature realized that *repealing* legislation that claimed to provide voters with *more* information about how much a bond would cost a voter might not be the swiftest of political moves, and the effort to bury the new AB 195 provisions quickly faded to gray.

Here's where the story gets interesting. The 2018 elections in June and November came and went, and there were 152 California K-14 GO bond elections on the ballot. Every one of them included this new – often tortured and indecipherable – AB 195 language describing the impact on taxes.

The impact? Murky at best. On the face of it, it appeared to have had zero impact. In fact, the percentage of California GO bonds that won in the 2018 midterm election (84%) was actually *higher* than in the 2014 midterm election (81%). However, voter turnout in November 2014 was only 42%. In 2018, voter turnout in California swelled to 65%. Some argue that were it not for the blue wave of democratic voters that turned out in 2018, the number of school bonds that passed would have nosedived.

There may be some logic to that argument. After all, nearly 95% of the California K-14 GO bonds were passed in the 2016 presidential election, in which voter turnout hit 75%. You would think that the passage rate in 2018 should have been closer to that of 2016 than 2014, given a 23-percentage point difference in those two elections – but who's to know?

The Plot Thickens

Even though the dire results that the anti-AB 195 pundits[13] had predicted failed to materialize in the 2018 elections, they nevertheless continued on with the battle into 2019. Early that year, a new bill – SB 268 – was introduced by Senator Wiener (D-San Francisco) that attempted to unwind the AB 195 disclosure requirements without being criticized for appearing to endorse *less* disclosure in ballot language. More *jujitsu* than *judo*, SB 268 allowed districts to strike the AB 195 tax rate disclosures out of the ballot language by requiring that they be moved into the tax rate statement (provided to all voters as part of the sample ballot). In place of these exiled words, a new phrase would be inserted: ***see voter guide for tax rate information.***

You have to admire the political deftness of SB 268. Instead of *replacing* the AB 195 language requirement, SB 268 sought to make this new wording an **option**, not a requirement. Those districts that still wanted to use the AB 195 language in crafting their bond measure ballot language could still do so; those who believed the AB 195 language to be confusing and harmful could run with the new language instead.

By allowing for a choice and pushing that choice down to the local level, it was hard to argue that anything was being taken away from anybody. But one of the perks of being governor is that when it comes to signing or vetoing a bill, you don't have to argue with anyone because the decision is yours and yours alone. And so, in mid-October 2019, nearly eight months to the day from when SB 268 had been introduced, Governor Gavin Newsom vetoed SB 268, citing his concerns that the bill would lead to "less transparency for bond tax and bond measures."

....

13 A Twitter-obsessed anti-school bond blogger who goes by the name *Big Bad Bonds* lovingly refers to this group as the *School Bond Cartel*. Even though I rarely agree with his opinions, he may be on to something in the case of the anti-AB 195ers. Made up of a loose coalition of school construction firms, bond lawyers, underwriters, lobbyists and financial advisors, the anti-AB 195 pushers were remarkable in both their lack of a formal structure and Ahab-like obsession.

Back to the Future

The fact is that AB 195 was a terribly drafted piece of legislation that should never have made it out of committee on day one. If its purpose was to better educate voters as to the cost of bond elections, it failed miserably. If, on the other hand, it was simply a political feint by those seeking to reduce the number of successful school bond elections, well, that also appears to have been a failure.

But for now, AB 195 isn't going away any time soon. So just grin and bear it.

BOARD PASSAGE OF THE RESOLUTION

All the planning, drafting, analysis and background work comes down to the board's action on the resolution calling for a bond election. For two-thirds elections, a simple majority of board members in attendance needs to approve the resolution. Prop. 39 elections, however, require approval of *two-thirds* of the board *seats*. For a five-person board, four "yes" votes are required; for a seven-person board, five "yes" votes are needed.

If everything goes according to plan, the board will have been part of the bond planning process from the beginning, and passage of the resolution is a foregone conclusion. But, as anyone who has ever worked with an elected board can tell you, sometimes getting those "yes" votes over the finish line can take a lot more effort and political know-how than is apparent from the outside looking in.

Getting It Over the Goal Line

Sometimes it's just dealing with a board member who is bound and determined to keep the item off the ballot (although why an elected official would want to deny citizens the right to vote "yes" or "no" on a proposed bond measure baffles me).

Other times, it happens when you walk into a board meeting thinking you've got all the votes nailed down, when suddenly – *wham!* – out of left field comes a sudden waffling of a board member who just days (if not hours) before had been 100 percent supportive.

The truth is that sometimes, even when you think it's a done deal, the votes just aren't there. But there are a few things you can do in advance to help get the resolution over the line. For example, as already mentioned, if the district already has a Citizens' Oversight Committee, it should make sure its members are briefed about the proposed bond and, if they are in support, arrange for one or more of them to make that support known at the board meeting. Not only are oversight committee members typically influential members of the community, their endorsement can subtly shift the calculus of the passage of the bond election resolution from being an internal board decision to a broad community mandate.

A roomful of supporters can also make a big difference. Having parents, members of local construction trade groups, representatives of the chamber of commerce, leaders of the PTA, etc. willing to stand up in front of the board in support of the bond measure is extraordinarily powerful.

The Role of the Superintendent

The role of the superintendent in this decision process cannot be overestimated. While I certainly understand the delicate position of a superintendent whose board members are split on such a major issue, in the end the superintendent is the professional leader of the district, and it is imperative that he or she be an active voice of support for the measure.

The importance of a superintendent's advocacy came home to me when I attended back-to-back school board meetings, one on a Monday evening in San Diego County, the other at a district in San Joaquin County the next night. Resolutions to place a bond on the upcoming November ballot were on both districts' agendas. Up until that week, both boards had shown medium-to-strong support for getting on the ballot.

At Monday night's board meeting, one board member announced he intended to vote against the resolution even before the board president had a chance to call for a motion. He'd had a change of heart, he said, and made an impassioned speech using the tried-and-true theme, "I'm not against the bond, but this isn't the right time."

When he'd finished, a second board member said she considered it critical that board support be unanimous. If any member had reservations, then the board needed to pull the item off the agenda.

The board chair, seeing the resolution about to go down in flames, turned to the superintendent. Did he have any thoughts or advice he would like to offer about the district's need for the bond measure?

"No," the superintendent mumbled, barely looking up from his papers. "I think we've already given the board all the information we can." And with that, the resolution died for lack of a motion.

Tuesday night at the San Joaquin County district, the meeting hadn't been going on long when it started to look like déjà vu all over again. One of the board members who had previously been highly supportive began showing signs of wavering. Was the district being too hasty, he wondered? Were they asking for too much from taxpayers? Had they really considered all the alternatives?

Without missing a beat, the superintendent jumped in. Speaking forcefully and frankly, he explained why the bond was critical to the educational mission of the district and laid out in detail what would and would not happen at the district's schools if the bond failed to be approved. One by one, the other four members also spoke in support and *each one* referred to the superintendent's remarks. When the vote came, it was 5–0 to proceed.

Finally, a comment on what I call the "*myth of the unanimous board.*" There is a deeply held belief among school and community college board members and many administrators that without a unanimous favorable board vote, the bond measure is sure to fail at the ballot box.

Based on my experience, this is simply not the case. Would it be nice to have 100 percent board support? Of course. But critical? No.

Think of your own voting behavior. When was the last time you voted against a bond measure because the vote by the board to place the item on the ballot was 4-to-1? For that matter, when was the last time you even knew what the vote was?

What really matters is how board members who oppose the bond behave after the board vote. If it's a simple matter of voting "no" on philosophical grounds, so what? Opposing members like these typically keep their opinions to themselves during the campaign, stay out of the way and then happily join everyone in a high-five at the victory party.

A bigger problem, however, is the board member who works loudly and publicly against the bond's passage. This situation, while rare, is dangerous, since voters are often looking for any reason to vote "no", and a vociferously opposed board member often provides that reason. Unless a board has polling data showing overwhelming voter support, it should consider waiting if an opposing board member promises to make his or her opposition clamorously public.

THE TAX RATE STATEMENT

The purpose of the Tax Rate Statement is to provide voters an estimate of the cost of the proposed bond issue. It is required under Sections 9400–9404 of the California Elections Code and is included as part of the sample ballot mailed to all registered voters.

The Tax Rate Statement is merely a projection of future tax rates, not a guarantee. However, this crucial difference is often forgotten or overlooked. Indeed, Tax Rate Statements generally incorporate language that spells out the variables its projections rely on.

Here's an example: "*Actual tax rates and the years in which they will apply may vary depending on the timing of bond sales ... and actual increases in assessed valuations. Actual assessed valuations will depend upon the amount and value of taxable property within the District as determined in the assessment and the equalization process.*"

The Elections Code requires that the Tax Rate Statement provide four tax rate estimates based on projected assessed valuations. These are:

- the average tax rate over the duration of the bond;

- the estimated tax for the first fiscal year *after the sale of the last series of bonds;*

- an estimate of the highest tax rate during any fiscal year; and

- an estimate of the total debt service, including the principal and interest, that would be required to be prepaid if all the bonds are issued and sold.

Although it is not legally required, we also suggest including the estimated *average* tax rate.

Even though the Elections Code stipulates that the stated tax rate estimates be provided per $100 of assessed valuation, it is now common practice to include the rate on a $100,000 basis. In addition, although it's not required, most Tax Rate Statements also provide an average tax rate.

The Tax Rate Statement is typically signed by the district's chief business official or superintendent. In the past, we always advised district officials to make sure they have written documentation specifying and justifying the underlying assumptions used to generate the estimated tax rates. The addition of the newly passed fourth requirement described below makes the documentation of assumptions even more critical.

FILING THE RESOLUTION WITH THE COUNTY

One of the most confusing and exasperating tasks associated with placing a GO bond on the ballot is the actual filing of the resolution with the county elections divisions. Even though there is a statewide election code, many counties impose their own rules and regulations. On top of this, recent budget cuts have reduced the ability of these offices to respond quickly to questions and concerns. While their employees do their best, the offices are often short-staffed, having lost many seasoned workers to early retirement.

For these reasons, give yourself plenty of time and be prepared for more than one trip to the county elections division. It seems that no matter how much advance preparation you do, you can never tell when the new person at the counter will suddenly discover an additional requirement that must be complied with.

Here are the major requirements needed to file a bond election resolution with the county:

- A certified copy of the resolution to the county Registrar of Voters, along with the cover letter explaining exactly what is to be done with the resolution. This should be hand-delivered if possible.

- A copy of the resolution, together with a cover letter to the clerk of the board of supervisors and the county superintendent of schools.

- A copy of the Tax Rate Statement. Although not every county requires that this document be filed at the same time as the resolution, it's simpler to file them together.

- If your district is in two or more counties, make sure you inform each of them. Determine early on which county will serve as "lead county" – usually, the county that contains most of the district; coordinate with the others and make sure they're all in the loop.

CHOOSING THE MEASURE LETTER

Campaign gurus make a big deal over the assigned measure letter (as in "Measure A") that appears on the ballot, imbuing the various letters of the alphabet with talisman-like qualities. "God help us if we get Measure T," they whisper, worrying over a subliminal connection to "tax." Equally bemoaned are Measure F (as in "failure") and Measure D (as in the grade – "near failure").

Some county election departments have simply dropped those letters altogether, probably out of fatigue from fighting with campaign consultants. While these letters might help an opponent concoct a hit piece against the campaign, the truth is the choice of a letter doesn't make much difference. Again, think of your own behavior. When did you last vote for or against any ballot measure because of its letter?

Still, there have been a few times when the assigned letter was so awful, we had to insist on a new one. We were once running a bond measure campaign for Pomona Unified School District. I've never figured out if the elections officials in Los Angeles County thought they were being funny or helpful (albeit clueless), or if they were simply diabolical. Whatever the case, they proudly informed us that Pomona Unified's bond measure would be on the ballot as Measure PU. After a few stern calls from the superintendent, it was changed to Measure PS.

YES ON "Sĺ"

Some consultants (including me) can get a little too clever. San Diego County once denied my request to name a bond Measure SI. It was for a district near the Mexican border and we figured it wouldn't hurt to name the bond "Sí," the Spanish opposite of "no." *Pero los funcionarios del condado dijeron, "No."* (But the county officials said, "No.")

THE ARGUMENT AND THE REBUTTAL

Second only to the ballot language in importance, the argument gives a district the chance to state its case for the bond measure to voters. In addition, it provides a vehicle for the endorsement of the measure by influential decision-makers in the community.

Drafting the Argument

Ballot arguments are limited to 300 words. Before spending too much time drafting the argument, make sure to contact the county elections division to obtain its style guidelines. Every county seems to have its own idiosyncratic method of how words are to be counted, and what may or may not be included in the formatting. For example, Ventura County counts each word in a district's name, but Santa Clara County treats a district's name as just one word. Words in boldface are allowed in San Diego County, can be used no more than 30 times in Los Angeles County, and are forbidden in Ventura County.

In fact, Ventura County stands as a leader in persnickety requirements. Here's an excerpt from the county's Argument Format Guide: *"Author(s) of arguments and rebuttals are required to type their statement, in block format, and upper and lower case letters. No centering allowed. The recommended type size is 12 point. Some words may be in ALL CAPITAL LETTERS or in any combination, to show emphasis only. The number of capitalized words is limited to ten. Bold and underlined words, graphics, and characters such as arrows, stars, asterisks and other symbols are not permitted."*

As with the ballot language, the argument should be easily understood by all readers and free of educational jargon. However, unlike the ballot language, which must be neutral, the argument should strongly advocate passage of the bond and explain why it is in both the students' and the community's best interests.

The argument is typically drafted by the political or financial consultant. Make sure they take the time to hand-tailor the argument to your community rather than simply recycling an argument from a past campaign. What issues and projects are seen as critical to your community? Look at the demographics of the voters. Republican or Democratic? Young households or retired couples? Urban, suburban, or rural? The answers should shape the overall arc of the argument.

For example, in a conservative community, the argument might stress how it's a conservative plan put together to provide fiscally sound management and protect the community's resources. In a suburban district, it may be more about preparation for higher education. In a rural community, it might be more about vocational education. In an urban environment, it might be more about having high-quality schools for the children. Communities with many retired people are much more supportive of school bonds than stereotypes would suggest. The key there is to present an argument that stresses reasonable tax rates and conservative, common-sense planning.

Beware of local landmines. For example, in one poll we recently conducted for a Central Coast district, the use of bond funds to repair student restrooms ranked dead last in voter support. In follow-up interviews with the district, we discovered that cost overruns on previous school restroom repairs had been a source of major controversy.

When drafting arguments for district bond elections, it's easy to fall into the "it's for the children" trap. Remember that in most districts a significant portion of voters do not have or *never have had* children in the local schools. These voters need to hear why the measure is in the best interests of the community at large, not just the students. Housing values? Safe neighborhoods? A better-educated workforce? These can all resonate with non-parent voters.

Also, remember that you're presenting an argument, not a civics lesson. Too often districts want to use the argument to educate voters about what a good job they've done with their past bond funds or balancing their budget. But unless these are hot-button issues, don't waste your 300 words. And don't forget that sometimes issues that have nothing to do with the bond measure can be the most powerful argument. For example, every California K–14 finance professional knows that bond funds cannot be used to fund administrators' pensions. But voters don't know that, and this may be just what they need to know to vote "yes".

Who Should Sign the Argument?

The argument can be signed by up to five people. Although the resolution typically authorizes the board and the superintendent to sign the argument, most people will already assume that the board is in support of the bond's passage. So, unless a board member is a highly visible and trusted member of the community, you'll get more mileage from having other civic leaders and opinion-shapers (rather than board members) sign the argument.

The best way to generate this list of potential signers is to ask your board members, administrators and union reps for recommendations. Who do they think are the most highly respected leaders in the community? Whose signature would make a difference to someone reading the ballot argument? Potential signatories should enjoy high *positive* name recognition.

For this reason, it's generally best to steer clear of elected officials, who tend to have detractors as well as supporters. Unless you can get a "balanced ticket" with signatures from respected Democratic and Republican officials, it's best to seek other signers. The only exception is for an elected official who is widely admired in the community, regardless of party. In that case, try as hard as you can to get her or his signature.

Other attractive signatories can be recruited from the ranks of respected professions, including:

- firefighters

- police officers and deputy sheriffs

- community sports league or high school coaches

- teacher of the year

- beloved retired principal

- clergy

- small business owner (especially an accountant)

Once you've assembled the list of names, pull together a small group of people who understand the dynamics of the community. Identify at least 12 potential signers, and then rank the names in order of their influence throughout the district, paying special attention to diversity in such areas as race, gender, neighborhood, religion, age and profession.

ASKING PEOPLE TO SIGN THE ARGUMENT

Even though you need only five signatures for the argument, it's a good idea to reach out to all twelve people on this list. Invariably, some will be out of town, some will prefer not to sign, and others won't meet your county's qualifications.

Most but not all counties require that the signatory be a registered voter in the district. If you identify the "perfect" candidate to sign the argument but find that he or she doesn't live in the district, check your county's regulations. And, as discussed below, if an argument is filed against the bond measure, you may need additional signatories, beyond the initial five, to sign the rebuttal.

There will probably be a handful of people on the list who will agree to sign the argument without any questions. But others will need some time.

Even though most people will be flattered to have been asked, they may also have concerns about putting their name in the public eye.

If you can, sit down with these people for a face-to-face in which you present all the reasons this bond measure is important to the community. Ask your financial consultant to prepare a short FAQ regarding the bond measure, including proposed projects, the term of the bonds, the cost to the taxpayers, etc.

In addition to a copy of the proposed argument, you'll need to bring each potential signatory a copy of the signature form required by the county. Each county has different regulations regarding this form but, in most cases, the signatures can be on separate pages that are then compiled for submission.

If possible, keep gathering signatures even after you've obtained the fifth one. This is partly so you can mix and match the signatures for purposes of diversity, and partly because the county will occasionally disqualify a signatory and you'll be happy to have a backup. Just make sure you circle back to those people whose signatures you don't end up using to explain why, and that you may be calling on them later if an argument is filed against the bond and a rebuttal is needed, or for a general endorsement.

The signature form will have a space to list the person's "title." This is a self-descriptive title that is instrumental in giving voters a better picture of a signatory's background and credentials. Some examples of these titles include:

- Building and Trade Counsel Representative

- CEO, Chamber of Commerce

- Chairperson, Community Development Corporation

- Minister and Founder, Christian Youth Network

- Parent and Citizen of the Year

- Past President, Optimists Club

Filing the Argument

And you thought filing the resolution was a pain. Every county in the state has its own idiosyncratic criteria for how it wants the argument filed. Some counties require that it be filed by one of the signatories. Others require the person who files the argument to also file an affidavit as the filer. We've had counties require the superintendent to file a statement taking responsibility for the authorship of the argument. We've had a county require that a certain form be filed by the signatories, and then change its mind and demand the district re-file with a different form.

Make sure you call ahead to find out exactly what needs to be filed, but don't be surprised if the instructions change again before you show up at the election department. In other words, be flexible and leave plenty of time for hiccups.

The Rebuttal

Anyone who wants to can file a ballot argument against the bond measure. (If more than one argument is filed in opposition, it is up to the county elections department to decide which will be printed.) The deadline for an argument in opposition is the same as the argument in favor.

If no argument is filed against the measure by the filing deadline, then no further action is required. If, however, an opposing argument is filed, then both the supporting and opposing camps have the opportunity to file a rebuttal to the other side's argument.

The rebuttal is limited to 250 words. It is typically due about two weeks after the filing date for the argument, but be sure to double-check that deadline with the county.

The rebuttal offers a chance to refute and respond to the claims made in the opposing party's argument. But even when an argument is filed against the bond measure, we rarely recommend using the rebuttal to respond directly to the opposition. Most opposing arguments are so poorly written, uninformed, shrill, and, at times, downright loony that they serve as their own best rebuttals. Trying to respond rationally is almost always a waste of time.

Better to ignore rambling denunciations and use the rebuttal to restate the case for the bond, emphasizing its benefits and adding any facts that wouldn't fit in the original 300-word argument.

In that rare instance when the opposition's argument is a well-reasoned, well-written attack on the management of the district, you need to quickly, deftly, and *calmly* refute the claims with facts (leaving emotion out of it), then quickly return to the theme of why the bond is in the best interests of the community's voters.

SIGNING AND FILING THE REBUTTAL

The signatories on the district's rebuttal to opponents' ballot argument can be the same as the original five, or they can be five new names. If the district has five new signatories for the rebuttal, when the ballot is printed voters will see the names of ten prominent citizens – five on the argument, five on the rebuttal – lined up in favor of the bond measure.

Here's where all the work you put into lining up those dozen signatures for the argument pays off. With just a few confirmation phone calls, you'll have five fresh signatures for the rebuttal. Better than that, it is almost certain that the opposition will not have it together enough to go out and find five additional signatures for its rebuttal in addition to the signatures on the original "no" argument. (In fact, more often than not, oppositions can't get five people to sign their original argument.)

The district's rebuttal to the opponents' argument needs to be filed separately with the county elections division. Once again, county offices differ wildly in what they require. Most counties are fine with the signatories of the rebuttal being different than the signers of the original argument. But in some counties, elections officials require one of the original argument signatories to give consent for people other than the original five to sign the rebuttal, and in other counties officials look askance if anyone other than the argument's original five sign the rebuttal.

In other words, be ready for a sleigh ride and, as always, be flexible and plan ahead when working with the county elections office. My advice to clients is to find a knowledgeable election official, stay in touch with that person, and use her or him as your main point of contact.

Chapter
SEVEN

....

THE DISTRICT AND VOTER INFORMATION

....

"Show me a good loser and I'll show you a loser."

~ Vince Lombardi

DISTRICT DO AND DON'T LIST[14]

Once the resolution calling for the bond election is filed with the county elections department, it's a whole new ballgame with new rules. The district is now officially on the ballot and with this new status comes a host of restrictions – and potentially severe penalties – regarding what district employees and board members may and may not do on behalf of the bond.

Note that the title of this chapter is The District and Voter Information. We'll get to the actual campaign mechanics in the next chapter, but don't overlook the critical need for the involvement – the legal involvement – of the district in providing voters with information on how the passage or failure

....

[14] Much of this section is based on analysis prepared by the law firm Jones Hall, to which I give special thanks.

of the bond will impact the educational mission of each district school or campus. This is of overwhelming importance to the outcome of the election.

Placing a bond measure on the ballot brings with it a heightened level of public scrutiny from both the press and opponents of the measure. District representatives must take special care not only to abide by all applicable laws but also to avoid even the *appearance* of stepping over the line regarding advocacy for the bond.

After the passage of the resolution, the district administration should immediately distribute a simple, reader-friendly memo to all district employees outlining a do and don't list pertaining to activities concerning the bond measure. (Bond counsel will typically draft this memo.) If possible, distribute the memo via email so there is a record of who received it. To be extra sure, ask each recipient to acknowledge receiving and reading the memo.

What District Activities Are Restricted?

Education Code Section 7054 specifically prohibits the use of school district resources (including supplies and equipment) "for the purpose of urging the passage or defeat of any ballot measure." In addition, the California Legislature strengthened these prohibitions in 1995 with the passage of SB No. 82 (Kopp), which makes such use of district resources a felony. SB 82 is no toothless watchdog: punishment for violations of these restrictions can include both hefty fines and jail time.

This prohibition includes the use by district board members, administrators and employees of district funds, equipment, facilities or any other district resources to advocate the passage (or defeat) of a measure. This includes the use of district copy machines, supplies, postage, etc.

If any activities related to the bond measure are undertaken during business hours (e.g., a lunchtime presentation), care must be taken not to advocate passage of the bond measure, but rather merely to provide information about the bond and election. Alternatively, district employees can participate in campaign activities during the workweek by taking vacation days (or hours). Keep careful records of any such time taken.

The prohibition also includes the indirect use of district resources, such as an administrator's or other employee's time, or the use of district vehicles to drive to meetings or rallies in support of the bond measure.

A district may not spend funds to hire a campaign consultant. Likewise, if a campaign consultant is hired by an independent citizens' committee, the consultant may not have free use of district equipment. Neither may he or she use the services of district staff during business hours.

The question often comes up whether district facilities can legally be used *after school hours* for meetings by the citizens' campaign committee. Although the answer is yes (as long as the committee is not given any special treatment and the district has a policy of making these facilities available to other community organizations), the district should weigh how holding such meetings on district property might be perceived.

Similar questions have also arisen regarding the use of district electronic information. For example, I recently received an email from a campaign volunteer who also happened to work in the district's IT department. He knew the district couldn't send pro-bond emails to the district's email list of student parents but thought he'd come up with a clever work-around:

"What if I requested the parent email list be sent to my personal email address, and then I sent emails about the bond to parents from my home computer? That way I wouldn't be using any district resources, right?"

"Possible," I responded. "Here's the question you need to ask yourself: If an opponent of the bond measure asked you to send him copies of all the parent email addresses, would you do it?"

"So much for that idea," he shrugged.

What District Activities Are Permitted?

The Education Code allows district resources to be used to provide information to the public about a ballot measure so long as the information is fair and impartial. In preparing such information, a district needs to be cautious not to cross the line into advocacy. For example, a district might send a press release to the local newspaper or insert an article into the parent newsletter explaining the purpose of the bond measure, but not calling for its support.

Likewise, a message reminding voters to cast a ballot on Election Day is permissible as long as the message is simply a reminder to "vote" and not about how to vote. Materials like these should be closely scrutinized by bond counsel before being published, to ensure their presentation is fair and unbiased.

School district administrators and board members may also appear before citizens' groups to discuss and explain the bond measure and answer questions about the use of bond funds, the cost to property owners, the timing of the projects, etc. However, if these talks are made by school district employees during business hours, the remarks must be limited to explaining the facts and not advocating the measure's passage.

What Personal Activities Are Permitted?

Board members and district employees have a First Amendment right to make their opinions heard regarding the proposed bond and to participate in campaign activities, so long as no district funds are used directly or indirectly. Likewise, board members and employees are not prohibited from soliciting donations for the campaign, so long as the money is raised on behalf of a citizens' campaign committee and fundraising activities are confined to after-business hours. Although board members and employees are free to contribute their own time and money to the campaign, the district cannot require them to do so.

DISTRICT COMMUNICATIONS

Communicating with District Employees

In every voter survey we conduct for a proposed bond measure, we ask people how they receive most of their information about their school district. While numerous sources are mentioned – e.g., local newspapers, the district's website, online news, and family and friends – a sizable percentage tell us they receive most of their information from the district's employees: teachers, administrators, and other staff members.

For this reason, it is critical that *all district employees* be fully informed as early as possible about the bond, including why the district has placed the measure on the ballot, and be given information regarding the proposed projects and the estimated cost to taxpayers.

For smaller districts, this can be achieved through an all-hands-on-deck meeting at the district office. Larger districts should organize a series of meetings with management teams, equipping them to cascade the information to their staffs. Regardless of the method, take care not to violate SB82's restrictions on use of district resources to advocate the bond measure.

Have copies of a "Do and Don't List" memo (drawn up by bond counsel) as well as an FAQ handout. Keep in mind that not all district employees will be bond supporters and that these opponents will pounce on any crossing of the line between legitimate dissemination of information and improper advocacy.

Communicating with Parents

Not surprisingly, voters with children in local schools are usually among the biggest supporters of a school bond measure. For example, in a voter survey we conducted for Bellflower Unified School District in 2012, 70 percent of the respondents with children currently in the schools supported the measure. Among parents who formerly, but no longer, had children in the schools, support fell to 55 percent.

In general, the challenge is not getting parents to support the bond measure; it's getting them to vote. Like many younger people, parents tend to be sporadic voters who generally turn out for presidential elections but often skip others.

Again, using the Bellflower USD as an example, we found that residents between ages 18 and 44 made up nearly half of all registered voters, but only 12 percent of those who had voted in all of the last three elections. People over age 65, however, made up only 17 percent of registered voters, but 45 percent of those who'd voted in all of the last three elections.

Accordingly, it's imperative for districts to communicate frequently, forcefully and effectively with district parents – not only about the objective facts of the bond issue but also how important it is to get out and vote. Use all available parental communications channels to get this message out, but be careful to advocate only *voting*, not support of the bond measure. A good parent turnout will be all the electioneering you'll need.

Communicating with District Voters

Districts also need to reach out to non-parent voters. Most often these communications are PowerPoint presentations made by administration or board members to local organizations and service clubs. Again, for employees of the district, these presentations must remain factual and free of electioneering, unless they are being made outside of work hours. ("Work hours" in the modern world is often any time at all, but for the purpose of following the law the traditional definition applies: approximately 8 a.m. to 5 p.m., Monday through Friday.)

Board members have more leeway in presentations like these, so long as no district resources were used in the preparation or presentation of a report advocating bond passage. In some districts, members of the board will organize themselves into a Speakers Bureau, where each board member meets with as many community groups as possible to urge passage of the bond.

Districts can also communicate with voters by mail. Mailings can range from a simple postcard listing relevant facts about the bond to a much fuller description of the measure, including the Project List and the overall facility needs of the district. Mailings may also include a letter from the superintendent or chancellor with photos of repairs to be made or architectural renderings of proposed projects.

The design and content of these mailings must be crafted carefully. They must be objective and factual – free of any campaign tone. They must be mailed to all voters, not just parents (that is, likely supporters). The design should be professional and clean, but not fancy or obviously expensive.

In choosing a printer, if possible have the job done locally rather than through a major print and mail house. The more dollars spent within the district the better, since the print shop and its employees might then talk positively about the bond election. Understand that in larger districts the production and mailing of such a piece can be quite costly, even when using standard postage rates. You need to balance the benefit of informing voters about the proposed bond measure with potential criticism of "wasting" district dollars on a "slick" piece of mail.

....

Special Topic #7
WHEN AND HOW VOTERS GET THEIR BALLOTS

Much of the information provided to the county elections office by a district that's putting a bond measure on the ballot is provided to voters in the run-up to Election Day. However, just exactly who gets what, and when, depends on what kind of voter you are.

The county elections department produces two official documents for each election: the *sample* ballot and the *official* ballot that is marked and cast by each voter. The sample ballot is more of a booklet than a ballot, and includes not only a copy of the ballot but also background information on the candidates, candidate statements, ballot propositions and bond measures, arguments in favor, arguments against, and rebuttals.

For a proposed school district or community college district bond election, the sample ballot also includes the Full Ballot Text, the tax rate statement, and any arguments and rebuttals filed favoring or opposing the measure. The sample ballot is typically mailed to all voters about a month before Election Day.

What day a voter receives the official ballot depends on how that person has registered to vote. A person can register either as a poll voter or a *permanent absentee voter* (PAV). Poll voters receive their official ballots at their polling place on Election Day. But PAVs receive their official ballot in the mail at roughly the same time as the sample ballot. After marking their selections on the official ballot, they mail it in any day before Election Day. (PAVs can also drop off their ballot at any polling place on Election Day.)

Prior to 2015, PAV ballots had to be received – not post-marked – by the county elections division by the time the polls close. That changed with the passage of SB 29 (effective January 1, 2015). Under this revision of the Elections Code, PAV ballots are to be counted if they are (a) received no later than three days after Election Day, and (b) postmarked on or before Election Day.

For most school bond elections, the impact of this change is murky. But for those few cliffhanger elections where victory hangs in the balance by a handful of votes, this change could be a lifesaver.

Chapter
EIGHT

....

RUNNING A CAMPAIGN

....

"There are many elements to a campaign. Leadership is number one. Everything else is number two."

~ Bertolt Brecht

A WALK DOWN MEMORY LANE

In the good old days (circa 1990), a couple of very bright campaign professionals developed a model of winning California K–14 bond elections that was quickly dubbed the *stealth campaign*. Although they adamantly denied (at least in public) that their program was anything close to a stealth campaign, it's pretty hard to come up with a better way to describe it.

The technique involved first picking the most obscure election date possible so the bond election would be the only item on the ballot – and on a day that no one associated with voting. Recall that this was before Prop. 39, and that two-thirds elections could be held on pretty much any Tuesday. Next, the campaign committee held a phone bank and asked every voter they could reach whether they would support the bond measure. "Yes" responses were put in a special file for subsequent contacts. "Undecideds" were sent a mailer explaining the bond program and its benefits and targeted for a follow-up call. "No" voters were crossed off the list and never contacted again.

By the time Election Day came around, the "no" voters had, in most cases, barely heard about the bond measure other than having received a sample ballot in the mail. But the "yes" voters had received a couple of pieces of campaign mail, an application to apply to vote absentee, and more than a few reminder calls to vote "yes" on Election Day. There were even people standing by to drive "yes" voters to the polls if they needed a ride.

Remember that you needed *two-thirds of the ballots cast* to win an election. If the district had, say, 50,000 voters and only 10 percent showed up to vote (and in some cases, that was a high turnout), the campaign would need just 3,334 "yes" votes to win. That works out to fewer than 7 percent of registered voters.

In most cases, the opposition never knew what hit them. I remember once running a don't-call-it-a-stealth campaign in a midsized school district in the middle of Los Angeles County. The week before the election, I was with the superintendent at Bingo night at the local senior center, chatting up some of the locals. I asked one of the players, a woman who was following five or six cards at once, what she thought about the school's bond measure on the upcoming ballot.

"Ain't gonna win," she said without looking up.

"And why's that?" I asked.

"Because," she said, looking up at me like I was the village idiot, "nobody's heard a word about it!"

The measure passed by 74 percent.

FAST FORWARD

The passage of Prop. 39 was the beginning of the slow death of the stealth campaign. Indeed, I think it's a safe bet that one of the main reasons Prop. 39 requires bond measures to be held only on regularly scheduled election dates is to put a stake through the stealth campaign's heart.

But on top of that, the world of school bond campaigns has changed dramatically over the years. A little over a decade ago, school bond measures weren't well understood by voters and could easily be overlooked by potential opponents. Not today. Keeping anything a stealthy secret in the world of 24-hour social media is impossible.

So, the game has changed. The stealth strategy of holding your cards close to the vest has given way to one of building a broad-based organization, capable of using a variety of media (direct mail, social media, newspapers) to stay on message.

Starting up a campaign today is similar to what business consultants would refer to as a *pop-up business*. In the beginning, there's no money, no staff, and no office space. You have only a handful of people (if that) who need to immediately jump in and build an organization from scratch in an atmosphere of intense deadlines, uncertain funding, a maze of state regulations, press scrutiny, and local politics. In the course of a few short months, a strategy needs to be crafted, funds raised, volunteers recruited, materials prepared, and the campaign launched.

And then, come Election Day, it all disappears.

FIRST STEPS

A few years ago, I was meeting with the chancellor of a small California community college district who was thinking about placing a GO bond on the ballot. He was optimistic about the chances of winning and eager to start improvements at the various campuses throughout the district. But I could tell that something was troubling him, some piece of the puzzle was giving him heartburn.

"I'm worried about the timing," he finally admitted. "Do you really think there's enough time to pull this off?"

Of all the things I could have imagined him obsessing about, this one caught me off guard. The election date we were discussing was over a year away.

But after we'd talked some more, I began to understand the source of his anxiety. A number of years before, he'd been a deputy chancellor at a much larger community college that had run a monster bond campaign – scores of volunteers, weekly phone banks, tons of slick mail and a budget the size of Kansas. He couldn't imagine how he'd be able to put anything like that together without months and months of preparation.

There Are Many Paths through Central Park

My conversation with the chancellor reminded me of an old New Yorker cartoon of an architect designing a skyscraper. He's hunched over his desk with a pair of scissors, cutting out the shape of a building from large roll of paper with pre-printed rows and rows of windows. Framed on the wall behind him are pictures of other buildings he's designed, each a different size and shape but all cut from the same roll of paper and looking exactly the same.

This tendency toward sameness also plagues a number of campaign consultants. But, as I told the chancellor, when it comes to K–14 bond elections, it's a mistake to assume there is only one way to run a successful campaign. I've run and won campaigns with six-figure budgets and others that could barely scrape enough money together to pay for a robocall. I've had campaigns with more volunteers than we knew what to do with and others without a single volunteer except for the superintendent using his vacation days to make calls to voters.

The fact is, there are many, many paths to success (although, to be fair, there are also a few strategies that will lead to certain disaster). The hard part is finding the one that works in your community's unique circumstances and with the amount of resources you can realistically obtain.

PULLING TOGETHER THE CAMPAIGN

The Professionals

Designing and running a political campaign is not part of your typical school administrator's skill set. For this reason, most districts are unwilling to risk placing an item before the voters without the help of a campaign consultant. Figuring out what firm – and what type of firm – to hire is the campaign's first challenge.

PROFESSIONAL CAMPAIGN ADVISORS

Over the years, California school district election consulting has split into two camps. On one side are the traditional campaign advisory firms that specialize in school bond campaigns. These firms are highly skilled in political strategy, produce excellent voter mail, and have a deep understanding of organizing a campaign. The downside is that they can be expensive. This is especially difficult for smaller and midsized districts whose campaign committees would typically be unable to raise enough money to hire these pros.

To deal with this problem, most campaign advisory firms now use a two-step fee process. While California law prohibits K–14 districts from spending public funds to advocate the passage of a bond issue, a district can hire a consultant to assist in the preparation and planning of a ballot measure before it is actually placed on the ballot. So, a campaign advisory firm often seeks to contract with the district for a monthly retainer in this preparatory period, often for $3,000 to $7,000 or more a month. Then, when the board takes action to get on the ballot, the consultant's contract with the district expires and it flips into a new and separate agreement with the campaign committee.

USING THE FINANCIAL ADVISOR TO RUN THE CAMPAIGN

An alternative approach is for the campaign to be run by the same firm that serves as the district's financial advisor. This method is offered by a handful of firms around the state (including mine). After the district passes a resolution to get on the ballot, the financial advisor signs a separate agreement with the campaign committee to provide election consulting services.

Under this approach, the financial advisor provides many of the same services offered by the campaign professionals in the period leading up to the district's passing a resolution to get on the ballot. However, unlike the campaign advisory firms, the financial advisor typically offers these services on a contingent fee basis; i.e., payment is made only if the election is successful.

The main advantage of this model is that the district pays the advisory fees only if the measure passes. While I still hear occasional sniping about this type of agreement creating a conflict of interest,[15] most of our K–14 clients

....

15 In July 1997, the Libertarian Party of Ventura County sued Dale Scott & Company and the Ventura Unified School District, alleging misuse of public funds. The case was dismissed on summary judgment due to lack of evidence.

appreciate the willingness of a private sector firm to tie its compensation solely to its performance.

THE ROLE OF THE CAMPAIGN ADVISOR

Regardless of how chosen, the campaign consultant plays a major role in determining if and when a bond package is ready to go to the voters. Consultants can help craft the project list, assess the impact of local political issues on the timing of a potential bond election, help interpret poll results, and talk with stakeholders and critics to ensure questions are answered and concerns are addressed.

Make sure there's clarity regarding any potential conflicts between your district's goals and the financial incentives of the election consultant. This is rare, but I have seen it cause problems now and then. If, for example, the election consultant is being paid a monthly retainer by the district, it's not necessarily in the consultant's best interest to get the district on the ballot as soon as possible. On the other hand, an election consultant who will be paid only after the election may want to push the district onto the ballot earlier than needed.

Building a Strategy

Before the first campaign meeting, before any thoughts about logos, Facebook pages or catchy slogans, you should spend time focusing on your voters – demographics, past turnout, party registration, and any recent significant changes in their makeup. As obvious as this sounds, it's amazing how many advisors skip this step in their rush to put a district on the ballot.

VOTER TURNOUT

Voter turnout is the *key driver* in determining the scope, direction and strategy of the upcoming campaign. More often than not, high turnout works in your favor since the less likely a person is to vote, the more likely he or she is to be your supporter. In other words, low-turnout elections tend to bring out the conservative voter who is usually – but not always – more likely to vote against a school bond. High-turnout elections (e.g., presidential elections) will attract younger, more casual, less conservative voters who are more likely to be school bond supporters.

However, the flip side is that while high-turnout elections tend to bring out more supportive voters, a larger turnout means you'll need a bigger budget to reach this larger voter pool. In addition, high-turnout elections typically have a lot of other hot-button issues on the ballot (e.g., presidents, senators, marijuana, gay marriage, single-sex bathrooms, etc.). These issues suck the oxygen out of the room and make it very hard to get your message across. Which means even more money.

WHAT'S THE BEST WAY TO COMMUNICATE WITH YOUR VOTERS?

Some districts are so spread out that the only effective method of communication is the U.S. mail. In others, it's ringing doorbells, plastering the streets with yard signs, setting up a table in front of the post office, or renting a booth at the local fair. Again, one size does not fit all, and you need to beware of campaign consultants that try to apply a cookie-cutter campaign strategy regardless of the local lay of the land.

I once visited a district in Monterey County that had just lost a bond election by a pretty sizable margin. Over 70 percent of the voters there were Hispanic and 10 percent requested ballots in Spanish. In glancing through the mail that had been sent in the losing campaign, I was stunned to see that it wasn't bilingual.

"I know," said the superintendent when I asked her why. "I kept asking 'Shouldn't we be printing the campaign fliers in English and Spanish?' but they said it would be a waste of time because, in their experience, most voters spoke English."

WHICH VOTERS SHOULD YOU FOCUS ON?

The best response to the question of which voters you should focus on is, of course, *all of them*. That's what Soledad USD did – to an extreme degree – with their 2012 GO bond election.

As part of the overall election strategy, we had scheduled a *Get Out the Vote* ("GOTV") walk a weekend or two before Election Day to hand out *Vote Yes* brochures. For most GOTV walks, we produce a "walk map" for each volunteer that lists the addresses of targeted voters: i.e., registered voters who are likely supporters.

"No maps," the campaign chair said, cutting me off as I started taking him through the logistics of the walk. I should add that the campaign chair was the town's former mayor. In other words, he knew the local politics inside out. He was also used to giving, not receiving, instructions.

"But without maps," I asked, "how will the walkers know what doors to knock on?"

"They're knocking on every door."

"*Every* door?"

"Every door."

"But why waste time talking to people who aren't even registered?" I asked. "Plus, you'll need an enormous number of volunteers to cover the entire town."

"You worry about the brochures," he said. "I'll worry about the volunteers."

"Okay," I said, then paused, reluctant to push him any further but still totally lost.

"Why are we doing this again?" I finally asked.

After a long pause, he said, "I want people to know that they can improve their kids' schools by voting. Hopefully, that's enough to turn a few of them into voters next time around."

The bond got a 75 percent "yes" vote, so it's hard to argue with the mayor's strategy. But unless, like the mayor, you can call on an unlimited supply of volunteers and you have plenty of campaign contributions, you're going to need a strategy for how to allocate your resources. And that leads straight to the question of which voters to focus on.

There are two schools of thought on this topic. By far the most common is the *preaching to the choir* strategy. By this I mean concentrating on those voters who you have every reason to believe are likely to vote "yes". This includes not only parents but also those demographics that have been identified as likely supporters (e.g., newly registered voters, middle-aged Republican women, younger independents, etc.).

This strategy works great in districts that tend to have more liberal voters, especially in a high-turnout election. So, for example, as of late 2019 over 80 percent of registered voters in the South Bay Union SD in San Diego County are registered as Democrats. So, when trying to reach voters in the district, it's pretty clear who the target audience is. But in the Bonsall USD, an hour up the road in northern San Diego County, the number of registered Democrats falls to 56 percent.[16] In other words, even if every Democrat and independent in the district cast a ballot in a bond election (which they won't) and they all voted "yes" (which they won't), you would just barely win without Republican voter support.

The contrarian strategy bears some risk but, in my experience, works well in high-turnout elections in the more conservative districts, especially when the campaign budget is tight. This approach turns the stealth strategy inside out. Voters you assume to be supporters are ignored. Remember, we're talking about high-turnout elections. The theory is that you can safely ignore these voters because all the excitement and publicity of a high-profile election will bring them to the polls. And once in the voting booth, they'll be voting for your school bond.

Instead, the focus is on the likely "no" voter, the one that stealth-election strategists treated as if they had rabies. Don't expect to convert this bloc into tax-and-spend liberals. The strategy is to explain why the bond is fiscally prudent, producing positive economic results for the entire community. The hope is to change enough likely "no" voters' minds, pushing the needle into "yes" territory. (Of course, it helps if your argument is true. Arguing like this for a Powayesque bond structure is not a smart move.)

....

16 Also, keep in mind that the independent voter can cover a wide spectrum. While I can't prove it, my bet is that the average independent voter in South Bay leans to the left while the independent in Bonsall considers the Republican party *too* liberal.

WHEN SHOULD YOU START THE CAMPAIGN?

A campaign consists of two parts. When most people talk about the best time to start a campaign, they mean the *campaign kickoff*. This and the activities that follow are the public face of the campaign – mailing information to voters, holding get-out-the-vote walks, putting up yard signs and everything else associated with communicating with voters.

The second part of the campaign takes place "beneath the hood." This *internal* campaign is the process of putting all the pieces of the puzzle – FPPC filings, fundraising, mail design, etc. – in place *before* launching the public campaign.

In my experience, almost everyone wants to begin the public part of campaign *earlier* than necessary. However, most voters don't focus on an election until a couple of weeks – at best – before sample ballots are mailed out. (See *Special Topic 7: When and How Voters Get Their Ballots*.)

Since campaigns have a limited budget, spending money to communicate with voters *who aren't listening* is a waste of resources. (This is not to be confused with informational mailers describing the potential for a bond sent out by the district. Better that these communications be sent before the campaign season is in full swing.)

Actually, starting the public campaign too early can be harmful. In addition to running out of money too soon, you risk losing momentum. Campaigns take a lot of energy, especially volunteer energy. Even though everyone is eager to hit the streets at the beginning, excitement eventually gives way to burnout. In addition, starting early can tempt opponents to organize against the bond measure.

Still, no matter how much I try to persuade campaign committees to keep their powder dry and resist the temptation of launching the campaign too early, I usually lose the argument.

Nobody knows anything about the bond!

The opposition is already putting out lies! We need to respond!

People keep asking why we aren't doing anything!

More often than not, an emotional, inexorable push by board members, parents, faculty, or city fathers creates so much pressure that the public campaign is forced to kick off earlier than it should.

The *internal* campaign is a different story. Even though, technically, the campaign can't begin until a campaign committee is formed and the necessary paperwork is filed, earlier is better for internal campaign planning. There is much to be done before the official creation of the campaign, including assembling lists of potential supporters and contributors, having exploratory conversations with potential volunteers, and reviewing voter registration demographics.

After you're official, this prep work really ramps up with mail design, volunteer coordination, fundraising, etc. My best advice is to get as much of the internal campaign out of the way as early as possible, because once the public campaign starts, it can be like trying to hold onto a tornado.

The Campaign Committee

Campaign committees come in all shapes and sizes. At one end of the spectrum, I've worked with committees with scores of enthusiastic, engaged members who quickly divided themselves up into subcommittees, each taking responsibility for a piece of the campaign.

At the other end, I've also worked on one campaign where the committee was comprised of the superintendent, the CBO and me. On a good day. (We still won, by the way.)

Campaign committees work best when they have a strong chair (discussed below), clear lines of authority, and access to enough resources (money, volunteers, or both) to communicate effectively with voters. When they fail, it's due to weak leadership (no surprise there) or when everybody wants to be in charge, but nobody wants to do any work.

NAMING THE COMMITTEE

Before you can ask for campaign contributions, you need to be registered with the California Fair Political Practices Commission (FPPC). And before you can register with the FPPC you need (a) a campaign treasurer (described below), (b) a mailing address (this can be a P.O. box, and (c) a campaign name.

That's why coming up with a name for the campaign committee needs to be one of the first assignments. Keep two simple rules in mind. First, the name has to make it clear that the committee is working in support of the ballot measure. Second, it should include the *measure letter* assigned by the county elections department.

So, for example, *The Committee to Save Our Schools* doesn't get you there. However, *Citizens for Measure A* makes the grade.

People sometimes go off the deep end when trying to come up with a name. But trying to stuff themes or broad descriptions into the name provides little benefit. Best to keep it simple (and legal) and move on.

THE CAMPAIGN COMMITTEE CHAIR AND THE TREASURER

I've worked with hundreds of school districts across the state over the past three decades, and I've never once walked away from a meeting with board members or administrators thinking *Wow, what a great district. Too bad the leadership's screwed up.* Organizations are great **because** of their leadership, not in spite of it.

The same holds true for campaign committees, which is why I try to have as much input as possible in selecting the person to lead it.

When people ask me what attributes to look for in the ideal campaign committee chair, I usually list three:

1. highly organized

2. understands and appreciates the political process, although not necessarily an elected official

3. not male

I'm kidding (kind of) about attribute #3 and have, of course, worked with some great guys as campaign chairs. But my experience has been that women generally take to this role better than men. Maybe it's their communication skills. Maybe they have more experience working in teams. Maybe they're just a little better at not letting their ego get in the way. Whatever the reasons, it's worth keeping in mind.

The campaign treasurer is another tough but critical role. Look for someone with accounting experience and a strong stomach for filling out arcane disclosure forms. Or, better yet, there are numerous campaign accounting firms that specialize in this area. More often than not, it's money well spent.

OTHER ROLES

There numerous other roles to fill in a bond campaign organization. While not all are critical (except for the fundraising coordinator), the scope and type of campaign will determine which are required.

- fundraising coordinator

- volunteer coordinator

- endorsement coordinator

- neighborhood walk coordinator

- yard sign coordinator

- special events coordinator

- parent liaison

- spokesperson

- social media coordinator

VOLUNTEERS

Volunteers are the lifeblood of some campaigns but less important in others. The number of volunteers you can effectively mobilize depends on the specifics of the campaign. A district that covers a broad expanse of mostly rural communities might have a hard time finding meaningful work for a large group of volunteers. On the other hand, for "walkable" districts (urban and suburban), a large corps of volunteers can be critical to success.

Money Money Money

Working up a draft campaign budget requires two skills: arithmetic and reality testing. The arithmetic part is simple. After you and your campaign advisor have decided on what pieces of the puzzle you want to include in your overall campaign strategy (e.g., direct mail, yard signs, phone banking), you (or, more likely, the campaign advisor) can pretty quickly calculate the cost of each line item.

For example, most campaigns today want their own website. That means paying someone (unless you can get the services donated) to design the site and register a domain name (the "URL" or web address) and also paying an internet service provider (ISP) to host the site. For direct mail, the cost is estimated by multiplying the postage by the number of households you want to reach by the number of mailings you want to send (or *"drop"* in Campaign-ese). Calculating how much you want to spend is the easy part. Getting the funds is the real challenge.

HOW MUCH CAN YOU REALLY RAISE?

Raising the funds for a school bond campaign will be among the most daunting tasks you'll face – if not *the* most daunting. But let's face it. No money, no campaign. That's why putting a full press on finding and nailing down contributions needs to be job number one when setting up a campaign.

Start by being brutally honest in answering the question of *how much money can you really raise*. The answer will determine what kind of campaign is run.

If the school bond is going to fund major construction or rehabilitation projects, then you can probably count on contributions from firms hoping to be hired for these projects.[17] However, be aware that increased media scrutiny of campaign contributions by architectural firms, developers, contractors, etc. has dampened the willingness of many such firms to contribute as generously as they might have in the past.

....

17 Note that asking firms such as these to contribute does not mean you are guaranteeing that they will be hired by the district if the bond wins. That's a felony. What you can guarantee them, however, is that **no one** will be hired if the bond fails.

Labor unions are another potential source of campaign contributions. Most unions understand that school bond projects mean jobs for their members. Local businesses that understand the connection between high-quality schools and a thriving local economy are another source of funding.

Surprisingly, given all the money schools are pumping into technology, the tech field has, by and large, been a non-player when it comes to campaign contributions. Also, as mentioned earlier, the days of large checks from underwriters and vendors are effectively over. (See *Special Topic #4: Pay-to-Play.*)

WHO IS GOING TO RAISE THE MONEY?

Almost everyone hates asking for money and it's a rare person who's good at it. However, the volunteer in charge of campaign contributions is so critical to the success of the campaign – every bit as much so as the campaign chair and the treasurer – that you need to do everything you can to identify the right person (or people) for this job.

Sometimes you get lucky. The chief business official of the school district is the obvious choice given his or her broad view of likely contributors. Other times, it's the superintendent or even a board member. (Keep in mind that campaign activities by district employees are only to be undertaken *off-the-clock.*)

Sometimes when the campaign comes up dry in identifying this person, it will be decided to spread the pain around and appoint a committee of (reluctant) volunteers with little or no fundraising experience. ("*I've never done it before but I guess I could give it a try.*") This is almost always a disaster, and you're better off to just keep hunting. As I said, it's a rare person who can handle this assignment, and it's not designed for on-the-job training.

When I get into this pickle, I'll try to meet with the entire campaign committee. As I'm running through the various volunteer roles that have yet to be filled, I'll slip in a pitch for a fundraising coordinator, letting them know how critical this position is to success and what the job requires.

At this point, pretty much everybody in the room begins studying the agenda or, if they've misplaced their agenda, making sure their shoelaces are tight.

But, with any luck, there will be one person who is looking straight back at me, and I can tell he or she is thinking, "*That doesn't sound so hard.*" That's my guy.

And, for the right person, the job *isn't* that hard. The campaign committee will put together the list of possible contributors, identify an "ask" amount and draft and mail letters with the contribution request clearly spelled out. All the fundraising coordinator then needs to do is get the targets on the phone (although potential donors are pretty good at making themselves scarce), make sure they understand why it's so important to contribute (after hearing them complain about how bad business has been lately), and walk away with a promise to mail in a check. Piece of cake.

IF ALL ELSE FAILS
In extreme cases, I've used paid fundraisers. For a cut of the action, these people will make the phone calls and dog donors for contributions. This has plusses and minuses. You don't have to spend time training professional fundraisers. They have a strong incentive to nail the contribution. The downside is obvious – they keep up to 30 percent of what they bring in.

Regulatory Issues

The requirements and regulations surrounding a bond measure campaign are too complex to cover here. Besides, they tend to change (or at least expand) with every election cycle. What doesn't change is my advice to avoid them at your peril, since neither the FPPC nor the IRS is known to have a sense of humor.

The required filings are primarily concerned with the contributions received by the campaign committee. For this reason, the responsibility for filing the required forms usually falls either to the campaign treasurer or to an outside accounting firm that specializes in political campaigns.

Unless the campaign treasurer is experienced in dealing with the FPPC, I recommend using an accounting firm. Although it means one more expenditure out of what is almost always a tight budget, the peace of mind is priceless.

Messaging

YOU TALKING TO ME?

Campaigns too often oversimplify voters' thinking on a bond issue. It's easy to divvy up voters as "yes", "no", or "undecided". Voter attitudes, however, are much more nuanced than these three tidy piles would lead you to believe. There are, of course, hard-core "no" voters who can never be convinced to vote in favor of raising their property tax. And there are staunch supporters of education who can't even imagine voting against an education initiative.

But what about everybody else? What about those voters not firmly entrenched in their positions, but leaning one way or the other?

The inclination of some campaign advisors is to preach to the group that leans "yes" and write off those who lean "no". I remember years ago sitting in on a presentation for school board members given by one of the state's top political consultants. He was standing in front of a pad propped up on an easel. He drew a big circle with a marker, then drew a line that divided it in half.

"Here are your supporters," he told the group, tapping his pen at the section of the circle nearest him. "But these people," he said, jabbing at the other section, "these are your opponents." He paused and looked around the room. "So, what should do with our opponents?" he asked. He paused and glared out at the audience, daring anyone to answer. "Forget about them," he said, slashing two lines through the opponents.

Okay, if I'm working in a district with poll results showing 70 percent support of the bond, I'd probably recommend the same thing. But in a close election, figuring out how a move a small slice of the *leaning "no"* vote in your direction – and, of equal importance, keeping most of the *leaning "yes"* voters in your column – can make the difference between winning and losing.

This means crafting different messages to address the often very different concerns of these groups. Sometimes it's a message of fiscal responsibility for the older, more conservative voter. Sometimes it's a message of expanded vocational education facilities for voters worried about job growth in their community. The point is that even though the campaign needs to speak with one voice and keep tight control over the messages being delivered, that doesn't mean it has to emphasize the same thing to every voter.

For example, we once ran a bond campaign in a very large high school district that included two highly different communities. One, largely Hispanic, had significant numbers of registered Democrats and young families. The other community was older, whiter, and more Republican. While there was support in both communities for improving local schools, the hot-button issues were very different. The first community's No. 1 issue was improved classrooms. The second community's No. 1 issue was increased school security. Although the proposed bond was going to address both these issues, the campaign mail sent to those two communities looked very different.

Bond opponents cried foul.

"*They're lying to us,*" they howled. "*Look how they're manipulating the facts!*"

Lying? No. Manipulating? Maybe. But every political campaign – from a local school district to presidential candidates – tries to connect with voters over the issues they care about.

THE LOGO

The campaign meeting had broken up at a reasonable time, but I'd spent the night at a hotel since I had a few morning meetings before flying back to San Francisco. As I was heading for the airport the next day, my cell phone rang.

"Are you still in town?" the superintendent asked. "We're having a bit of crisis about the direction of the campaign, and we're wondering if you could join us."

It was hard to imagine what kind of crisis could have erupted in less than 24 hours. The previous evening's campaign committee meeting had gone great. The campaign chair was getting her sea legs. Everyone agreed that making budget seemed doable. As we broke for the night, I'd handed out a proposed logo that our designer had come up with and asked people to email me their comments.

Walking into the conference room where we'd met the night before, I saw the campaign chair and superintendent hunched over a single sheet of paper, staring intently.

"It's the logo," the superintendent said, looking up at me. "We hate it."

Actually, most school bond campaign logo designs are pretty awful. Apples.

Little red schoolhouses. ABC building blocks. Their kitschy sameness makes me want to scream.

But does the design really matter that much? It clearly did to the superintendent and campaign chair, so we spent the next two hours pulling logo examples off my laptop, tossing around ideas, and doodling on the white board until they were happy with the new direction.

But, by and large, what matters most about the logo's design is that it be readable (especially from a moving car when the logo is printed on a yard sign) and that it can't be confused with the logos of other ballot measures. You also need to pay special attention to the colors. For example, if the district has only one high school, it makes sense to use the school's colors. But if there are competing high schools in the district, should some colors be avoided?

While you don't need to obsess, it's still important that someone take the time to review the logo with a critical eye and think about what message is being delivered. For example, if you're running a campaign for a technology bond, does it really make sense to have a chalkboard as part of your logo? On the other hand, some voters still equate the funding of educational technology with kids playing games on iPads. As cool as that screen might look on a tech bond logo, is that the message you want to be sending voters?

SLOGANS

I feel the same way about slogans as I do about logos. Most of the slogans I see on school bond campaigns around the state are clichéd and overused:

> *Save Our Schools*
> *Help Our Children*
> *Our Children Need Your Yes Vote*

Slogans should capture the purpose or theme of the campaign. That's easier said than done and, in my experience, the best ones are created organically from within the campaign. For example, we were working on a campaign whose primary purpose was classroom remodeling and earthquake safety at an older campus. At one of my first meetings with the campaign committee, we all struggled to find words that could sum up the need for the bond. Out of nowhere, a volunteer blurted out:

> *"Safer Schools. Better Classrooms."*

Boom. Four words that encapsulated the purpose of the campaign.

Other times, slogans just come from blind luck combined with sudden inspiration. A few years ago, Hemet USD had a GO Reauthorization Bond on the ballot that would not only allow the district to continue improving local schools, but would also provide for a tremendous reduction in the cost of the borrowing.

I was sitting in a sandwich shop with the campaign chair and a few members of the committee when I received a text from my office. The county had just released ballot letter designations. Hemet's bond would appear on the ballot as *Measure U*.

"Measure U?" I said, looking around the table. "What the hell do we do with Measure U?"

"U Saves Money?" the campaign chair laughed. Maybe not grammatically correct but it stuck because it perfectly captured the campaign's message.

But slogans like that are the exception, not the rule. Unless you get lucky and the perfect slogan jumps up and bites you on the nose, better to stick with the tried-and-true *Vote Yes on Measure A!*

The Endorsement Drive

In the first weeks of the campaign, there is a fair amount to do under the hood – logo design, putting together a donor list, developing a campaign strategy, appointing a campaign chair, etc. At this stage, there are often a number of people eager to get involved, but there's just not a lot for them to do. This is a perfect time to get everybody working on the endorsement drive.

Two types of endorsements are needed. The first comes from the community's A-list: major organizations (e.g., the local chamber of commerce, the county taxpayers association); large, well-known employers; and widely recognized civic leaders.

Obtaining A-list endorsements requires careful discussion among the campaign chair, the superintendent, and any other campaign committee members who are dialed into local politics. Getting some will be a slam-dunk (e.g., people who signed the argument in favor). But it may take some strategic thinking to figure out who should contact other potential A-list endorsers and what concerns they might have.

The second group of endorsers includes everybody else. There are a number of ways to gather these endorsements. Some campaigns get them through online signup. Others pass clipboards around at PTA meetings. What I've found works best is to have endorsement cards printed on hard-stock paper, four to a page. The printer can cut them into four 4.25-by-5.5-inch cards. At a minimum, the card must allow space for name, title (this needn't be a formal title: "resident," "homeowner," "alum of NAME School," "business owner" and many others will work fine), and signature. Some campaigns also want space for a phone number or mailing address. Others want check-off boxes indicating willingness to volunteer or contribute. It's up to you. To me, the important thing is one card per person, legible handwriting and a signature at the bottom. [18]

These endorsements can be used in a variety of ways, including posting on the campaign's website, newspaper ads, and direct mail. But their most important function is to get people involved and committed to supporting the bond measure.

Pictures

Last, but not least, on the to-do list as you get ready for the campaign is assembling images to be used on mailers, the website, and other campaign communications. This is trickier than it sounds.

Almost every district has great pictures of its students and facilities. But that's the problem. They're the district's pictures, not the campaign's. Special

....

18 I learned this lesson the hard way. Years ago, we were running a campaign in a small town in Santa Barbara County. The volunteers collected endorsements by calling people on the phone, rather than having them sign an endorsement card. We aggregated all the endorsements and bought a full-page ad in the local weekly paper. The names ran into the hundreds and we thought we'd hit it out of the ballpark. That is, until, the campaign chair got a call from one of the more prominent older residents of the community, who was very, very upset. She had seen her and her husband's names listed in the paper as endorsers. First of all, she was most definitely not an endorser of the bond, and she was going to make sure everyone knew this. Second, her husband had passed away more than two years before.

care needs to be taken to make sure that no laws are violated by using these photos and, obviously, signed releases need to be obtained from the students' parents or guardians.

A quick work-around of this problem is to use stock photography. Stock photos are easily purchased online and have a professional quality often lacking in local photos. But there can also be a certain sameness and lack of emotion in these photos that makes me want to curl up in a ball.

Regardless of which path is taken, make sure to give yourself plenty of time to find photos that match the demographics of the community.

Communicating with Voters

DIRECT MAIL

Direct mail is that stream of glossy mailers and endorsement recommendations crammed into your mailbox in the weeks before Election Day, courtesy of the U.S. Postal Service.

It is a rare person who will admit to reading these mailers. When I first bring up direct mail, I usually get an earful of how terrible they are. Some of the nicer comments:

A waste of money. I never read them.

I dump them straight into the recycling bin.

I don't even bring them into the house. I toss them in the garbage the moment they arrive.

So, if everybody thinks direct mail is a waste of money that no one bothers to read, why use it?

Quite simply, because it works. Except for knocking on a front door, handing a voter a campaign brochure, and asking him or her to join you in voting "yes", direct mail is the most effective campaign tool available.

Direct mail allows you to target your message to a specific voter without requiring anyone to go to a rally, pick up the phone or answer the doorbell. And claims that no one even looks at direct mail are simply untrue. Time and again, I have heard the very people who swore they never read campaign mail discuss in detail what they liked and disliked about a particular mailer or bring in other direct mail pieces for comparison.

However, the *timing* of direct mail makes a large difference in its effectiveness. Remember, as of 2019, the statewide average for vote-by-mail (VBM) registration is 67 percent. This requires dividing the voter mailing list into two files, so VBM residents start receiving mail at the same time they get their ballots.

For the voters, it's deceptively attractive to try timing their mail to hit just before Election Day. There are two problems with this approach. First, every other political race is timing its mail too. This means a flood of campaign mail is going to hit at the same time as your piece.

Second, even though the Post Office pledges to make its deliveries despite rain, sleet or snow, it won't guarantee *when* it will deliver your critical mailer. Years ago, we were working with a small elementary district in Kern County that had a bond on the ballot. Because the district was mostly rural, the campaign committee threw most of its limited resources into a direct mail program and hired one of the state's top school district campaign firms to oversee it. The campaign firm laid out a timetable with the last, most important piece of direct mail timed with military precision to arrive in mailboxes the weekend before Election Day.

"Worst case," the campaign consultant assured me, "it hits Monday."

The mailer was delivered on Wednesday.

NEWSPAPERS

The impact of the press on a bond campaign is remarkably uneven and needs to be analyzed on a case-by-case basis. In some communities, the local newspaper will actively report on the progress of the campaign, at times even more than you might prefer. But elsewhere around the state, there is no significant newspaper presence and coverage of the bond campaign is effectively zero.

Even districts in those areas with a robust newspaper might face difficulty in getting "free media" (i.e., a news story about the campaign). Only so many column inches are available in a newspaper, and during the campaign season the competition can be fierce. If you hope for newspaper coverage during these times, it's best to contact the reporter or editor early on and give him or her an "angle" on your bond measure that will make for a compelling story that is likely to interest readers – this is the only way to get, at best, more than an inch or two buried in an inside page.

The same goes for newspaper editorials. Because of staff reductions, it can often be extremely difficult to get a face-to-face meeting with the paper's editorial board. In fact, some newspapers no longer provide editorial endorsements for local campaign issues. Check your local paper's policy early on and try to schedule a meeting with the editorial board as soon as possible.

As you might expect, getting someone to answer the phone at the newspaper is a lot easier if you are looking to place a paid campaign ad. Unfortunately, in most cases, placing an ad in the local paper is not very effective. When considering this expenditure, ask yourself how many voters you think will even notice the ad. In smaller communities, that number can be quite large. But in larger districts, it's usually not worth the money.

In any case, in any self-respecting newspaper, the journalists have a strict arms-length relationship with the advertising department. Buying ads will get you nowhere with an editor or reporters. In fact, pointing to your status as an advertiser (should you choose to buy ads) is likely to paint you as an ignorant boor who likes to throw his weight around. It could easily cost you good will from editors and reporters.

SOCIAL MEDIA

There has been a lot of buzz about trying to use social media to spread the message about a school bond with voters and, at first glance, it seems like a natural fit. After all, it's a rare person who is not on some social media platform (Facebook, LinkedIn, Twitter, Pinterest, Instagram, etc.); and the ability to target ads by region, age, and gender is impressive. Better still, compared with direct mail, the ads are dirt cheap.

So far, however, the jury is still out on how effective social media ads are as a campaign tool for local bond elections. In smaller, affluent communities, they can be a great tool for communicating and scheduling volunteers. But their effectiveness in "getting eyeballs" remains in doubt. Here's how one of the savvier campaign consultants put it when I asked whether they included a social media component in their school bond campaign plans.

"Do I use social media on a campaign?" he asked. "Sure. It's part of the campaign plan we show to clients when we're being interviewed so I can say *here's our social media plan*. Beyond that, I haven't figured out what good it is."

I will, however, add two giant caveats to my slightly skeptical view of social media in bond campaigns. New email products are in development, that could be game changers in this field. Time will tell. Also, the use of social media as a tool *within* the campaign can be very powerful – and very inexpensive – when created and run by the campaign committee itself. Using platforms like Facebook to coordinate campaign events, schedule volunteers, share thoughts and concerns, and post pictures is highly effective from an internal organizational rather than a campaign messaging point of view.

PHONE BANKS

If I had to name one thing that has caused the biggest change in how school bond campaigns are run, I'd choose *caller ID*. It's easy to forget but there was once a time when people actually answered their phones without knowing who was calling.

What an amazing world that was. You'd just be sitting down for dinner or watching TV, and the phone would ring. Literally. Not beep. Not buzz or vibrate or meow like a cat. It would ring, and you would walk over, pick it up, and say "Hello" without any idea of who was calling.

For school bond campaigns, this was nirvana. Entire campaign plans consisted of not much more than nightly phone banks with volunteers dialing number after number in the search for bond supporters.

Caller ID destroyed this entire system. If you want proof, just think of your own behavior. When was the last time your telephone rang, flashed a message *caller unknown*, and you still answered the call? I know there are still a number of campaign advisors out there who recommend phone banks, but I'm convinced the payoff has become so meager that it's just not worth the time or energy.

YARD SIGNS/WALK CARDS

My appreciation of yard signs, on the other hand, has grown deeper with every campaign cycle. Not too long ago, yard signs were a mixed bag. They looked great for the first few days but, being made of cardboard, they would dissolve into a floppy mess after one good rainstorm. Today, however, they're typically made with a plastic laminate that holds up in the worst of weather. Not only that, there are now plenty of local print shops that can produce yard signs cheaply and quickly.

In districts with a lot of yards (and volunteers), I like to target a specific weekend for yard-sign installation. When you can pull it off, the sudden eruption of brightly colored signs in neighborhood after neighborhood sends a strong statement throughout the community that the campaign has widespread support.

Of course, it's not all a bed of roses with yard signs. Problem number one is that opponents like to steal them. Creepy, I know (not to mention illegal), but it happens.

Second, signs don't work well in rural, sparsely populated areas. The lone yard sign on the side of the country road isn't going to build much enthusiasm. On the other hand, I've worked with some campaigns in these areas that morphed the yard sign concept into billboards and placed them at major intersections or turn-offs near the center of town.

But hands down, the biggest problem with yard signs is what I call the *trunk issue*. Too many yard signs are picked up by volunteers or supporters and thrown in the trunk of their car, never to see the light of day again. Paying for a yard sign that no one sees is a total waste of money. If possible, try not to hand out yard signs one by one, but have a group of volunteers assigned to yard sign installation.

My favorite yard sign installation story took place in a small elementary district where the superintendent encouraged all of his principals to volunteer for yard-sign installation duty. He then asked them to walk (on their own time) to every home within their school's attendance boundaries, knock on the door, introduce himself or herself, and ask if they would like a yard sign. If the homeowner said yes, it was the principal's job to install the yard sign and then (my favorite part) take a picture of it with a smart phone and email it to the superintendent. That's what I call accountability.

Walk-cards (sometimes referred to as *palm-cards*) are another underrated and inexpensive campaign tool. These cards can come in a variety of shapes and sizes but all have the same purpose. They give voters a quick overview of the bond measure by providing a few bullet points that highlight the strongest arguments for voting "yes". They will typically have the campaign logo, one or two pictures, perhaps an endorsement quote, and the campaign's website address.

While the main use of these cards is as a handout during neighborhood walks, they can be used in any number of venues to give voters a quick pitch for the bond measure.

ROBOCALLS

If you are a registered voter, you've probably received at least a few robocalls. These are prerecorded telephone messages of support, often taped by well-known politicians or celebrities, urging you to support (or oppose) a particular candidate or ballot measure.

Robocalls can also be purchased by a local bond campaign committee and, as with social media and direct mail, they can be targeted to particular demographics. For example, you send a message from a well-known fiscal conservative to households with at least one registered Republican and a different message to a more liberal community member.

You can also program the calls to be made in the middle of the afternoon (when fewer people are at home) so there is a greater chance of being able to leave a message on an answering machine. (Although care needs to be taken with this option. In a notorious screw-up, one campaign firm apparently checked the wrong box when it put in a robocall order. A few weeks before Election Day, every voter in the district received a pre-recorded phone call in support of the bond measure – at 3:30 a.m.)

Besides being able to target specific voter blocs, the only real virtue of robocalls is that they are fast and cheap. The script can be turned around in an hour or less and the recording made by phone from the home of the endorser.

Unfortunately, after fast and cheap, the list of advantages of robocalls is pretty short. In fact, the only time I think they make sense is when you received an unexpected contribution at the last minute and have no better way of spending the money before Election Day.

LETTERS TO THE EDITOR

Assuming your district has a local paper (even a weekly), don't drop the ball on letters to the editor. As part of the campaign planning process, line up between six and a dozen community members who are willing to write letters in support. If no opposition to the campaign develops, you probably won't need them. That doesn't mean you shouldn't send them to the paper. Just don't be surprised if they aren't published.

But if organized (or, for that matter, disorganized) opposition develops, having these letters in your pocket will be a big help for two reasons. First, with rare exceptions, organizations that come together to oppose a bond campaign rarely have two dimes to rub together. So, they're forced to go cheap. They'll start a Facebook page but quickly figure out that the only people visiting it are their comrades in arms. They might try to put up some yard signs but typically ask people to make a donation to the *Vote No* campaign to cover the cost. You can guess how many signs go up.

But the one place they can get traction is with letters to the editor. Newspapers love a fight and will usually be willing to print a few of their letters. Having a few already-drafted letters of support in your back pocket will alleviate the need to scramble when the editor calls and asks if you want to respond.

The Ground Game

East Side Union High School District has 215,000 voters and over 13 high schools spread across the eastern half of Santa Clara County. Given the size of the district, campaign leaders have avoided trying to run any kind of ground campaign and have instead focused on voter communication through direct mail, free media, and the like. (With great success, I should add. Since 1991, district voters have approved seven bond measures totaling over $1.5 billion.)

HERDING CATS

For districts that are less spread out than East Side Union HSD, a well-thought-out ground game can make a huge difference. In general, this boils down to preparing a walking map of *specifically* identified voting households in *specifically* identified neighborhoods. These voting households are targeted based on a number of factors, including the walkability of the area, party registration, frequency of voting, etc. These maps are then divided into walking lists and distributed to volunteers on the day of the walk.

The reason this strategy is so effective is quite simple. There is nothing – *nothing* – as effective in a bond campaign as knocking on a person's door, introducing yourself as a fellow community member (or taxpayer or parent) and telling that person why you support the school bond.

However, pulling off a successful walk requires a certain alignment of the stars that may or may not be possible in your district. Let's start with the most obvious. The area has to be walkable. That rules out most rural and semi-rural districts. It also generally rules out gated communities or dense urban areas with large apartment buildings.

Next, you need volunteers willing to walk. I've worked on some campaigns where people were so eager to be involved we almost had to turn away volunteers on walk day. But in other districts, finding volunteers to walk is next to impossible. Typically, it isn't because the parents in these districts don't care. It's because they're already working as hard as they can just to make ends meet and don't have the time and energy to donate to a campaign.

Finally – and by far the most critical factor – you need a tough, no-nonsense walk coordinator who's willing to help structure a walking strategy with military precision and then enforce it. This is because walking door-to-door is hard work, and volunteers will constantly try to change the rules to make it less arduous.

Can't I just take the pamphlets and hand them out on my own? (No. They need to be handed out to registered voters who've been previously identified.)

Can't I just walk with my friend? (Possibly, but two people walking together cuts the number of contacts in half.)

Do I have to follow the map? Wouldn't it make more sense to hand out information to all voters? (No. Except in rare situations like the Soledad USD bond campaign described earlier, there is no reason to waste time and resources handing out information to people who aren't interested.)

Managing a volunteer campaign walk is an exercise in "herding cats." This is why having a no-nonsense/no-excuses walk coordinator is pure gold.

ONE-OFFS

One of the hardest tasks for a school bond campaign manager is keeping people from wandering off the playbook. This is especially true when it comes to the overwhelming desire of some volunteers to have the campaign participate in special one-off events such as back-to-school-night, town fairs, football games, etc.

I get the logic behind why volunteers press so hard to have the campaign be a part of these events. They usually bring out lots of parents, are a good place to recruit other volunteers and involve minimal effort. Why not wave the flag at these functions? It's also a lot easier to have people walking over to your table or booth than to get them to answer a knock on the door on Saturday afternoon.

On the other hand, no matter how you slice it, participation at these events means devoting campaign resources – volunteer time and, typically, printed material – that might best be expended elsewhere. Whether to participate or not is a judgment call that requires weighing the use of these resources against the potential benefit.

There are two litmus tests that help clarify these tough decisions. The first is what I call the *likely voter test*. By this, I mean how many participants at the proposed event are likely to be voters on the school bond? If it's a regional fair, probably not too many. But if it's the local farmers market, okay, possibly a fair number.

The second litmus test is the *appropriateness of place*. By this I mean is the venue an appropriate place to discuss the school bond? Back-to-school-night is a great example. It's filled with parents and you can reasonably assume many of them are voters. While the event is a school function and therefore off-limits to political activities, campaigns can still set up tables on the sidewalk outside or have the teachers' union hand out campaign materials at its table inside.

I recognize that I am in the deep minority on this issue, but I feel uneasy about trying to push the campaign message at back-to-school-nights. A short mention from the principal in his or her welcoming remarks? Okay. An FAQ in the packet handed out to parents? No problem. But I think parents who take the time to go to back-to-school-night do so to meet their child's teacher, hear about the year ahead, and meet other parents. Is talking about the school bond the right message to be delivering at this venue?

On the other hand, some venues are perfect opportunities for a campaign to jump in with both feet. For example, Atascadero's annual Colony Days event in October celebrates the town's founding. Part parade, part fair, it is the perfect venue for a bond campaign booth.

Again, while many will disagree with me on the issue of appropriateness, I believe the most successful campaigns are those that adapt to their local community, rather than follow a paint-by-the-numbers formula.

VOTER REGISTRATION DRIVES: ARE THEY WORTH IT?

Although they have fallen out of fashion in recent years, voter registration drives used to be a core component of many campaigns. I remember distributing thousands of voter registration cards to parents through PTAs, adult education classes, and preschools.

As optimistic and energetic as these efforts were, by and large the results were meager at best. Registering new voters is fairly simple. But getting them to actually vote is next to impossible. The sad fact is that voting behavior is an acquired habit that is tough to change. People are perennial voters who never miss an election, non-voters or those who show up for a presidential election (and maybe the governor's race) but rarely any other election. You can beg, cajole or offer a ride to the polls but, unless your name is Obama, turning a non-voter into a voter is a tough slog.

Opposition

What is the best way to handle opposition to a school bond campaign? Most people's reaction to being attacked is to defend themselves. But that's not always the best course of action in a school bond campaign. How a campaign responds to criticism – or if it even responds at all – depends on a number of factors that need to be carefully thought through.

THE BEST DEFENSE IS A GOOD OFFENSE

The saying may be overused but it's still true. In most cases, the best reaction to school bond critics and opponents is to ignore them and stay on message as you implement the campaign plan. That's because, by and large, no one is listening to them except their friends. Here's a good example.

A few years ago, we were running a campaign in Riverside County. This particular measure was widely popular throughout the district except with a small but vocal group of parents and homeowners from one particular neighborhood. I don't know what had happened, but there was a history of bad blood between this group and the district.

As the campaign was being rolled out, the neighborhood group came out in opposition to the bond. They kicked it off with a community meeting meant to fire up the "no" voters. It drew a modest crowd but certainly not a mob. They then had *VOTE NO* yard signs printed up but, due to lack of funds, made people buy them instead of giving them away. Here and there, a few *VOTE NO* signs popped up but they were a rare sight.

Then they struck gold. Somehow, they got their hands on an email list of district employees and a smaller number of district parents. (Our guess was that a disgruntled employee had leaked it to them, but we could never prove it.) They began sending out a flurry of *VOTE NO* emails to this list, urging recipients to forward the emails to their friends.

Like most correspondence sent out by opposition groups, these emails were filled with half-truths and, at times, complete lies. But as the campaign wore on, the attacks became much more scathing and personal. The board's honesty was impugned in highly personal terms and the administration's competence mocked.

As we entered the final days of the campaign, both the board and the superintendent had grown bitter and angry. They wanted to punch back, even though they knew it would be a mistake to engage. Showing extraordinary willpower, they kept their cool and bit their tongues. But by Election Eve they were thoroughly demoralized.

"I've got a bad feeling about this," the superintendent said to me on Election Day.

"You're going to win," I assured him.

"I don't know," he sighed. "Did you see their last email?"

I had a copy of it on the screen in front of me. After yet another long screed attacking the district, the superintendent, the board and its "high-priced San Francisco consultant" (me), they concluded with this:

"Please join the undersigned in opposing this bond. Vote NO."

I scrolled down and counted the names. There were 13.

"How many voters in the district?" I asked the superintendent. "Roughly."

"I think you said there were about 70,000," he replied.

"So, out of 70,000 voters, these guys can only come up with *13* signatures? You're going to win."

And they did, with a 64 percent "yes" vote.

The lesson? When you're in the foxhole and people are shooting at you, it's important to know whether it's a couple of nuts or an entire army. In this case, it wasn't even a platoon.

BUT WHAT IF IT IS AN ARMY?

Most of the time, the opposition to a bond campaign is a toothless tiger. Most of the time. But what should you do if it's not? More importantly, how can you tell when it's not?

Just because the opposition is organized doesn't mean it's a threat. The group that I described above with the purloined email list is a great example. They had a few committed volunteers. They were good at raising hell (and stealing yard signs). But, in the end, they were talking to themselves because no one – not the press, not other community groups, not taxpayer organizations – was listening. This was partly due to the fact that it was a presidential election and scores of other issues pushed their message aside. But mostly, it was that their leadership wasn't viewed as credible. Most of the community saw them as a group of disgruntled parents and neighbors with an ax to grind.

Two factors stand out as warning signs when it comes to opposition. The first is whether the opponents have a source of funding for their campaign. This funding can come from any number of sources: e.g., conservative political groups, realtors, apartment owners' organizations, etc. The source is unimportant. What's important is to keep your ears open and be ready to react if you get wind of opposition money being raised. The reaction will depend on the election date, the resources available to you, and the magnitude of the opposition.

For example, you may need to step up your game with the media to refute the misinformation that the opposition will likely start spreading. Maybe the superintendent needs to reach out to more service organizations. Additional mailers addressing opposition claims might make sense. Throughout the process, the campaign needs to make a tough judgment call as to whether refuting the opposition is needed or if it just amplifies their messages.

The second warning sign – and by far the most threatening – is active opposition by current or retired board members. Note the word *active* in describing this opposition. I've worked with plenty of districts where one of the board members votes "no" on the resolution to place the bond on the ballot. This can be due to any of a range of reasons, including personal opposition to the bond or having aspirations for higher office and not wanting a vote to raise taxes on his or her resume. No biggie.

But I've also worked in a handful of districts where a sitting board member takes it upon himself or herself to run or participate in an active opposition campaign. It seems inconceivable that a member of a school board would take on a battle that is sure to create ill-will and anger among the other members of the board. Yet, remarkably, it happens.

So, what to do? Unfortunately, having a sitting board member campaign in active opposition to a bond measure is so damaging there are few good options available. The reason is that most bond elections are won or lost by which way voters in the center swing. Strong supporters of education are not going to be put off by the opposition's arguments against the bond, regardless of how vitriolic the opposition may be. And the hard-core "no" voters are and always will be opponents.

But the voter in the middle is a complicated character. In my experience, undecided voters are, by and large, "yes" voters so long as they are not given an excuse that lets them vote "no" in good conscience. And what better rationale than a sitting board member – an insider who has attended the meetings, studied the issue and weighed the options – telling the voters that the bond measure is a bad idea.

If you think there is a possibility of active opposition to a bond measure by a member of the board, the best course is to manage around it, if at all possible. For example, can you delay the measure until the next presidential election in the hope the board member's opposition gets little attention in the maelstrom of pre-election messages? If there is one particular geographic area where the board member is particularly influential, can you structure the bond measure as an SFID? Also, reach out for endorsements from as many former board members and other local officials as possible to show voters that this board member is an outlier whose views are not shared by those in the know.

The hardest thing of all, however, is to stay above the fray. Getting into a public debate is a bad idea. It just serves as an echo chamber that adds resonance to the opposing viewpoint. Still, holding your tongue is almost impossible because all the other board members are going to be furious and ready for a fight. However, no matter how much the bond is needed, no matter how strong the arguments in favor of passage, the board opponent will destroy you with a maddeningly passive-aggressive strategy of denying being against the bond, but claiming only to be concerned either that (a) it's not the right time, (b) more study is needed, or (c) the cost to taxpayers is simply too high.

It's a fight you're almost guaranteed to lose.

....

Special Topic #8
THE HIDDEN IMPACT OF VBM

Near the end of September 2014, at the end of a long day filled with one campaign meeting after another, I looked up from my laptop and gazed out the airplane window as we began the descent toward Oakland airport.

"I just can't seem to catch up," I said to myself, then looked back at my laptop, hoping to sneak in a few more minutes before the cabin attendant reminded me to turn my computer off.

I'd been through plenty of campaigns but there was something different about the 2014 cycle. Unlike previous years, this time we were working twice as hard to keep on schedule as deadline after deadline hurtled toward us. Had I just forgotten how intense campaigns were, or had something changed?

Gazing at the San Francisco skyline, I did the math in my head. Before the passage of Prop. 39, state law required a district's resolution calling for a GO bond election to be delivered to the county election department at least 123 days before Election Day. For a November general election, that meant a district needed to pass its resolution in late June or the first week of July at the latest. The campaign would then stretch out over a leisurely four months.

In 1999, this requirement was amended to an 88-day filing deadline so it conformed to the time required for city GO bond elections. (As already mentioned, some counties, such as Ventura and Santa Barbara, have opted to ignore this change and continue to require a much earlier filing deadline.)

This change shaved five weeks off the election schedule. Although losing these 35 days was far from ideal, people generally took it in stride, recalibrated their timetables, and got on with it.

By 2012, a new change had crept into the calendar. But this one wasn't the result of legislative action. It was a change in human behavior – voting by mail.

I remember a time, not that long ago, when people who were healthy enough to get to the polls but instead opted to vote by mail were viewed with a touch of suspicion. Real Americans (so the feeling went) marched down to their polling place, stood in line for their ballot, stepped into the voting booth, pulled the curtain behind them, and marked their ballot.

Not today. In fact, it's the people who *don't* vote by mail who are beginning to be seen as a little odd. Statewide, VBMs are quickly becoming a majority.

But while it's great to have the convenience of voting by mail, it plays havoc with the campaign schedule. The reason is that VBMs get their ballots about a month *before* Election Day.

In other words, while our collective brain remained locked into thinking that Election Day means the *day of the election*, two-thirds of voters can now vote up to 30 days before everybody else.

When VBMs were only 10 to 15 percent of the electorate, you could get away with a slightly sanguine attitude toward this 30-day head start. We'd bifurcate the mail, making sure the first pieces were sent to VBMs a little earlier than everybody else but that was about it. There was no need to stress out since the common belief was that the only VBMs who actually mailed their ballot back the day it arrived were the ones who had already made up their minds.

But when the number of VBMs started pushing 50 percent (and in some counties as much as 70 percent), mass panic set in. Direct mail is now targeted to arrive in VBMs' mailboxes on the same day – if not earlier – as their mail ballot.

The arithmetic isn't pretty. What was once a four-month campaign cycle had already shrunk to three months in the late 90s. And now, with vote-by-mail taking hold across the state, it is shrinking again, down to a sleep-deprived two months.

....

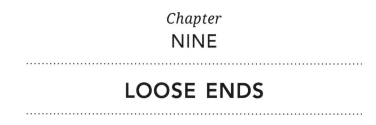

Chapter
NINE

....

LOOSE ENDS

....

"The more difficult the victory, the greater the happiness in winning."

~ Pele

YOU WON. NOW WHAT?

Except for high-fives earned by a fine team doing a great job and the opportunity, finally, for everyone to get back to a normal life, not much actually happens after a district wins a bond election. A few financial advisory firms and investment banks might use the morning after Election Day to put a heavy squeeze on districts to issue the bonds right away (claiming lower interest rates, the ability to arbitrage the tax rate or anything else they can think of), but that's more about managing their own cash flow than the district's. No matter what you hear from the outside pros, a district rarely faces a time constraint or deadline as to when the bonds must be issued.

Authorized but Unissued Bonds: A Line of Credit

With the approval of the bond measure, the district's bonds are now referred to as authorized but unissued bonds. As mentioned earlier, think of this bonding authority as similar to a line of credit. A bank provides a maximum amount you can borrow and may even specify some terms for the loan. But it's up to you when the loan is drawn down, and until you actually borrow the money there are no payments required.

Authorized but unissued GO bonds work somewhat the same way. Although the voters have approved a certain amount of bonds that the district can sell, there's no cost to the taxpayers until bonds – some or all of them – are actually sold to investors. Once bonds are sold, taxpayers must begin gradually paying principal and interest on the amount of bonds issued.

Here's an example of how the next steps happen: In November 2010, Atascadero USD (San Luis Obispo County) voters passed a $117 million GO bond with a 65.3 percent "yes" vote. After the election, the district board and administration took additional time to review the proposed Project List and consult with the community on the priority of the proposed projects (all of which were on the voter-approved Project List, remember).

In June 2011, more than six months after the bond election, the district sold $25.5 million of bonds through a competitive bid process. This left the district with $91.5 of authorized but unissued bonds. The $25.5 million bond was structured with level debt service payments, amortized over 30 years with an optional call feature in 2022. The payments are fixed and the repayment schedule for the $25.5 million will not change unless the district refinances the bonds at some future date.

After the sale was completed, we provided the San Luis Obispo County Treasurer-Tax Collector's Office with the annual repayment schedule for this first series of bonds. The county then computed the tax rate required to make the bond debt service payments for the fiscal year. (In calculating a bond's first levy, county treasurers will routinely over-assess in order to produce a surplus that can be used in future years, in case future tax payments come in lower than expected.)

The tax rate calculated by the county was placed on district secured-property owners' tax bills and sent out in October. (Owners of unsecured property must also pay this tax, but these bills typically lag by a year.) The first installment of the property tax bill was due in December and the second the following April.

The county assessor computes the assessed valuations for all property in the district at the end of each fiscal year. The assessor's office sends this information to the treasurer's office, which then calculates the tax rate to be levied for the next fiscal year to pay the upcoming interest and principal payments.

Certification of Election Results and Reporting Requirements

Once the county finishes counting the ballots and issues a final and official voter tally, the district board needs to pass a resolution certifying the election results. There is no required timing for the passage of this resolution. However, Prop. 39 requires the board to form an independent Citizens' Oversight Committee within 60 days of passing the certifying resolution. For this reason, some districts delay passing the certification resolution to gain time to form the committee and determine how members will be selected.

Prop. 39 contains two specific reporting requirements regarding a district's general obligation program:

- an "annual, independent performance audit" to ensure the funds have been expended only on the specific projects listed;

- an "annual, independent financial audit" of the proceeds from the sale of the bonds until all of those proceeds have been expended for the approved school facilities projects.

These audits are to be undertaken by an organization independent of the district. In these cases, the district's auditors are considered acceptably "independent" under the law. The purpose of the performance audit is to ensure that bond proceeds have been spent on facilities specified in the Project List provided to voters in the Full Ballot Text. The purpose of the financial audit is to review how the bond proceeds have been spent, including a review of the amount and purpose of individual expenditures.

The Citizens' Oversight Committee

As noted, within 60 days of certifying the election results, the school district or community college board must establish a Citizens' Oversight Committee (COC) and appoint its members. Despite early concerns by many (including me) that COCs would hamper districts by second-guessing everything a district does, most COCs have proven to be hard-working, diligent, and strongly supportive of the long-term goals of the districts they serve.

Indeed, to my complete surprise, it is often the COC members who are the most supportive of a district returning to the voters for an additional bond authorization after the funds from the first measure have been expended. As you would expect, all is not sweetness and light in COC-land and a few districts have suffered from attempted micro-management of building programs by runaway COCs. However, these are few, and the vast majority of COCs have been strong district partners, not adversaries.

FORMATION OF THE COC

The school or college district board resolution establishes the Citizens' Oversight Committee and approves its bylaws. (Bond counsel typically drafts this document.) The committee must consist of at least seven members, each serving a term of two years without compensation. Members may serve no more than three consecutive terms.

The law is specific about who is to serve on this committee. (Restrictions and requirements regarding the COC are found in Assembly Bill 1908.) The committee must include the following members:

- a person active in a business organization who represents the business community located within the district;

- a person active in a senior citizens' organization;

- a person active in a bona fide taxpayers' organization;

- for school districts, a parent or guardian of a child enrolled in the district;

- for community college districts, a student who is both currently enrolled in the district and active in a community college group (this member may, at the discretion of the board, serve for up to six months after graduation);

- for school districts, a parent or guardian of a child enrolled in the district and active in a parent-teacher organization;

- for community college districts, a person who is active in the support and organization of the community college, such as a member of an advisory council or foundation.

The law also specifies who may *not* serve on the committee: any employee or official of the district or a vendor, contractor, or consultant to the district. With all these requirements, the law is strangely silent as to how these committee members are to be selected, so districts have had to figure out the selection process on their own.

In some districts, applications are sought from community members, and the board makes the final decision as to whom to appoint. In others, the administration goes through a screening process and makes recommendations to the board.

A bigger concern for many districts – especially the smaller ones – is finding people who are both qualified and willing to serve, especially the individuals needed to fill the specifically mandated slots. For example, the Kern High School District, with roughly 250,000 registered voters, can easily find a person who is a member of a "bona fide taxpayers' organization" and willing to serve on the COC. But it's a different story for districts like Dehesa School District in San Diego County, with only 1,355 voters.

For this reason, COC members who represent organizations (for example, the senior citizen representative) may live outside the district boundaries. Even then, many districts still find it difficult to fill each mandated position. In these situations, a district needs to maintain a record of its attempts to locate and recruit appropriate members, including website postings, newspapers ads and recruiting letters to organizations and clubs.

PURPOSE AND LEGAL DUTIES OF THE COC

It's not uncommon for members of newly formed Citizens' Oversight Committees to believe they'll be involved in developing district policies regarding the use of bond funds or in determining the priority of bond projects to be funded. They are mistaken. The purpose of the COC, as stated in the implementation legislation of Prop. 39, is limited to *"inform[ing] the public concerning the expenditure of bond revenues" and "actively review[ing] and report[ing] on the proper expenditure of taxpayers' money for school construction."*

The purpose of the COC is not to set policy, but merely to make sure the bond funds have been spent in accordance with state law on projects specified in the Project List. To this end, the law says COCs may engage in any of the following activities:

- receive and review copies of the annual, independent performance and financial audits;

- inspect school facilities and grounds;

- receive and review copies of any deferred maintenance plans or proposals developed by the district;

- review efforts by the district to maximize bond revenues by implementing cost-saving measures.

Finally, the committee must issue reports at least once a year. As public bodies, COCs operate in total sunshine – all COC proceedings are open to the public and public notice of meetings must be posted. In addition, all minutes of COC meetings as well as documents and reports, must be made available on the district's website.

YOU LOST. NOW WHAT?

One in five Prop. 39 elections ends in failure. So, what happens if you lose? From a legal and administrative point of view, not much. While there are some cleanup forms to be filed by the campaign committee, there are no notices, documents, or resolutions required of the district.

But from a political point of view, a loss requires the district to ask itself, "What's next?" Yes, losing after putting in so much effort and emotion can be devastating, but too many districts let their emotions get in the way of making what should be a purely business decision about how to maximize chances for success next time.

Losing districts often make one of two critical mistakes. The first is to fall into the "nobody loves me" trap. This may actually be true for some districts. There was, for example, a district on the November 2012 ballot that received a horrifically low 38.5 percent "yes" vote. With that lack of voter support (and on a presidential election ballot, no less, when support is usually highest), this district came face-to-face with the need to find out why nearly two in three voters said "no," and to fix the problems before going back to those voters.

Losses of that magnitude can usually be traced to a recent report of fiscal mismanagement by the district, a local scandal, an election claim on the district's part that was shown to be false, or a grudge against the district held by an influential citizen. Whatever the cause, lopsided losses must be understood, and the underlying problem(s) solved. Negative outliers aside, most losing districts "win" with more than 50 percent support but "lose" because they don't make Prop. 39's 55 percent threshold. (One of our clients once lost a Bay Area election by an agonizing two votes.)

The second critical mistake referred to above is trying again without making an effort to analyze what caused the loss. More on this in the next section.

Getting Back on that Horse

If a private-sector company were to lose a major piece of business by just a handful of votes, it would stand up, dust itself off and start thinking about Round Two. But many school districts and community college districts aren't that resilient and go into a self-defeating sulk after a loss, even a close one.

For example, I once met with a district in the Monterey Bay area that had run a GO bond campaign on the June 2008 ballot. In general, this was a terrible ballot to be on because it didn't include a presidential primary (it had been moved to February) that would draw a large number of favorably inclined voters. That the district had still managed a 54 percent "yes" vote – just 1 percent shy of victory – among the small number of conservative voters who turned out was pretty impressive, but it was still a loss.

I met with the superintendent shortly after the election and suggested she go back to the voters quickly. I told her the district had chosen the wrong ballot date. With Democratic registration nearly double the Republican in her district, it was easy to see that the huge Democratic voter turnout in the November 2008 presidential race – just five months hence – would put the district over the 55 percent finish line.

"You'd have to move fast to get on the upcoming ballot," I told her, "but the data is overwhelmingly in your favor. This upcoming ballot is perfect for a district like yours."

She picked up the flipbook I'd prepared and thumbed through a few pages listlessly. "The truth is," she sighed, "I think we're just too emotionally worn out to do this again so soon."

Too emotionally worn out? For the past three months, the campaign had been telling voters this bond measure was critical to the education of the community's children. Had that changed overnight? You can't spend months telling voters your bond projects are absolutely critical, then curl up in a ball when you lose. Either they're critical or they're not. And by not getting back on the ballot quickly, the district would only reinforce the opposition's charge that the bond projects weren't really needed.

In fact, the district failed to get back on the ballot immediately and spent the next four years wandering in the wilderness. New board members were elected. The "emotionally worn out" superintendent resigned. Finally, four years later, the parents had had enough and demanded that the board place a measure on the 2012 presidential election ballot; it won overwhelmingly.

The second mistake losing districts make is just the opposite of what happened in that Monterey Bay district: They rush back onto the next ballot without taking the time to analyze the underlying causes of their loss. Was the problem low voter turnout? A bad ballot choice? Was it a strong opposition? Was there something that should have been eliminated from – or added to – the Project List? Is the district held in low esteem in the community? If so, why?

Instead of digging into the data to understand what went wrong and what should be changed, these districts instead focus on such superficial or tangential items as reducing the dollar amount of the bond, eliminating projects from the list, or appointing a new campaign committee chair. And they ignore deeper, more systemic questions. Did we ignore certain segments of our community? Did we effectively communicate our message to all key voting blocs in the district?

Remember the district that lost by just two votes – one of the tightest squeakers on record? After losing, it proceeded to do just about everything wrong. It spent the next two years grumbling about the loss instead of making the effort to reach out to hear the community's concerns.

All it really needed to do was hold onto its supporters and locate a handful of additional "yes" votes. Instead, it convinced itself the problem was one of strategy. It tossed all its advisors overboard, hired an entirely new team and rewrote the ballot language, in the belief that the problem could be solved by tweaking words rather than talking to voters. On Election Day, it was handed a humiliating defeat, dropping from a near-win two years prior (just two votes!) to a resounding loss, with less than 48 percent voting "yes".

....

Chapter TEN

THE BOND ISSUE: LAYING
THE GROUNDWORK

....

"It's tough to make predictions, especially about the future."

~ Yogi Berra (attributed, but possibly apocryphal)

Compared to the struggle required to win a GO bond measure, the issuance of K–14 district GO bonds is relatively easy. Nevertheless, the stakes involved in their issuance are enormous, as long-term GO debt will affect taxpayers for generations to come.

If the debt is structured correctly, the district and its taxpayers can be confident that the annual payments made by property owners are the result of a fair and well-reasoned financing plan. But if the financing plan is built on overly optimistic projections, complicated financing structures, and lack of thorough review, all hell can break loose and, in some cases, even the fiscal solvency of the district can be put in jeopardy.

It's therefore critical that district administrators and board members take the time to understand the bond financing process, and to probe the underlying assumptions on which their debt structure is being built.

THE FINANCING TIMETABLE:
HOW LONG IS THIS GOING TO TAKE?

Bringing a K–14 tax-exempt GO bond to market involves hundreds of decisions and actions by district administrators, board members, financial advisors, underwriters, lawyers, rating agencies and other bond professionals.

In general, assume that a typical GO financing will take at least three to four months. The major components, discussed in greater detail below, are:

- preparation of the documents, including the financing resolution, offering statement (the "Official Statement") and, if sold through competitive bid, the notice of sale

- the rating presentation

- board passage of the financing resolution

- sale of the securities

- the closing of the transaction

COMPETITIVE OR NEGOTIATED?
HERE WE GO AGAIN

Although the debate over whether bonds should be sold through a competitive or negotiated sale was covered in Chapter 5, it deserves a revisit. There really is no simple, hard-and-fast answer. In some cases, a competitive sale makes financial sense, while at other times, having an underwriter on board to pre-sell the financing to investors is critical. Choosing between the alternatives requires districts to make thorough analyses of their unique situations rather than accepting the (too often self-interested) preference of the financial advisor or underwriter.

There are many advantages to a competitive sale. It's politically attractive and financially efficient. Firms that wish to underwrite a district's bonds are required to bid against one another, and whoever submits the lowest cost of interest wins the bid. Period. There are no RFPs. No interviews. No gray areas. And, in general, no questions from the press, concerned citizens, or government officials as to why the competitive sale method was chosen.

But there are also financially sound reasons why a district might opt for a negotiated sale. Credit issues, such as a poor rating, a declining tax base, or a general fund that is under significant stress, may lead to a scarcity of investors willing to submit a bid on the bonds. There may be issues regarding the structure of the financing that make it more advantageous for a district to sole-source its bonds to an underwriter rather than go through a competitive sale.

For example, capital appreciation bonds (CABs), because they often require investors to wait 10 years or more for payments and often require convincing "stories" told by underwriters, can be very difficult to sell through a competitive sale. Smaller financings (less than $5 million) may also fail to generate much bidder interest and can often be better served by having a dedicated underwriter.

In addition, a negotiated sale does not have the same timing restrictions as a competitive bid. Competitive sales require bids to be submitted on a fixed date and time that must be decided anywhere from five to 10 days in advance (although they can be rescheduled with 24-hour notice). Negotiated sales, on the other hand, can be brought to market on any date the underwriters suggest. This can be advantageous during periods of high volume or market turmoil.

Two Districts: 50 Miles and a World Apart

Let's look at two examples from districts that are less than an hour's drive from each other. Palm Springs Unified School District benefits from having an internationally recognized name and a strong local economy. In addition, the district's GO bond credit rating is AA – due, in part, to the district's years of stable management.

In January 2010, the district brought $110 million of GO bonds to market through competitive bid. Eight bids were received, with the difference between the winning interest rate and the second-place finisher – known as the cover bid – coming in at two-hundredths of 1 percent.

By contrast, consider the Nuview School District, about 50 miles west of Palm Springs. With just slightly more than 2,500 students, it is the second-smallest district in Riverside County. Unlike Palm Springs USD, it is hardly a household name, and thus less attractive to potential investors. And even though Nuview is rated A+ by S&P, its assessed valuation – though beginning to stabilize as of mid-2013 – had fallen more than 30 percent in the previous five years.

The district's small size and falling assessed valuation necessitated a financing offering that combined current interest bonds (CIBs) and capital appreciation bonds (CABs). All these open-market investor impediments – small district, falling AV, the use of CABs – led us to recommend a negotiated bond sale to ensure that the district would get the money it needed for its projects.

Ultimately, your financial advisor or investment banker will need to make a recommendation as to whether your bonds should be sold through a competitive or negotiated bid. There are some key questions that need to be asked of the financial advisor and/or underwriter – and answered credibly – to establish whether their recommendation is truly in the best interest of the district. Among them:

- What are the issues and concerns regarding the district's credit quality that led to this recommendation? Districts with strong credit can usually do better in a competitive sale. Yet there are financial advisors who seemingly always come in with a recommendation for a negotiated sale, and they just happen to have a banker on hand to be the underwriter. If financial advisors or underwriters recommend a negotiated sale, it's wise to make them defend that recommendation with specific proof points drawn from the district's situation.

- Are there structural issues regarding the financing that led to the recommendation, such as the use of CABs?

- What political pluses and minuses might result from the recommendation? For many districts, public perception is just as important as getting the best deal. Since competitive financings are totally transparent, no one can ever accuse a district that opts for a competitive sale – as opposed to a negotiated one – of "back room dealing."

STRUCTURING THE BOND

A properly structured bond issue:

- meets the district's funding needs;

- complies with federal securities regulations;

- complies with state regulations, including bonded indebtedness limits and tax-rate limitations;

- meets (or at least attempts to meet) any political promises made to voters during the campaign;

- is attractive and marketable to investors;

- sets a fixed number of years over which the bonds will be amortized;

- identifies a maturity date to repay principal; and

- determines if the bonds will be callable and, if so, sets the penalty.

Besides that, it's a piece of cake.

Further complicating the process: the success of a bond measure at the polls seems to trigger an odd form of amnesia among many K–14 business officials who suddenly want all the money right away.

Before a bond measure is placed on the ballot, hours will be spent working with a district to develop a *bond issuance schedule* that will allow the district to comply with the tax-rate limitations found in Prop. 39. So, for example, a $30 million bond measure might be separated into three $10 million bond issues to be brought to market one at a time over a nine-year period.

If the financial advisor/investment banker is doing a proper job – and not all do – the underlying structure and assumptions of this proposed issuance timetable will have been described, discussed, debated, and documented with district officials before the bond measure was taken to the voters.

But after the campaign is over and the bond measure has been approved by voters, it's not uncommon for districts to lose all memory of these timing discussions. Within days after the election results are announced, I'll often get a call from a district CBO asking how soon they can sell *all* the bonds.

"All?" I ask, scrambling to open the tax-rate assumptions report on my computer. "You're only scheduled to sell about a third of the bonds in the first year. Do you want me to send you a copy of the assumptions sheet you signed off on?"

"No, no, that's okay," the CBO says. "But do me a favor, will you? Take another look at those numbers and see if we can speed up the schedule. I've got the superintendent breathing down my neck."

Bond Sizing and the Tax Rate

Putting aside these occasional bouts of amnesia, the starting point for the structuring of any bond financing is the cash flow the district needs to complete the next phase of construction. Recall that U.S. Treasury regulations require that at least 85 percent of bond proceeds from a financing be spent within a three-year timeframe (with certain exceptions). So, the first and simplest question is the timing of the district's bond expenditures.

The second and more complicated issue is the impact of the financing on the tax rate. Bond authorizations passed under Prop. 39 must have projected tax rates of no more than $60 per $100,000 of assessed valuation for unified school districts, $30 per $100,000 for high school and elementary districts, and $25 per $100,000 for community college districts.

For this reason, most financial professionals begin the structuring process by reviewing the original assessed valuation growth projections developed before placing the bond measure on the ballot. Since the original estimates may have been made up to a year earlier, assessed valuations for the most recent year need to be obtained and used to recalculate projected tax rates.

The impact of assessed valuation projections on tax rates was discussed in detail in Chapter 6. While there is no need to plow this ground again, it's worth noting that the stakes are much higher in putting these numbers together for an actual financing than for an election. Overly optimistic AV-growth assumptions made before an election will lead only to delays in the actual timing of the bond sales. The district will need to wait for assessed valuation to increase.

But if you blow the assumptions on the bond sale, it won't be long before the tax rate is climbing over the soft tax-rate cap, your bond program is half completed, and angry taxpayers are wanting to know what happened.

Political Tax-rate Caps and Other Promises

Any political promises made during the election must be kept in mind when structuring the numbers for a bond financing. During a bond campaign, some districts will commit to a *political tax-rate cap* – they'll "promise" voters the tax rate won't go over a certain amount even though the rate is allowed to go much higher under Prop. 39. For example, even though a unified school district can take the tax rate up to $60 per $100,000 of assessed valuation, it might "promise" voters it will hold the rate at, say, $25.

This commitment, which is almost always triggered by voter survey results, is extremely perilous. There is a huge political difference between *informing* taxpayers that the average tax rate to finance this bond is estimated to be $25 per $100,000 of assessed valuation, and *promising* them that the rate will not exceed this amount.

Many districts have learned the hard way. They promised a specific tax rate and then watched as their assessed valuations began to fall. Suddenly, they had to face a painful choice among unpleasant options: (a) delaying their school improvement projects until assessed valuation returned to former levels, (b) using costly capital appreciation bonds to remain under the political cap even though the interest cost of these securities is sky-high, or (c) breaking their political promise.

The question then becomes: Which is the more important promise to voters – the one about tax rates or the one about school improvement projects? I've seen debates on that thorny question get extremely heated.

Experience leads me to urge districts never to make promises about the tax rates or when a project will be finished, since these are outside of the district's control. Estimates? Yes. Plans? Of course. But hard promises, such as "this bond won't raise your taxes" or "you'll have a new middle school in three years," are asking for trouble, even when made in the best of faith.

TRANSPARENCY AND THE EX-PRESIDENT

A few years ago, I was working with an elementary district north of Los Angeles. The district board was getting ready to vote on the final resolution to place a bond on the ballot. The board had three specific projects it wanted to fund. In helping the district draft the Project List, I made sure there was enough wiggle room so that – should the district's needs change in the future – the district could reallocate some of the funding to other projects.

When the board president read the Project List, he exploded in anger when he saw the bond language was broader than the three specific projects he wanted funded.

"This is what people hate about politics," he raged. "They need to hear the truth! They deserve to know exactly what they are voting for! They need transparency!"

And so, at his insistence, the rest of the board agreed that all of the "wiggle-room" language should be tossed out of the resolution, and the bond measure went to the voters with only three projects. No more. No less.

Within two years, the president had been voted out of office (surprise, surprise), and – you guessed it – the district was calling up, saying one of the three projects was no longer a "district priority" and wondering if it was possible to use bond proceeds to fund a project that wasn't on the Project List.

Repressing a deep urge to yell "I told you so" into the phone, I referred the question to bond counsel who, after reviewing the Project List, responded that the answer was, unfortunately, no.

Callability

A bond's interest rate is fixed on the day of sale and cannot be altered afterward. This rate lock-in feature is an enormous advantage to taxpayers, who are insulated from future increases in tax rates due to rising interest rates in the marketplace.

But what if market rates go the other way? Can taxpayers benefit from lower rates in a *falling* interest rate market?

The answer is yes, so long as an optional call feature has been included as part of the bond structure when first sold to investors. This ability to call and prepay all or a portion of the bonds prior to their maturity (also known as an optional redemption right) holds tremendous future savings potential for taxpayers. If rates fall significantly, the bonds can be refinanced at lower interest rates (or "refunded" in the jargon of municipal finance), with the resulting savings flowing directly back to taxpayers.

Frankly, because a bond's later maturities will tend to have higher interest rates than earlier maturities (also known as a positive yield curve), interest rates don't even need to fall in order to provide savings to taxpayers through a refunding. Just by letting time go by, maturities that were once on the higher end of the yield curve will shift to the lower end – assuming rates remain stable.

Although an optional call is now a standard feature of most K–14 GO bond transactions in the state, the terms, limitations and costs associated with this redemption right can vary from deal to deal and should be carefully scrutinized. The most common limitation for an optional call is known as *call protection*. This feature requires that a certain number of years must elapse before the bond's optional call can be executed. For example, a bond issued in 2012 with 10 years of call protection cannot be refinanced until 2022.

CURRENT REFUNDINGS/ADVANCE REFUNDINGS

Bonds that are refinanced (refunded) after or within 90 days of their call date are known as *current refundings*. The number of tax-exempt current refundings allowed under IRS regulations is unlimited.

Bonds that are refunded earlier than 90 days before their call date are known as *advance refundings*; i.e., they are being refunded in advance of their call date. So, for example, even though a bond may not be callable for two years into the future, it can still be refinanced into lower interest rates using an advance refunding structure. However, due to recent changes in tax law, advance refundings with tax-exempt bonds are now prohibited and can only be structured using taxable bonds – a huge disadvantage.

Advance refunding bonds involve placing the proceeds of the refunding bonds (the bonds being sold to refund the outstanding, higher-interest bonds) into an escrow account. Funds in the escrow are held until the refunded bonds become callable.

Note that because the interest earned on the funds put into an escrow will almost never be invested at a rate that will equal or exceed the cost of borrowing the money in the first place, an advance refunding will produce what is known as *negative arbitrage*. This is essentially the cost of carrying the money sitting in the escrow. This cost – which is really lost savings – is often conveniently left out of presentations made by underwriters and financial advisors. Make sure you ask its amount, since it may be worth delaying the refunding until closer to the call date, in order to reduce this cost.

A bond's call feature might also come with a *prepayment penalty*. This is an amount to be paid to investors should the bonds be called prior to maturity. Taking the earlier example, a bond issued in 2012 with 10-year call protection might also come with a 2 percent prepayment penalty if the bonds are called before 2022. This penalty typically declines after the first call date, eventually falling to zero.

CABS AND CALLS

Oddly enough, even though an optional call feature provides tremendous potential future savings for taxpayers, there is one type of bond financing where, until recently, optional call features have been more the exception than the rule: capital appreciation bonds. This practice makes no sense to outside observers (as well as many insiders), given that CABs are such an expensive form of financing. (Note: AB 182 requires that all CAB deals with maturities of 10 years or more include an optional call feature.)

So, the question arises: given that having a call feature on a bond is a great deal for taxpayers and that CABs bear such high interest costs, why would anybody structure a bond *without* one?

In defense of making CABs non-callable, I've heard investment bankers argue that a call feature on a CAB will make its interest rate even higher because of the "thinness" of the investor pool that is willing to buy callable CABs.

There's some truth to this argument. A bond investor views interest rate risk from a point of view opposite to that of a taxpayer. If general interest rates rise, the investor has to accept the fact that the value of his investment in this bond is going to fall.

But if general interest rates *fall*, the value of his investment in this bond will rise. If the bond has an optional call feature, then the investor is at risk of being refunded out of what was beginning to look like a pretty smart investment. In response to this risk, the investor is going to want to be compensated. And the only way to do this is by offering the bonds with a higher interest rate.

How much higher? Obviously, the spread is going to move around depending on the market. However, I can't remember ever seeing a deal where the differential between callable and non-callable rates justified recommending the non-callable structure. The potential savings from being able to someday refund the CABs into CIBs is overwhelming.

Although there are certainly significant exceptions, when it comes to the structuring of K–14 GO bond CAB deals over the past decade, a number of investment banks have, I believe, spent more time worrying about their investors than their public-sector clients. Indeed, some of the most egregious CAB deals have been put together by investment banks that were strongly opposed to their district clients hiring an independent financial advisor who could have warned them what was going on.

Which is not to issue blanket praise to every financial advisory firm in the state. For reasons I still don't really understand, too many of these firms were active and willing participants in putting these non-callable deals together, and totally failed to warn their clients about the monetary and political risks of these transactions.

(By the way, my firm has recently developed a system of unwinding these non-callable CAB deals. This is covered in detail in *Special Topic #9*.)

Bond Anticipation Notes (BANs)

A month or two after the Poway USD CAB story hit the headlines, I was invited by the San Diego County Taxpayers Association to speak at a forum on the current state of school funding and finance. In response to a question from the audience regarding the increasing use of BANs as part of districts' GO financing plans, I got a little carried away and, Warren Buffett-style, called BANs a financial weapon of mass destruction when it comes to school finance.

I might have been a little over the top, but interestingly enough, at the end of the breakfast a board member from a San Diego County school district walked over and shook my hand.

"I couldn't agree more with what you said about BANs," he offered. "We thought we were geniuses when we first issued them. But looking back, once we jumped off that cliff, there was no turning back. We really had no choice. We had to issue CABs or go under."

Back in the good old days, BANs were generally issued for one reason: to front the state's portion of the district's school construction program. A district might be in line to receive $10 million in state funding, but for some reason the state was slow in making payment. So, the district would issue a BAN as a bridge loan to cover this delay in funding. Today, BANs can be an effective tool when structuring a tax rate extension by serving as a bridge between the soon-to-be-gone old tax rate and the newly approved replacement rate.

Other uses should be approached with caution. For example, some professionals tell clients they can use BANs as an arbitrage play to lower borrowing costs because a BAN's short maturity normally carries a lower interest rate. Others tout BANs as a way for a district to sell bonds even though its assessed valuation doesn't currently support such financing.

All of these creative uses of BANs are, from my point of view, dangerous ventures that should be avoided without a careful review of the underlying assumptions and risks inherent in these short financings. What impact does the potential for rising future interest rates have on taxpayers? What happens if assessed valuations fail to grow at the projected rate and the district is unable to issue take-out GO bonds? What is the actual cost to taxpayers of pushing payment on the bonds into the future in order to maintain today's previously promised political tax-rate cap?

Importantly, is the board aware that BANs – uniquely among financing methods – leave a *district's general fund* on the hook for financial shortfalls? Every other financing method makes taxpayers liable, while BANs make districts liable. Without a full and complete discussion of these issues, do yourself a favor and avoid the use of BANs as a substitute for long-term GO bonds. It's just not worth rolling such potentially explosive dice.

....

Special Topic #9
CAB RESTRUCTURING BONDS: CONFRONTING THE MESSY CLOSET

One afternoon in the summer of 2014, I got a call from Ron Bennett, the CEO of School Services of California. Ron's company is the state's premier K–14 financial management and advocacy firm. Districts often bring him in to help solve all types of complex and seemingly intractable problems. He'd just been handed a big one.

"You need to find a way to refinance some non-callable CABs," he said.

Sure, I thought. And then I'll turn to world hunger.

Ron explained that he'd just met with a newly hired superintendent of a southern Californian elementary district. She'd recently learned that about 10 years earlier, the previous administration had issued a whopper of a CAB. Even though the debt ratio was over 10-to-1, the deal had somehow slipped beneath the radar when the Poway CAB fiasco blew up. But it looked like this lack of scrutiny was about to change.

"There's a new taxpayers' representative on the Citizens' Oversight Committee," Ron said, "and he went ballistic when he discovered the CAB's debt ratio. Plus, the CABs are non-callable. He's on a rampage and demanding that the superintendent figure out a way to unwind the deal."

I knew Ron was well aware of the CAB facts of life but I ran him through the drill anyway. AB 182, the legislation that required CABs to be callable, restricted to a term of no more than 25 years and have debt ratios of less than 4-to-1, was solely limited to CAB deals issued after its enactment date of January 1, 2014. The bill did nothing about the hundreds of CAB deals issued in the decade or two before the legislation went into effect.

As the Poway/CAB mess unfolded in the press, politicians huffed and puffed in righteous indignation over these previous non-callable CABs, all pledging to turn their sights on these prior deals as soon as AB 182 was passed. But, like shutting the door of a messy closet, the bill's passage let people think that the problem had been solved. But just because a closet door is closed doesn't mean the mess is gone. The sad truth is that, if a pre-AB 182 CAB is non-callable, a district has no legal recourse whatsoever to get the bonds back from investors in order to refinance them.

"I know, I know," Ron said. "But you're going to have to figure out something. The superintendent wants to meet with you as soon as possible and I told her she could count on you."

Nothing like a little pressure, I thought to myself.

Ron's call provided the creative spark behind our CAB Restructuring Bond ("CRB") program. By the time I got together with the superintendent a few weeks later, we had the outline of a plan for refinancing non-callable CABs (even though it took another six months of research, development and legal review before it was ready for prime time).

In developing a solution that allows districts to refinance non-callable CABs, we had to unhook our brains from a number of commonly held assumptions and myths surrounding non-callable CABs. The first was that it's impossible to locate the owners of these CABs. Actually, there is a grain of truth to this statement. Many CAB deals have been sold to retail investors, and finding these people is next to impossible. But many CABs are owned by a handful of investment firms and mutual funds. These owners and their investment holdings are easily identified.

The second myth was that, even if you could find the owners, no one would ever voluntarily sell a non-callable CAB. "Why would anybody in their right mind sell such a great investment?" I heard over and over again from board members, administrators, journalists and competitors.

Ironically, it only takes about five minutes on a Bloomberg terminal to discover that California K–14 CABs get bought and sold regularly. It's a thin market, I'll grant you, but it exists.

So, why do investors sell these CABs? The answer is *what difference does it make*? Maybe they need the money. Maybe they've found a better investment. Maybe they've decided that waiting around 30-plus years to get paid on their investment wasn't such a great idea.

In the end, it doesn't matter. When you buy shares of Apple stock, you don't ask your broker why the previous owner sold them. They have their reasons to sell just like you have your reasons to buy.

Myth number three was that even if you could find the owners and even if they were willing to sell, the price they would demand would be so high it wouldn't make financial sense to buy the CABs back. This was an easy one to take down. By working with a team of highly competent underwriters who know the California K–14 CAB market inside and out, we're able to calculate market rate prices for these CABs that fairly compensate the owner while still making financial sense to the district. This is done *before* we approach the investor. Once we enter into a negotiation with them, if they are willing to sell their investment within our pre-established range, we've got a deal. If not, we walk away.

It doesn't work all the time. But when it does, the savings to taxpayers can run into the tens of millions of dollars. And, the closet ends up a bit tidier.

....

Chapter
ELEVEN

···

PREPARING FOR THE SALE

···

*"If you can't explain it simply, you don't understand it
well enough."*

~ Albert Einstein

In many ways, a bond financing is similar to buying a house. The financial
terms need to be specified. Everybody needs to take out his or her calendar
and agree to a timetable. Reams of legal documents need to be drafted,
reviewed, haggled over and, ultimately, approved. And piles of documents
must be signed, many of which are unintelligible to all but the most expert,
and yet the lawyers insist they are crucial to the closing.

Rather than delve into minute detail, I've listed below the major steps
in bringing a GO bond to market. Note that, as with the election process,
each county can have its own particular requirements, but any experienced
financial professional or bond counsel will know enough to check with the
various agencies to find out what exactly is required.

Preparing for the Sale

After the general structure of the financing has been developed (including the timing of the sale, principal amount, amortization schedule, call features, etc.), the following steps are required:

- Development and distribution of a *financing timetable* by either the financial advisor or the underwriter;

- Drafting of the preliminary official statement by either *disclosure counsel* or the financial advisor;

- Submission to one or both of the *rating agencies* of the preliminary official statement, plus the district's two most recent audits and three most recent budgets;

- Submission of similar information to *bond insurers;*

- Scheduling of a meeting (either in person or by phone) of the financial advisor or underwriter with one or both of the rating agencies;

- Appointing a *paying agent* to distribute principal and interest payments to investors.

Also, contact must be made with the board of supervisors of the county in which the district is located if the supervisors' approval is required for the issuance of the bonds. Some, but not, all counties have passed a blanket resolution allowing for direct district issuance without county involvement. But some require that each financing be approved by the board. This requires contact with both county counsel to review the resolution and the clerk of the board to schedule its passage.

The treasurer-tax collector's office also needs to be contacted and added to the distribution list and timetable. This office's level of involvement in the transaction differs from county to county, with some wanting to be deeply involved in both document review and the final pricing of the bonds. Others simply want to know when the funds are going to be wired into their account.

Finally, if the district's financials have a qualified or negative certification, approval by the county office of education may be required. Determining whether such approval is required is a bit of a gray area that depends on such factors as whether the bonds are being issued through the Government Code or the Education Code, as well as whether they are being issued through competitive bid or by negotiated sale. In these cases, it's best to rely on bond counsel to guide you through the maze.

BOARD ACTION: THE AUTHORIZING RESOLUTION AND THE OFFICIAL STATEMENT

The district resolution authorizes the sale of the bonds (either through competitive or negotiated sale) and approves the financing documents. This resolution is critical to everything that the district has been striving for since it first thought of passing a bond, and all parties should carefully review it. The resolution not only authorizes the district to sell a certain amount of bonds, it outlines the terms under which those bonds can be sold and directs the county treasurer to levy a tax of *whatever amount is necessary to repay the bonds* for years into the future.

Unlike the passage of a Prop. 39 resolution calling for a bond election, the finance resolution needs only a simple majority of the board for passage, not two-thirds. It also must be approved by a roll-call vote and cannot be placed on the consent calendar.

In passing the authorizing resolution, the board is also approving the publication of the Official Statement (the OS). This document, which is prepared either by disclosure counsel or by the financial advisor with review by legal counsel, provides investors and potential investors with the details of the bond financing, the repayment structure, the use of the bond funds, and the underlying credit of the district.

It will also include information on the bond's rating, whether bond insurance (a policy purchased upfront from bond proceeds to upgrade the bond issue's credit rating) has been purchased, and where the various funds created by the bond financing will be invested.

Technically, the Official Statement becomes "official" only *after* the sale of the bonds, and in passing it the board is giving authority to publish the OS upon completion of the sale. Prior to the sale, the document is known as the *Preliminary Official Statement (POS)*, also called a *red herring*. (A red herring doesn't refer to an intentionally misleading clue, but rather to language printed in red along the left-hand side of the cover to alert readers that the document remains in draft form.)

Read the Documents

As boring and tedious as the POS/OS may be, each board member needs to take the time to read it carefully, paying special attention not only to statements made about the district but also to the underlying assumptions used in developing the deal.

Many school and community college board members feel frustrated that those parts of the OS that detail the principal and interest payments remain blank prior to being approved by a board. While this frustration is understandable, these blanks cannot be filled in until the bonds are actually sold. Regardless, this should not deter board members from requesting that draft numbers be provided for review as part of the final resolution item.

If you doubt the importance of reviewing these assumptions, consider the hell a number of board members in districts around the state have gone through because of their highly-leveraged CAB deals. I don't know this for a fact, but I'd bet that few of them took the time to carefully read the OS and the supporting documents before making a commitment that would bind their district's taxpayers for years into the future.

Many of these board members claim they had "no way of knowing" how onerous these deals were, that they were misled and never told the total costs. Perhaps they are right. But I've been at this long enough to know it doesn't take much digging to figure out whether a deal is grounded on rational assumptions or froth.

Take just one example: a paragraph from an Official Statement for a general obligation BAN issued just a few years ago by a district that will remain nameless. Remember that this document was approved by the district's board when it approved the financing resolution. As background, the assessed valuation in this district dropped 10 percent in the two years prior to the board approving the resolution to issue BANs. Here's the description of what must occur for the district to issue a new series of GO bonds to repay its BANs:

"In order for the District to issue a second series of General Obligation Bonds ... and comply with the $30 per $100,000 limitation, the 2014–15 assessed valuation in the District would need to be ... **approximately 41.9 percent higher than the 2010–11 assessed valuation.***"* (Emphasis added.)

In other words, even though the district's AV had been plummeting for two years, this district's plans for paying off its BAN hinged on AV growing about 10 percent annually for the next four years. What would possibly induce an elected board member or administrator to read the paragraph above and say, *"Oh yeah, that makes sense"*?

My bet is the board and administrators didn't read the document but, instead, relied on the assurances of their financial advisor that everything was going to work out. And I can guarantee that when angry taxpayers start yowling, each board member will claim he or she was never told about the potential risks of the deal.

These denials by school boards across the state remind me of words of wisdom I was given years ago when I was just starting out in municipal finance. "When a deal goes bad," one of my first bosses on Wall Street told me, "there's no such thing as a sophisticated investor. Get everything on paper and get everybody to read it. It's our only protection."

Description of the Bonds

The most important sections of the POS/OS are presented below. (Different lawyers may use different names for these sections, put them in different order, combine sections, add new sections, etc. This is meant to be a general overview of the type of information included in the POS/OS.)

GENERAL OVERVIEW

This section provides information on the mechanics of the transactions, including:

- **Authority for Issuance**. A description of the legal authority under which the bonds are being issued, what amount of bonds have been previously issued under the authorization (if any), and what amount of bonds will remain authorized but unissued after the current sale.

- **Type of Debt Instrument**. A description of the type of bonds to be sold (e.g., current interest bonds, capital appreciation bonds, etc.).

- **Optional Redemption**. Although the year in which bonds can be called will typically not be listed in the POS, this section will make clear whether the bonds can be prepaid in the future or not.

DEBT SERVICES SCHEDULE

As noted above, the debt service schedule and interest rates are usually not provided in the POS. However, the OS presents a blank table where repayment information is to be filled in. From this blank table, you can generally see the number of years over which the bonds are to be amortized, plus whether the repayment is to include any capital appreciation bonds. In addition, the debt service from any previous financings under the authorization should be included in this section.

APPLICATION OF BOND PROCEEDS

As described in Chapter 14, funds from the sale of the bonds are almost always held by the county treasurer-tax collector. However, it's worth a quick check of this section of the OS to make sure this is the case with your financing.

SECURITY FOR THE BONDS

Since the security for the repayment of the bonds is the payment of taxes by property owners within the district, this section describes how property taxes are calculated, assessed, collected, and appealed. In addition, any potentially significant future changes would be described in this section, such as a large amount of property being taken off the tax rolls. In addition, this section generally includes three very interesting tables that give an overview of a district's assessed valuation.

HISTORICAL ASSESSED VALUATION

Typically stretching back at least five years, this table gives a quick view of the total assessed valuation of the district by year. The annual percentage changes are also included.

ASSESSED VALUATION BY LAND USE

A breakdown of properties within the district's boundaries by type of use (e.g., agricultural, commercial, single-family homes, mobile home parks). Both the total assessed valuation and the number of parcels for each category are included.

PER-PARCEL ASSESSED VALUATION OF SINGLE-FAMILY HOMES

People tend to misunderstand the difference between assessed valuation and market valuation. A table is provided to investors that shows just how far apart those two numbers can be (and how drastically Prop. 13 has kept assessed valuations artificially low over the years). The table typically breaks down the number of homes assessed in $25,000 increments, starting at $0 to $24,999 and working its way up to over $500,000. So, for example, thanks to Prop. 13, in the 2011–12 fiscal year, there were nearly 24,000 single-family homes on the tax rolls of the Kern High School District with an assessed valuation of less than $50,000 – nearly 12 percent of all the single-family homes in the district.

TOP 20 TAXPAYERS

The credit analyst uses this table to determine if there is a significant concentration of property taxpayers in one industry segment. Turning again to the Kern High School District, six of the top 20 property taxpayers in the district are involved in oil and gas production. This table is also often interesting for pure conversational value, because you never know who might pop up. Michael Jackson was the second-largest property taxpayer in the Santa Ynez High School District, and Oprah Winfrey's home in the Montecito hills has an assessed valuation of $100 million (and that's not even the highest valuation in that district).

DIRECT AND OVERLAPPING DEBT

The Statement of Direct and Overlapping Debt gives the most comprehensive view of not only the district's outstanding debt (including lease financings) but also the debt – borne by taxpayers – of other public agencies within the same boundaries. So, for example, even though the Dehesa School District in San Diego County has only a small amount of GO bond debt outstanding, its taxpayers also are responsible for the repayment of a portion of the GO bonds for Grossmont-Cuyamaca Community College District, Grossmont Union High School District, and the Grossmont Healthcare District. Overlapping general fund debt (e.g., certificates of participation) is also included.

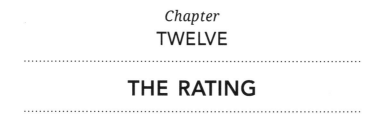

Chapter
TWELVE

....

THE RATING

....

"No sensible decision can be made … without taking into account not only the world as it is, but the world as it will be."

~ Isaac Asimov

The rating process is both easily understood and maddeningly opaque. The ratings agencies Moody's and Standard & Poor's (S&P) go out of their way to help districts understand what information is needed to rate the district's creditworthiness. They do a great job of streamlining the rating process so that it does not turn into a burden but, rather, is simple, clear, and highly efficient. Still, the entire rating process of GO bonds is so counterintuitive that it continually leads K–14 districts to question whether either of these agencies really understands what it is rating.

ONE OR TWO (OR THREE) RATINGS?

A financing's rating is the most important factor in determining its interest rate. The higher the rating, the lower the interest rate. For example,

TABLE 11
DISTRIBUTION OF CALIFORNIA K-14 GO BOND RATINGS 1/1/01 – 7/1/19

Ratings Assigned By:	Number of Ratings	Percent
Moody's and S&P	2,058	44.1%
S&P	1,713	36.7%
Moody's	597	12.8%
S&P and Fitch	218	4.7%
Moody's, S&P and Fitch	68	1.5%
Fitch	15	0.3%
Total	4,669	100%

Source: California Debt and Investment Advisory Commission

on July 10, 2019, a 5.00% coupon bond maturing in 10 years which was sold through competitive bid by the Stanislaus Union School District (underlying rating: "A+") had a yield 3 basis points above the MMD AAA curve. In contrast, a 5.00% coupon, 10-year bond sold through competitive bid six days later by the higher rated Santa Cruz Elementary School District (underlying rating: "Aa2") had a yield 23 basis points below the MMD AAA curve.

For this reason, going through the rating process (and paying the rating agencies' fees) is clearly necessary. Less clear is whether it makes sense to pay for two (or even three) ratings. And if a district chooses to seek just one rating, which one?

Most experienced underwriters prefer two ratings because, they say, most buyers prefer two ratings, which in the end translates to a lower interest rate for the district. As shown in Table 11, about half of the California K–14 GO bonds sold from January 1, 2001, through July 1, 2019, carried two ratings, usually from Moody's and S&P.

However, given that a nearly equal number of issues go to market with only a single rating, and that obtaining a rating can cost anywhere from a few thousand to tens of thousands of dollars, it's fair to ask if it's worth spending the money for a second rating.

It makes sense to apply for two ratings if the district's credit is weak, due either to internal finances or to the local economy. In these cases, having two ratings can help allay market fears of a district perceived as financially troubled. In addition, many large institutional buyers prefer two ratings because this extra layer of security helps them resell the bonds in the secondary market (where investors can buy and sell bonds after they have been issued, but before their maturity date) in the future.

But applying for a second rating doesn't always make sense. A district with strong, well-known credit (e.g., Palm Springs USD) probably doesn't need a second rating. Moreover, the rating agencies don't always see eye-to-eye on a district's circumstances, so requesting a second rating can sometimes result in a "split rating," in which one agency gives a lower rating than the other. (You can guess which one rating investors will point to when haggling over the interest rate.)

For districts with smaller financings (under $10 million), any interest rate savings that might result from a second rating might or might not justify the additional fee that would need to be paid.

There is also a third rating agency, Fitch Ratings. However, as noted in Table 11, Fitch's market share for providing "stand-alone" ratings (i.e., providing the only rating) of California K–14 bonds is close to zero. Fitch mostly provides second ratings, combined with those of either Moody's or S&P. While having a Fitch rating may make sense for especially large (or especially distressed) K–14 GO bonds, for most districts it's hard to justify a second (or third) rating from Fitch.

If only one rating is being applied for, the next question is how to decide between Moody's and S&P. In general, if a district has already been rated by one of the agencies (and the rating appears relatively accurate), it makes sense to stick with that agency. Still, investors tend to give more weight to the S&P rating, so if the choice is a toss-up, the tilt is usually – but not always – to S&P.

APPLYING FOR THE RATING

The process of applying for a rating starts with a phone call from either the financial advisor or the underwriter to a rating agency analyst. The focus of this call is to impart such basic information as the name of the district, the type of financing, the amount, the date by which the rating is needed, and the date of the sale. Also discussed is whether an in-person presentation is needed or a telephone interview will suffice. (See *Special Topic #10: The Rating – How Important Is a Face-to-Face Meeting?*)

After the schedule is agreed to, the financial advisor will send a packet of information to the rating agency that will include:

- a draft of the Official Statement, as well as legal documents

- the preliminary debt service numbers

- the last three audits of the district

- the most recent budget of the district

The financing is assigned to one particular analyst who is responsible for sifting through the information provided, as well as reviewing data the rating agency already has about the district. This will include credit reports and notes from previous financings completed by the district, as well as in-house data sources maintained by the agency.

Theoretically, the rating analyst reads all the documents in preparation for an interview with district officials. An analyst who's truly prepared will use the interview to get a better feel for the district. Unfortunately, analysts are occasionally unprepared, and in the course of the interview it may become clear that your analyst simply hasn't had the time to review the information submitted. While frustrating for district officials having to walk the analyst through material available in previously submitted documents, this lack of preparation will have little impact on the final rating. One way or the other – either in the initial interview or in follow-up phone calls – the analyst will eventually obtain all the information needed to complete the rating.

Major areas that analysts ask about include:

- unusual trends in the district's budget (e.g., a declining ending balance over the past few years)

- enrollment trends

- the status of current contract negotiations

- a better understanding of the audit, especially any significant concerns noted in the audit

- forecasts of the current year's ending balance

- contingency plans for potential future reduction in revenues

- an overview of the capital facility needs of the district

The absolute best district rating presentations convey a strategic sense of where the district is headed and how it plans to deal with potential adversities. In addition, ratings agencies want to see that a district has the administrative and political willpower to make hard decisions when faced with difficult circumstances. More than anything, rating analysts are looking for straight, honest answers. In more than 30 years of attending rating meetings, I've only seen one district official attempt to lie his way through an uncomfortable question. (The district was downgraded.)

Let's look at two examples – one good, one miserable – of how tough questions should be addressed in a rating meeting.

Special Ed and the Budget

The cost of providing an education for children with special learning needs is rapidly increasing. In both districts, the rating analyst noticed that special education costs were rapidly rising and asked what the district planned to do about this in the future.

In the first district, the superintendent answered, "We've been aware of this problem for some time now and are working to reduce the growth of this expense. We're doing this internally by making sure our expenditures are in line with the law, yet delivered efficiently. The truth is, our special education program is the best in the region. So, we also are making sure that the children who need this special care are, in fact, residents of our district."

An answer like that signals to the analyst that the district administration is aware of the problem and is working to solve it. The analyst might probe a little bit more to determine what specific actions are being considered but, in all likelihood, he or she would then move on to the next issue.

When the second district was asked this same question, the official hemmed and hawed for a while as if little thought had been given to this question. Finally, the superintendent sheepishly answered, "Well, I guess we're just going to hope that a lot less of these children show up next year." You can imagine what kind of confidence this answer inspired in the analyst, who, for a number of reasons, ended up putting that district on credit watch.

THE RATING PROCESS

The analyst will formulate an initial rating recommendation after compiling documentary information and conducting an in-person or telephone interview. This initial rating recommendation is then run by the analyst's manager and, if the manager agrees, the analyst will schedule a presentation to the firm's ratings committee.

The ratings committee is made up of senior rating agency officials. I've always thought of ratings committees as something like the Politburo in the former Soviet Union. Where they meet, when they meet, who's on the committee, what they talk about, and how they vote are all cloaked in secrecy. In addition, arguing with the committee after its members have made their decision is, in almost all cases, useless.

After hearing the analyst's presentation, the committee may accept the proposed rating, overrule the analyst and assign its own rating, or ask the analyst to obtain additional information before a decision is made. Sending the analyst back to answer additional questions is reputedly a veiled criticism of the analyst for not bringing enough information to the table. Analysts work hard to avoid being sent back for more information, which is why districts sometimes feel analysts are asking more questions than necessary.

TABLE 12 RATINGS		
Description	Moody's	S&P
Highest Rating Quality	Aaa	AAA
Very Strong Quality; Low Credit Risk	Aa	AA
Strong Upper Medium Quality; Low Credit Risk	A	A
Medium/Adequate Quality; Moderate Credit Risk	Baa	BBB
Modifiers	1, 2, & 3	+/-

Who Should Make the Rating Presentation?

The district official closest to the main problem(s) facing the district should be present to answer the analyst's toughest questions. If a district's problems stem from local politics (or, in the case of a community college, the accreditation process), it's critical that the superintendent or the chancellor make the presentation. If the problems are budgetary, then the CBO should be ready to handle most of the meeting. If the district's labor contracts are at the root of major financial issues, bring the assistant superintendent for personnel. In the end, the presentation should be about what makes your district special.

A Ratings Guide

As interest rates have fallen, the spread, or distance, between the interest rate on a highly rated bond versus a poorly rated bond has shrunk. However, a lower rating will still cost taxpayers more.

Both major agencies use a letter grading system with AAA at the top of the pile. The letters differ slightly between the two agencies, but the general sectors are about the same. Both agencies have imposed more and more granularity within the system by adding either numbers (Moody's) or plus/minus signs (S&P) to the letter rating. So, for example, an A1 at Moody's is higher than an A3 but not as high as an Aa3. Similarly, at S&P, an A+ is higher than an A- but not as high as an AA-. A guide to the various ratings is provided in Table 12.

S&P and Moody's have yet another level of gradation. When they feel a district is moving in the wrong or right direction, but it's too soon to lower or raise the rating, they will place the district on or take the district off negative credit watch. Negative credit watch status is announced to the market and tells the district, "Get it together or you're looking at a downgrade."

....

Special Topic #10
THE RATING: HOW IMPORTANT IS A FACE-TO-FACE?

How important is a face-to-face meeting with Moody's or Standard & Poor's? Both agencies welcome these meetings (at least, they say they do), but are the meetings actually necessary?

Let's start by differentiating between first-time issuers and a district that's on its second, third or fourth financing. For the repeat issuer, unless something has materially changed with the district (such as receiving a negative certification from the county office of education, getting ready for a strike, expecting a major lawsuit, etc.), you can probably save time and money by handling the rating interview over the phone.

But, for the first-time issuer (or a district that's been out of the market for many years), most financial advisors strongly advise setting up an in-person meeting with the rating analyst. Face-to-face meetings allow analysts to explore in depth the challenges facing the district.

While the basis for a rating remains the analysis of a district's financials and economic underpinnings, hearing first-hand about the background behind the district's challenges will give the analyst more to draw on when recommending a rating. Meeting with the analyst won't change the unemployment rate, but it might help shape the way the analyst views the administration's ability to deal with current and future financial problems.

In certain situations, a sit-down meeting with the rating analyst can benefit the district indirectly as well. While a district's fiscal officer will know his or her district's budget and audit inside out, as well as the short- and long-term challenges, that's (surprisingly) not always the case with the superintendent or chancellor. For some district administrators, listening to the questions and financial concerns of the rating agency analyst can be an eye-opening experience.

This is even more the case for board members. While some board members have been at it long enough to deeply understand the budgetary intricacies of their district, they are the exception to the rule. For the remainder – and especially for newer members – the rating presentation can be a tremendous learning experience about not only their district's finances, but also about the connection between a district's financial performance and its treatment by the capital markets.

Unlike many financial advisory firms, I prefer not to turn the rating presentation into a parade of charts and facts to try to overwhelm the analyst (and, I suspect, the client) with information. This usually has more to do with stagecraft than credit analysis.

I am also dubious about the benefit of scheduling rating agency dress-rehearsals to make sure everyone knows her or his scripted "part." A better idea is a pre-presentation conference call to make sure district officials know what they'll be asked, that being honest is the most important thing of all, and that if they're asked a question they can't answer, they should say, "I don't know, but I'll make sure to find out and get back to you."

Having sat through hundreds of rating presentations (and also having conducted numerous off-the-record interviews with rating agency analysts to hear what they're really looking for in these presentations), I've come to see that the most successful rating presentations are short, concise and candid. The absolute best results are achieved not through a rehearsed presentation but through open, free-flowing dialogue between the analyst and the district.

Which reminds me of a story. As mentioned above, over the years I've had a number of confidential conversations with rating analysts. In one discussion, I asked a former analyst her opinion of the usefulness of a particular competitor's presentations, which have a reputation for being tightly scripted and so deeply detailed that they sometimes even include student test scores at the districts' schools.

Was this level of detail really useful, I asked? Should we be providing the rating agencies this type of information? From an analyst's point of view, how did she feel about sitting through such a presentation?

She turned and stared out the window for a moment, silently thinking over her many years as an analyst. When she looked back at me, there was a slight smile on her face.

"Honestly, I'd rather stick a fork in my eye," she sighed.

....

IF GOS ARE BACKED BY TAXES, WHY KEEP ASKING ABOUT MY BUDGET?

It's clear the rating agencies are a critical component of the tax-exempt market. They provide investors with an independent, third-party review of a financing's creditworthiness. They employ trained analysts to review a district's budgets and audits with an eye to their short-and long-term financial health. Analysts take the time – which most investors don't have – to dig into the details of a district's transaction, reviewing a variety of topics that could affect the financing's strength, including a district's assessed valuation growth, the underlying economics of a region, the status of contract negotiations and the size of and year-to-year changes in the general fund ending balance. Their ratings can mean millions of dollars – plus or minus – in interest costs to taxpayers.

And yet, with all the power wielded by the agencies, with all their publications, seminars and client meetings, with their increasingly granular system of ratings, why is it that – at least with general obligation bonds – nobody seems to understand what exactly is being rated?

After a district's first interview with a rating agency, the superintendent or CBO will inevitably turn to me in the elevator and ask, "Do they always spend that much time on the budget?"

"Always," I'll nod. "And they'll probably be following up by phone with a few more questions in a day or two."

"But…" the client will ask after a pause, "what difference does my budget make? Don't they understand these bonds are being paid off by the taxpayers, not the district?"

And it's not just K–14 officials who are confused. I was once interviewed by a reporter who was convinced that GO CABs created the potential for future financial disaster for school districts.

"Look," I said to the reporter, "after a district issues a GO bond, the taxpayers, not the district, are responsible for its repayment. Every kid in the district could move to Arizona, the district could shutter its classrooms and its playgrounds could be paved over, but its taxpayers would still be required to make annual property tax payments to repay the bond." So, if a district's general fund isn't on the hook for a GO bond's repayment, why all the focus by the rating agencies on the district's finances? (By the way, this doesn't apply to BANs, as a few unlucky districts are slowly figuring out. BANs are, in fact, typically guaranteed by the district's general fund.)

DEFAULT RISK VS. VOLATILITY

It's a good question and one I've struggled to answer over the years. If the purpose of the rating is to analyze the risk of bond repayment, and the district has no responsibility for repayment, why spend so much time rooting around in a district's budget and audit?

The Rating

I'll admit my answer is a bit idiosyncratic, and I doubt you'll find it in the rating agencies' promotional materials. But, over the years, I've come to believe that a K–14 GO bond rating has very little to do with the potential for default. Rather, I think the rating provides an assessment of the risk of volatility in the future price of a bond in the secondary market.

Those of us who assist school and community college districts in the issuance of debt financings tend to forget about the secondary market. But the secondary market is not only vast, it is exquisitely sensitive to changes in interest rates as well as concerns regarding a particular credit.

Take, for example, an investor who buys a $100,000 GO bond from the XYZ District maturing in 10 years with a 5 percent interest rate. This means the owner of the bond will receive a $5,000 interest payment every year for 10 years and then, in the 10th year, be repaid the $100,000 principal.

But what happens if the investor decides she no longer wants to own this bond and wants to get back her $100,000 now rather 10 years from now? In this case, the investor needs to sell the bond to another investor through the secondary market.

But just because she paid $100,000 for the bond when it was issued doesn't mean she can sell it at par (the original purchase price) in the future. Just as the value of a house rises and falls, the value of the bond may rise or fall from its original purchase price, depending on the current interest rate market as well as any changes in the bond issuer's creditworthiness.

A bond's interest rate – in this example, 5 percent – is locked in when the bond is issued. Regardless of what happens to either interest rates in general or the district's credit rating in particular, this bond's interest rate remains fixed.

Going back to our example, let's say current market interest rates have fallen from 5 percent to 4 percent since our investor bought the $100,000 bond. That makes the bond more valuable, since it is paying 5 percent per year compared to newly issued bonds that are paying 4 percent. And because it is more valuable, the price of the bond (the amount investors are willing to pay for it in the secondary market) will rise. Conversely, if interest rates rise, the price will fall below $100,000.

The effect of credit quality on the value of a bond in the secondary market is complicated and, as shown in the example above, is about more than just the ability of an issuer to make timely interest and principal payments. The impact of a bond's credit quality on its price in the secondary market is more about how others will perceive the issuer's creditworthiness, rather than the actual ability of the issuer to make the required payments.

Let's return again to our investor who bought a $100,000 bond issued by the XYZ School District. Remember that this bond is due in 10 years and pays 5 percent interest per year. Repayment is guaranteed by the obligation on the part of the county treasurer to levy a tax on all the taxable property within the district's boundaries sufficient to repay the bond's interest and principal. In other words, although it is theoretically possible, it is hard to imagine a set of circumstances in which this investor will not be paid.

And yet, if bad news about the district suddenly occurs (for example, a negative qualification of its budget by the county office of education, a financial scandal within the district or the bankruptcy of a major employer), investors will react negatively, even though these events have no impact on the repayment of the XYZ District GO Bond's principal and interest. The more bad news there is about a district's finances (or management), the more volatility there will be in the price of its bonds in the secondary market.

(It's worth noting that changes in a bond's price in the secondary market have no impact on the district that issued the bond. Once again, the rate of interest on the bonds to be repaid by taxpayers is locked in on the date of sale.)

I think this explains why the rating agencies spend so much time in their evaluation on issues that would appear to have nothing to do with the repayment of the bond. My view is that a GO bond's rating has only a little to do with the actual risk of its repayment. What's really being rated is the potential volatility of a bond's price in the future. Even though issues such as the stability of a district's budget, the status of its employee agreements, the quality of its administration and the stability of its board may have nothing to do with repayment of a bond's principal and interest, they can have an enormous effect on the future price of that district's bond in the secondary market.

Chapter
THIRTEEN

....

THE SALE AND THE CLOSING

....

"I'm extraordinarily patient provided I get my own way in the end."

~ Margaret Thatcher

In the good old days (there he goes again!), the opening of bids and the bond closing were filled with arcane ritual and drama. We'd hold the bid openings for a bond sale in our offices in downtown San Francisco, and it was quite the scene with a cast of characters (and I do mean characters) rushing into our conference room at the last minute to deliver their bids. Most of the time, these guys would have just hung up from a pay phone down the block and would show up out of breath from running up the street with a scribbled interest rate bid crammed into a sweaty, wrinkled envelope.

There were twists and turns over who had or had not made it to the opening, yelling matches over whether or not a bid was late, missing good-faith checks, and the final drama of envelopes being ripped open to announce each bid.

And the closing? That entailed an all-day meeting in the lawyers' offices, documents strewn across conference tables, and phones jangling off their hooks with confirmations of funds being received. And then, as dusk began to fall, everybody would troop off for a formal dinner with toasts and roasts.

Today, I hardly know when a client's bonds are sold or deal closes. Tap, tap. Click, click. Bids are received on computer screens. Pricing is handled via conference call or "real time" websites. A successful closing rarely even warrants a phone call. Word of the receipt of funds is now sent by email. And dinner? I honestly can't remember the last closing dinner I attended. And I'm the one who usually picked up the check.

HOW INTEREST RATES ARE SET

The Ins and Outs of Competitive Sales

Although a competitive sale of municipal bonds involves a little more upfront work, the setting of the interest rates is surprisingly simple. This simplicity is its greatest political asset. Regardless of a board member's level of financial sophistication, the concept of "the cheapest bid wins" is about as simple as it gets, and the political cover provided by requiring competitive bids is highly compelling.

Not only is the form of the sale easy to understand, the steps involved are equally straightforward. A sale date and an exact time to receive bids are chosen when the financing's initial timetable is put together. It's traditional to avoid Mondays and Fridays (though you see them occasionally), and the time for bids to be received is typically mid-morning. So, for example, a bid might be tentatively scheduled for Tuesday, May 24, at 10:00 a.m. Pacific Time.

The chosen sale date is inserted into the Notice of Sale, the format of which has already been approved by the district's board as part of the authorizing resolution. Listings are published in various periodicals, letting the market know that a sale is planned. About a week before the sale date, copies of the Notice of Sale and the Preliminary Official Statement are posted on a special online site that can be accessed by underwriters throughout the country.

Once the Notice of Sale has been posted, the sale date is engraved in stone and cannot be changed without 24-hour notice. Although language is typically added to the authorizing resolution allowing the district to take new bids at a later date if none are received or accepted on the sale date, this lockdown of the sale date is a feature that's baked into the competitive sale process.

Bids are received electronically on the day of the sale. Although the services that host the bids calculate the winning bids, it's the responsibility of the financial advisor to recheck the bid calculations and make sure they have been correctly computed.

As mentioned above, the lowest cost of money wins the bid. This calculation is more complex than just adding up the total amount of interest to be paid. (Although, remarkably, this was how the Los Angeles County Treasurer's Office calculated winning bids through much of the early 1990s.) The bid calculation is "time-weighted," meaning it takes into consideration the time value of money, rather than treating a dollar owed in Year One the same as a dollar that needn't be repaid for 20 years.

A call is then made to the client to announce the results and decide whether the low bid should be accepted and awarded. Although the legal documentation typically provides that the district has up to 24 hours to award the bid, as a courtesy to the financial institutions we typically try to award the sale as soon as possible.

As a side note, I've always believed one of the strongest arguments in favor of bringing bonds to market through a competitive process is the ability to reap the rewards of mistakes made by others. Every once in a while, you'll see a winning bid that is 10 to 20 basis points (one basis point equals 0.01 percent) below all the others. Although I can't prove it, I've always suspected that the gap was due to some type of screw-up on the part of the "winning" bidder and that their mistake was the district's gain.

The biggest possible hiccup in issuing bonds through a competitive sale is the potential failure to receive any qualified bids. This happens rarely; nonetheless, it's the financial advisor's job to avoid these situations. For example, a small, poorly rated bond might get pushed aside if it comes to market on the same day as one or more significantly larger financings. The financial advisor should look sharp and keep the client's offering out of the shadow of larger deals.

In other cases, a competitive sale might be challenging if a district's credit is widely *perceived* as a piece of junk regardless of the facts (such as a strong investment-grade rating). For example, Stockton USD needed to get into the bond market around the same time the City of Stockton was declaring bankruptcy. Even though there was no connection between the district and the city, and Stockton USD's credit had a solid investment-grade rating, we anticipated the market would avoid anything with the word "Stockton" in it. So, we recommended the district sell its bonds through a negotiated sale with a single underwriter, so the underwriter's sales force could educate investors about the financing.

In cases where clients reject our recommendation for a negotiated sale and insist on a competitive sale, we make sure the resolution contains back-up language allowing a move into a negotiated sale in case no bids are received.

Finally, sometimes you can just sense that getting a qualified competitive bid might be iffy. Maybe the number of bidders registering is way below normal. Maybe you're hearing rumors of market concern about the structure of the credit. (In one case, I had a board member quoted in the paper—the day before bids were to be received—saying he believed his district was about to go bankrupt. Funny how a comment like that can spook an underwriter.) In these cases, a savvy financial advisor will get on the phone and start calling underwriters, making sure they are aware of the deal and responding to any concerns.

Although it is rare, there are times when the market in general simply has no appetite for the risks associated with a competitive sale. In the months following the meltdown of 2008–09, finding a competitive bid for all but the best of credits was tough sledding. While the competitive bid market eventually came roaring back, those districts that insisted on a competitive sale during the dry months paid a price. For this reason, I always urge our clients to be open-minded in the war between advocates of the competitive vs. negotiated sale and always be ready to embrace change when necessary.

Once you let the underwriter know theirs is the winning bid, the process from that point on pretty much kicks into autopilot. Plenty of work is being done. There are documents to be drafted, notices to be filed, final number runs to be completed, debt service tables to be sent to the county treasurer's office, closing memos to be prepared, wire instructions to be drafted and reviewed, and so on. But, from the point of view of the district, the heavy lifting is over. Besides the signing of a mountain of documents, the financing is essentially complete.

The Ins and Outs of Negotiated Sales

As described earlier, the negotiated sale does not involve the receipt of bids but is, rather, a sole-source sale to either a single underwriter or a group of underwriters. As with a competitive sale, a sale date is chosen when putting together the financing calendar.

But unlike a competitive sale, there is much greater flexibility in changing this date if there is a sudden spike in interest rates or the general tone of the market is unsettled. Indeed, even though we have long been and remain strong advocates of the competitive sale of new-money GO bonds, the ability to easily and quickly shift the sale date is the one clear and major advantage of a negotiated sale.

The underwriter will typically schedule a "pre-sale" conference call with all the participants on the day before the sale. This will usually include the district CBO and other financial staffers, the district's financial advisor (if there is one) and occasionally bond counsel.

Some other rituals in the pricing and closing of municipal bonds may have disappeared or become e-streamlined – as I made clear in my nostalgic grumblings at the start of this chapter – but the pre-pricing conference call (and the following day's sales call), managed by the investment bank's underwriting desk, remains among the most stylized, opaque, and cryptic rites in the securities industry.

After everybody gets on the line and introductions are made, the lead investment banker typically turns the call over to the underwriter. This is the person responsible for pricing the deal at interest rate levels that are aggressive (i.e., low) enough to stop the bonds from sailing off the shelf, but not so aggressive that his employer, the investment bank, ends up retaining ownership of the bonds.

As the call starts, you can hear the din of a trading desk in the background, sales men and women barking out orders as everybody tries to stay on top of the frenzy. After being introduced, the underwriter will typically take a deep breath, hold it for a beat or two, and then launch into a usually unintelligible review of market conditions. This is usually a tour-de-force that weaves together not only current interest rate levels (including Treasuries, state bonds, recent deals in the markets, and Bond Buyer averages) but can also include housing starts, currency levels, speculation on upcoming Federal Reserve actions, recent natural disasters, etc. – all spit out at breakneck speed.

At the end of the report, there's usually a short pause. "Any questions?" the lead banker will ask.

More often than not, there's a stunned silence on the phone until the investment banker turns the conversation to the proposed rates for the deal being proposed. This is what everybody has been waiting for. It's the most fraught part of the call.

As mentioned, the underwriter needs to come up with a scale that is aggressive enough to test the market's limits but not so much so that he ends up eating the deal for lunch. Here is where the underlying conflict of the negotiated sale gets laid bare: the district issuing the bonds is the investment bank's client, but so are the investors to whom the bonds are being pitched.

One transaction. Two clients, with opposing goals. The district wants the lowest interest rate possible. The investors want the highest. How can the bank fairly represent the interests of both parties?

Even though most (and I emphasize *most*) investment banks I've worked with do their best to thread that needle, the potential for conflict cannot be ignored. This is why, as already mentioned, MSRB now requires investment banks to tell their public sector clients that the bank does not represent their fiduciary interests. It's also why investment banks are now prohibited from trying to dissuade their municipal clients from hiring a financial advisor, who does have a fiduciary duty.

Let's review the role of the financial advisor during the negotiated sale's pricing and pre-pricing calls. The financial advisor has three main tasks on these calls:

1. **Produce, Review and Interpret Comparable Interest Rates.**
   The municipal market is messy and disorderly. Unlike the U.S. Treasury market, there is no easily accessible "real time" source of tax-exempt rates. This has partly to do with the decentralization of the market, but it is also a function of the wide variety of tax-exempt bonds. So, the only way you can get a read on the "fairness" of the proposed interest rate scale is to look at recent comparable financings. It's important that this list of other transactions be

prepared by the financial advisor and not by the underwriter, to avoid the potential for cherry-picking.

2. **Make Sure the Client's Questions Are Answered**. As I indicated above, the underwriter's pricing spiel can be pretty intimidating, and not all school district officials feel comfortable asking questions – especially when they feel they should already know the answer. The financial advisor often needs to challenge the underwriter's claims or ask for clarification in order to create an atmosphere of dialogue so that the client feels comfortable asking questions about the transaction.

3. **Make Sure the Underwriters Act Like Underwriters.** Even though underwriters like to talk about how they are paid to take risk, in reality they do their best to minimize it. I'm not criticizing them: theirs is a fairly rational business model. Still, the job of the underwriter is to underwrite the bonds (i.e., to guarantee to buy, for their bank, any that remain unsold to investors), not just be a clearinghouse.

That's why it's important for the financial advisor to press the underwriter to tighten up the scale (i.e., lower the interest rates) if the deal is oversubscribed. Truth be told, good underwriters will do this without being asked, but that doesn't mean they all will. And even the good ones can use a push now and then.

All of this presumes an arm's-length relationship between the underwriter and the financial advisor. However, when the financial advisor and the investment banker have a hazy symbiotic business relationship, it makes the financial advisor's ability to provide independent advice questionable.

For example, the financial advisor on one of the most egregious CAB deals done in the state in the past few years – its debt ratio was in excess of 10:1 – was brought into the financing by the underwriter. This was the first bond deal this financial advisor ever handled, and he failed to give the school board any warning about the deal being proposed. He simply didn't have the tools or the credentials to stand up and ask the hard questions.

Once the interest rates have been established and agreed upon, the closing procedures for a negotiated financing and a competitive deal are nearly identical.

Private Placements

There is one other method of selling bonds that, although seldom used, can be highly effective in certain circumstances – or incredibly costly if not carefully analyzed. A *private placement* (sometimes referred to as a direct placement) takes place when the bonds are sold directly to a buyer instead of an underwriter for resale. There are a number of advantages that can result from a private placement. The first and most obvious is the cost savings. There's no need to pay an underwriter, although districts still pay reduced *placement agent* fees. And, since the deals are not going to be sold or reoffered to the public, there's no need to produce an Official Statement or purchase a rating, since these deals are rarely rated.

On the other hand, private placement interest rates offered by some financial institutions can be way off the market. For example, we were recently asked to look at the financing package being proposed for a small district planning to install a solar/energy-saving project. The energy equipment provider claimed to be providing a turnkey package that included the private placement of the bonds. With one call to a competing financial institution, we cut the proposed interest rate nearly in half.

COSTS OF ISSUANCE

Years ago, when I ran the Public Finance Department for Crocker Bank (later Wells Fargo), I attended an all-day strategic planning meeting with the managers of the various departments that made up the bank's Capital Markets Division. These included Treasury bond sales, tax-exempt bond underwriting and trading, asset-backed lending, and so on.

The purpose of the meeting was to give the division's newly promoted manager – Fred – an overview of the challenges faced by each department.

Fred had been a manager of numerous bank departments and had worked inside the bank his entire career. He was a complete straight arrow – I don't think I ever saw him wearing anything but a starched white shirt with a striped tie and a gold Cross pen in his pocket. Despite his warm, easy smile, he had little tolerance for poor performance and even less for excuses. The bank was going through a pretty rough patch financially and Fred's mandate was to raise his division's revenues and cut expenses.

Each department head was required to give Fred a thorough briefing on his or her business model, short-term and long-term projections, and any outstanding issues. Fred's smile slowly faded over the course of the day as he worked his way around the conference table, grilling each manager about his or her plans and challenges.

Unfortunately, the news was rarely good, and Fred was getting more and more exasperated. Toward the end of the meeting, the head of the foreign currency department – the section of the bank that tried to make a profit by trading one country's currency against another – weighed in with a particularly bearish report. When he concluded, Fred, ticking another report off his list, asked, "Anything else?"

Currency traders, in my experience, tend to have a bit of pirate roguishness in their attitude, a certain swagger that comes from getting paid for what to me always seemed like legalized gambling. This fellow definitely fit that mold.

"We could use a new currency trader," he drawled, giving Fred a big opening-bet card-game smile. "Our last one died a few months ago, but I can't get approval for a new hire."

"Okay," sighed Fred. "And just exactly how much will a good currency trader cost?"

"About $300,000 a year."

Fred winced. "What about a bad currency trader?"

"A bad one?" he laughed. "Well, that'd cost you about $2 million a year."

I think of that story whenever I run across a district that wants to hire its financial advisor or bond counsel based on lowest fees. While I'm certainly sympathetic to the need for district officials to keep an eye on costs, I've seen too many situations where taxpayers get the shaft because the "least expensive" financial advisor turns out to be clueless.

The Sale and the Closing

Putting together a bond deal is expensive. That's neither a defense nor an apology. Even the simplest deals involve hundreds of moving parts and hours upon hours of work from financial advisors, investment bankers, rating agency analysts, tax lawyers, and paying agents. But if the main goal is to reduce costs, the result is too often a bond deal put together by B-team players who have no idea what they're doing. Or – worse – know exactly what they are doing, and are doing it to you.

To see how misleading it can be to focus solely on costs of issuance, let's contrast the experiences of two Southern California school districts.

District A in San Diego County passed a $95 million bond in 1998. Even though this was a pre-Prop. 39 bond election (and therefore had no tax rate limitation), the district took a very conservative approach in bringing its bonds to market. Each bond was sold through competitive bid with a term of 25 years or less, and the underlying assessed valuation assumptions were kept purposely low and carefully reviewed each year. In addition, the district took a very slow and steady approach to issuing the bonds, dividing the authorization into six separate series over an eight-year period.

District B in Los Angeles County passed a $75 million bond four years later in 1992. Although District B also took eight years to issue the entire authorization, unlike District's A's issuance of six series of bonds, it issued all the bonds in only two sales.

On the surface, it would be easy to assume that District B – which went through just two sales cycles instead of District A's six – got a better deal because such costs of issuance as financial advisors' fees were lower. Think again.

In a bond deal, the real nut isn't what is paid to the professionals; it's what is paid to the investors. Total interest paid by District A's taxpayers came to $67.7 million on a $95 million bond. In other words, for this bond, nearly 60 percent of every tax dollar paid by taxpayers was destined for the repayment of principal and only 40 percent for interest.

Though District B might have saved money on professionals' fees by having just two sales, its taxpayers weren't so lucky. They'll end up paying more than $287.5 million interest on the district's $75 million bond – nearly four times as much interest and principal. Who got the better deal? District B with its low cost of issuance? Or District A, which certainly paid its advisors a whole lot more than District B did?

I'm not suggesting that the more you pay your financial advisor, the less your taxpayers will pay in interest. It's just that too many districts fixate on lowering the cost of issuance while ignoring the enormous cost of interest payments. Just like a bad currency trader, it's not always the smartest move to hire the cheapest financial advisor.

Open the Pod Bay Doors, Hal

So how *do* you find out if the fees being proposed are reasonable? That's a tough question. After all, one man's *reasonable* is another's highway robbery. I recently had an experience on this very subject that reminded me just how hard it must be for public officials to assess if they're getting a fair deal. I was meeting with the superintendent and CBO of a midsized suburban elementary district to discuss a proprietary financing program we'd developed that I knew would be perfect for that district's needs.

The superintendent immediately saw the value in the program and was all over it. I think he would have started work on the financing at that very moment if his CBO had let him. But the CBO quickly reached over and pulled the handbrake.

"Before we begin anything," he said coolly, "We'll need to run this plan by our current financial advisor. Would you have a problem with that?" he asked, turning to me.

"Oh sure," I thought to myself, "And, while you're at it, why don't you give her the online password to my checking account?"

I smiled, took a deep breath, and explained to him that, yes, this would be a problem because the district's current financial advisor was also one of my competitors.

"I know," he persisted. "But she's also our current financial advisor. So why wouldn't we want her opinion?"

"Because," I answered, trying to remain calm. "Most businesses generally try to avoid sharing their best ideas with their competitors."

"But how else would we know if your fees are fair?" he asked in a flat logical tone of voice. I was beginning to feel a little like the astronaut in *2001: A Space Odyssey* who's been locked out of the spaceship and is trying to talk the computer into letting him back in. (*"Open the pod bay doors, HAL." "I'm sorry, Dave. I'm afraid I can't do that."*)

Just then, it dawned on me that he was actually asking a pretty good question – one that I was at a loss to answer. He could see how much the superintendent wanted to get moving on this project, but his job was to make sure the district didn't get taken for a ride. And the reality is that it's damn hard to figure out whether the underwriting, financial advisory, or legal fees that are being quoted are indeed reasonable compared to the rest of the market. This guy just wanted to do what seemed rational – check out the fees with someone he trusted. (We ultimately agreed that the current financial advisor could be consulted about the fairness of our fees but wouldn't be given any proprietary details regarding the financing package.)

What this CBO was doing – and I give him credit for it – was not falling into the trap of simply assuming that there's an industry standard for underwriting, financial advisory, or bond counsel fees. True, the fees for most firms fall into roughly the same range. After all, we all know each other, watch each other, complain about each other, and compete with each other. But I've also seen cases where the investment banker, financial advisor, or both charged their clients two to three times the going rate without batting an eye. Just remember, public finance remains a largely unregulated industry and, in the end, it's up to you to protect the hen house.

Although getting a second opinion on fees is generally a good idea, I think it's more effective if the opinion is not coming from a direct competitor but from an unrelated market participant whom you know and trust. For example, if you've worked with another bond counsel firm in the past, you might contact them to run through financial advisory or underwriting fees. Similarly, if you know a financial advisor other than the one you are about to hire, you might give him or her a call to discuss proposed legal fees.

If you still question the reasonableness of the proposed fees, call up a few other districts that have used different firms. Don't rely on the comparables or references handed to you by the firm that's trying to sell you, since they've probably been cherry-picked.

You should also realize that different financial advisors view their roles quite differently. Again, until recently, public financial advisory is an almost wholly unregulated industry. While most people in this field get deeply and legitimately involved in the structuring and analysis of the financing and running of the deal, some advisors are, shall we say, a little more sales-focused.

Their *modus operandi* was perhaps-too-colorfully described to me recently by a young financial advisor I was interviewing for a job.

"They're bond pimps," he said. "All these guys do is drive around the state, buying everybody lunch, trying to convince them to get onto the ballot. When one of them finally bites, they swoop down, promise them the moon, get 'em to sign some outrageous contract, then pimp them off to some poor schmuck investment banker to do the heavy lifting."

Colorful language aside, he pretty well captured the business model of a few of the more notorious public finance advisory firms around the state. Again – *caveat emptor*.

How Costs of Issuance Are Paid

Fees – including all costs of issuance and underwriting – can be paid one of two ways: you either take a slice out of the pie (thereby reducing the money available to fund projects) or you make the pie bigger so the amount of project funds remains unchanged. These two methods can, by the way, be mixed and matched, as will become clearer as we go on.

In "taking out a slice," the underwriter is compensated by buying the bonds at a *discount*. (In the trade, this is referred to as an *underwriter's discount*.) For example, a $10 million bond with an underwriting fee of 0.50 percent, or $50,000, would be purchased by the underwriter at 99.5 percent. At closing, $9.95 million would be wired to the district and the underwriter would retain the $50,000 fee.

The remaining costs of issuance (financial advisory fee, rating, etc.) would be paid out of the $9.95 million wired to the district. Let's say those costs come to $150,000. This would leave $9.8 million for projects.

That's all well and good, some would argue, except that voters approved $10 million worth of *projects* and now they're getting only $9.8 million. As an alternative, sometimes costs of issuance are paid by making the pie bigger. This is achieved by selling the bonds to investors at a premium, also referred to as OIP or *original issue premium*.

In this situation, the investor must pay more for the bonds than their face value. So, for example, instead of paying $10 million for $10 million of bonds, she pays $10.2 million. Of this $10.2 million, $50,000 goes to the underwriter, $150,000 goes to a "cost of issuance fund" set up to pay the various professional fees and expenses, and the remaining $10 million goes to the district.

So far, so good. The district gets the full $10 million and everybody gets paid. But where, you might ask, does the extra $200,000 come from? Hint: Not from the investors. No, ultimately, it's paid by the taxpayers. Because the investor is going to have to pay $10.2 million for a bond that's only worth $10 million, he's going to want a higher interest rate to compensate for the extra cost. And that higher interest rate translates into a slightly higher tax rate.

Mind you, we're not talking about huge tax rate increases. In most cases, the impact is negligible. But it's still money that comes out of the taxpayer's pocket.

Here's the problem. On one side (I tend to agree with this side), people argue that voters voted for $10 million of *projects*, they didn't approve a tax rate. The full amount of the approved project funding can be obtained by selling the bonds at a slight premium.

Others say, "Not so fast." Voters approved $10 million of debt and by selling the bonds at a premium, you're essentially creating an additional $200,000 of debt without voter approval.

POWAY AGAIN?

This issue would have probably remained on the sidelines had it not been for some financial advisors, underwriters, and bond counsel who decided to push it to the max. "Gee," they said. "If we can generate a premium on a bond sale and use it to pay costs of issuance, why couldn't we use it to pay all sorts of other things?"

So that's just what they did. They started using it to raise funds to pay the interest on BANs that were coming due. They used it to pay off previously issued COPs and lease deals. They used it to reimburse costs of issuance from previous bond deals that had already been paid from bond proceeds.

One of the most aggressive examples of this method of raising extra cash was by Poway USD. In 2009, Poway sold $74 million of bonds and generated a premium of $9.5 million – 13 percent more in funding than was actually being sold. In 2011, when Poway was getting ready to sell its $105 million deal (the one that pushed it over the $1 billion mark in repayment costs), it wanted to raise an additional $21 million in premium – a 20 percent mark-up.

Apparently the financing team, worried that this was too much of a stretch, filed what is known as a *validation action* – essentially a legal CYA maneuver – in the local Superior Court. The way judicial validation actions are supposed to work is that the concerned party files papers with the court indicating its intentions and allowing anyone who might object to challenge those intentions. In almost every case, nobody shows up to object, and the judge awards the filer what is known as a *default judgment*. With the judgment in hand, the filer can proceed with whatever action it wants to take with pretty strong confidence that no one can raise a challenge in the future.

Even though nobody showed up in court to object to the Poway deal, it did catch the attention of Kamala Harris, California's attorney general at that time. Her office wrote a letter to Poway USD's lawyers citing "significant concern" over the proposed bond issue and saying, "the law is clear that any premium … must be deposited into a special fund applied to pay debt service, and therefore cannot be diverted to pay costs of issuance."

Despite this strong letter, the attorney general's office didn't file any opposition to the Poway validation action in court. Nor did anyone else, and the day after Poway's lawyers received the AG's letter, the judge issued a default judgment in favor of the district allowing it to proceed with the sale of the bonds.

This left the entire industry in doubt about the proper way to pay costs of issuance. While the attorney general's letter threatened to "scrutinize proposed bond issues such as this in the future," it wasn't a formal legal opinion that could be cited by a court in any legal challenge.

This lack of clarity left everyone groping around in the dark for the next few months over how to pay costs of issuance. There's no statutory or case law that said it was okay to use premium but, then again, there was nothing that prohibited it. A number of costs had been traditionally paid through premium, and it made no sense to start paying out of the project fund. For example, the purchase of bond insurance only benefited taxpayers, since it produced a net savings in the interest rate.

Most bond lawyers have been able to see their way out of this problem by applying a strict interpretation of Education Code Section 15147(f), which states that *"any premium or accrued interest **received from the sale of the bonds** shall be deposited in the interest and sinking fund of the district."* (Emphasis added.) Since bonds have been sold for decades with original issue premium that is retained by the underwriter and used to pay costs, many lawyers now believe that this Education Code provision does not apply to OIP, which is never paid to the district. Accordingly, when a district wants its cost of issuance paid out of OIP, it's important to make certain that these funds are not a part of the purchase price of the bonds and, therefore, are never *received* by the district.

Comfort can also be taken from the *lack* of legislative action on this issue during the 2013 session. Although AB 182 (the CAB legislation) placed severe limitations on the structure of school bonds and went through numerous rewrites, amendments and hearings, there was no significant discussion addressing the issue of paying costs of issuance out of premium.

Reviewing Costs: The Good, the Bad and the Contingent

Almost all the fees and expenses associated with a general obligation bond sale are billed on a contingent basis. If the bond doesn't pass, or even if it does pass but the district decides not to issue the bonds, no fees are paid, with the few exceptions noted on the following pages. When the deal finally closes, the fees and expenses are included as a cost of issuance and are paid from bond proceeds.

Some argue that this method of payment ends up costing taxpayers more because districts spend less energy reviewing and negotiating the fees, since they know they won't have to pay them directly. I'm sympathetic to this argument, and I'm sure our fees would be lower if we were able to shift the risk of not getting paid onto the district. However, I'm willing to bet that the alternative of sending a district an invoice for our services, either on an hourly basis or as a set fee, regardless of the outcome of its election, would find few fans among district business officials.

The strength of the contingent fee agreement is that it encourages all the players in a bond deal to work as efficiently as possible. Not only are the professionals only paid upon the success of the financing, there's no incentive to produce unnecessary reports, slow the process down, or create nonexistent problems in order to increase the number of billable hours.

So, assuming you've structured your deal so that costs of issuance are paid at closing, here's a review of what you should be looking for in terms of fees and what to keep an eye out for:

UNDERWRITING/COMPETITIVE SALES

Because the computation for a winning competitive sale bid includes the underwriter's fee, there's no need to worry about whether this cost is too high. It could be the most outrageous fee in the history of the tax-exempt market but if, when rolled together with the interest rate, it produces the lowest net interest cost, what do you care?

UNDERWRITING/NEGOTIATED SALES

This one, on the other hand, you should really pay attention to. Since underwriters charge a percentage based on the par amount of bonds being sold, this number can add up quickly. And unless you have a financial advisor willing to step in and play referee, you have little chance of being able to "negotiate" fees with the underwriter.

Here's an example: One particular underwriter had been working with a district in southern California for many years. The underwriter routinely charged a fee of 1 percent on the par amount of the bond. That doesn't sound like much, but on a $50 million bond that comes to $500,000. On the final sale, the district hired us to serve as financial advisor. In *one telephone conversation* with the underwriter, we got the fee chopped 50 percent.

Was it because I'm a great negotiator? Probably not. All I did was point out the average underwriting fees on similar deals for the past year or so were much lower – and made clear this information was going to be shared with the client – and the underwriter immediately found a way to lower its fee.

FINANCIAL ADVISORY FEES

State law prohibits financial advisory fees from being calculated solely as a percentage of the size of the deal. This makes a certain amount of sense in that it removes any incentive to boost the size of the deal to increase the fee. However, it is still common for financial advisors to tier their fees so that issuers of smaller deals pay less than those with large financings.

We've already spent plenty of time discussing financial advisory fees, but there are a few curveballs you should look out for. Beware of any financing plan that involves BANs. Especially ones in which the financial advisor is pitching the idea as a way to lower borrowing costs. I'm not saying BANs are never justified. Just make sure you completely understand what is being proposed and precisely what the risks are. In far too many cases, it seems to me, advisors recommend BANs simply to boost their fees.

Be leery of new players suddenly showing up at the table. There are a few firms that seem to have developed "strategic alliances," which basically consist of each firm shoehorning the other into some bogus slot in the final financing. A very few mammoth districts in California could probably use more than one financial advisor looking over the details of a financing. But it's hard to see why any but these giant districts need to double-team a financing.

BOND COUNSEL FEES

Bond counsel fees are typically calculated on a diminishing percentage scale. So, for example, the fee for the first $5 million of par will be calculated at one percentage rate, the next $10 million at a lower percentage, the next $25 million at an even lower percentage, and so on.

UNDERWRITER'S COUNSEL FEES

This is one of the squishiest areas of the bond closing. In negotiated deals, some underwriters will want to hire their own lawyer; others are willing to rely on opinions by bond counsel. In addition, some underwriters' counsel will take on a fair amount of work (e.g., drafting the official statement), while others seem to view their role as marking up other people's documents with often illegible comments in the margins.

In addition, the prices are all over the map and, worse still, even though these lawyers represent the underwriter, they are generally paid out of the deal's cost of issuance and not out of the underwriter's pocket. The financial advisor can be helpful in sorting this out, and a good one will nail down all these particulars early in the process.

DISCLOSURE COUNSEL FEES

In certain cases, the drafting of the Official Statement is fairly straightforward and involves little more than updating the last document. Other times, it can be a remarkably arduous task that you wouldn't wish on your worst enemy. (All right, maybe some of them.) Oddly, however, the price doesn't seem to vary much.

RATING AGENCY FEES

Much has been made lately of the inherent conflict embedded in the rating agencies' business model. Critics charge that because they're paid by the issuer of the debt being rated, the agencies are unable to provide an independent unbiased evaluation.

Without getting too deeply into this argument (which, at least, in the case of the subprime mortgage crisis, may have some merit), let me say that almost every analyst I've met at both Moody's and S&P has been incredibly hard-working, diligent and highly professional. The rating agencies provide a remarkably useful and efficient service to both investors and issuers. Because investors look to them to vet a credit, their efforts provide enormous interest cost savings to both districts and taxpayers, and the cost of their rating is worth every penny.

ELECTION REIMBURSEMENT

The bad news is that county elections departments have become more and more aggressive about billing bond measure election costs to districts. The good news is that if you win, this is a recoverable expense paid from bond proceeds. If you lose, election costs are yet another sad result.

THE CLOSING

As I mentioned at the beginning of this chapter, closings just aren't what they used to be. Sure, there's still tons of paper floating around, signatures to be obtained, Fed-wire transfers to be checked, and final sign-offs to be done. But over time the need for the direct involvement of district officials has been greatly reduced.

During the closing, the heavy lifting is the responsibility of the financing team. This is the moment for everybody else – board members, campaign volunteers, district staff – to savor. All the planning, the uncertainty, the worry, the arguments, the emotional rollercoaster of the election, the rating, the sale … is over. The money's in the bank and now the hard work – overseeing the spending of the bond funds – is about to begin.

Chapter
FOURTEEN

....

AFTER THE CLOSING

....

"Coming together is a beginning; keeping together is progress; working together is success."

~ Henry Ford

THE CASH FLOW: FUNDING THE DISTRICT'S PROJECTS AND REPAYING INVESTORS

After the bonds are sold and the transaction closes, three distinctly different activities take place in relation to bond funds. These cash flows are completely independent of one another, but they often get muddled together in the minds of board members, district administrators, and the general public. Herewith is a guide:

Depositing Bond Funds into the District's Project Fund

The first cash flow occurs with the wiring of funds from the underwriter to the treasurer's office of the county in which the district is located. Over the years, there's been a fair amount of grumbling over the requirement that districts invest the bond's project fund with their county's treasurer. While this may not be the greatest system in the world (one county, in fact, lost an enormous sum by investing in Lehman Brothers right before it tanked), it's the system we've got, and trying to fight it without a legislative fix is futile.

Before the close, a member of the financing team will prepare a closing memo that details the county wiring instructions and what amounts are to be sent to which accounts. Most of the money will go into a project fund held by the county, although there may also be other short-term funds set up and held by a commercial bank to handle smaller sums, such as a cost of issuance fund.

Once the bond proceeds are in the county's custody, the county takes responsibility for their management and investment. Investment earnings remain in each specific fund and are not commingled or transferred among the various accounts.

Drawing Down Bond Funds for Project Funding

The second cash flow is the drawdown by the district of money in the project fund to pay for the projects approved by voters. Occasionally, a district will voice concern over how quickly the counties will be able to process their requests, but, by and large, this system works remarkably well, even though it may take a while to convince the district that everything is going to be just fine.

Some years ago, we worked with one of the state's larger community college districts in passing its first general obligation bond. A few weeks after the election, one of the board members called and asked if we could schedule a meeting to discuss the district's role and responsibility regarding the bonds. He had discussed many of his issues with the district's CBO but wasn't able to get the answers he was looking for. He had, he said in a grave voice, "many concerns."

The next morning, the board member, a retired president of the local community bank, arrived in a three-piece suit holding a worn briefcase.

"My concern," he said, launching right in after a few pleasantries, "is the oversight of the investment of the funds. Who sets this policy? How do we choose our investment manager? How do we determine the correct mix of investments to meet our cash flow needs?"

All good questions, I assured him, and then took him through how California K–14 general obligation bond funds are handled.

"On the day the financing closes," I explained to him, "all the funds are wired to the county treasurer's office."

"Then what happens?"

"They're held by the county treasurer until needed by the district."

"But who decides how they're invested?"

"They're invested in the county's investment pool. All the funds in the pool receive the same blended rate."

"And where's the interest go? Who gets it?"

"It stays in the Project Fund and is applied toward whatever projects you're funding."

He paused for a moment, running over the cash flow in his mind. "And when we want the funds, how much advance notice do we need to give the county? Is there a penalty for early withdrawal?"

"Of course, the county would prefer as much notice as possible. But they're your funds and you can draw them down whenever you need them."

"Even overnight?"

"Even overnight."

"Without penalty?"

"Without penalty."

"I see," he said after a longer pause. "So, you're saying the college has no responsibility for these funds?"

"You're responsible for spending them wisely."

"But what about repayment of the investors? How do we do that?"

"That's also handled by the county."

"I see," he mused lost in thought. After a few more cursory questions, the conversation drifted into the pros and cons of different San Francisco restaurants, who was going to win the next governor's race, and how early he needed to leave in order to beat rush-hour traffic.

Repaying Investors from Tax Receipts

A *debt service repayment fund* is also created at the same time the project fund is set up with the county. When the financing is completed, the financial advisor or underwriter will forward a copy of the final annual debt service schedule to the county assessor's office. Using these numbers, the county assessor will annually set whatever tax rate is required to raise sufficient funds to repay investors.

The reality is a lot more complex than that, and there are a number of seeming anomalies. For example, because levies on unsecured property lag behind levies on secured property by a year, counties routinely overassess in the early years of bond repayment to build up a payment reserve, and the tax-rate computational method differs from county to county. But these are technical side issues.

Once the tax rate is set, it is applied to each property owner's assessed valuation and tacked on to the semiannual property tax bill. As the funds come in, they are deposited in the debt service repayment fund and used to make annual principal and semiannual interest payments to investors.

Here's where people most often get confused. Let's quickly retrace the first two steps. First, the bonds are sold and the money is wired into the project fund and other various accounts held by the county. Second, a district draws money out of the county treasury to pay for the projects approved by the voters. Both of these steps deal with the generation and spending of funds for the completion of projects approved by the voters.

This third cash flow, however, is concerned not with project funding but with the repayment of investors who loaned funds to the district by purchasing the bonds. It's not uncommon to hear a board member or citizen wonder why taxes levied by the county assessor and placed into the debt service fund can't be used to fund the construction or rehabilitation of one of the projects instead of going to the expense of paying investors.

It's a good question but, fortunately or unfortunately, there is no legal authority to use these tax revenues for any purpose other than the repayment of debt service. These funds are collected solely for the repayment of the principal and interest on the bonds.

Making it a little more complicated is the fact that some bond funds might also be deposited into this account. For example, if there is a mismatch due to timing between the receipt of the first tax payment and the disbursement of the first interest payment, we might require the underwriter to sell the bonds at a slight premium to generate enough money to make that first interest payment. On the day of closing, these funds would also be wired into the county treasury but would be deposited into the debt service fund, not the project fund.

CONTINUING DISCLOSURE

Many of us who work in the field of K–14 financing tend to focus on the sale of new bond financings while forgetting that there is an enormous secondary market for these bonds that continues for years after the original sale.

Let's say your district sells a $25 million GO bond with a 25-year final maturity. Let's imagine that the final maturity had an interest rate of 4.50 percent payable on a semiannual basis. If an investor were to buy a $100,000 piece of that maturity, he'd receive $2,250 in interest (tax-free) every six months until the bond matured.

But what happens if the investor wants the money back before the final maturity? This could happen for any number of reasons. A mutual fund might need to liquidate some of its holdings because its investors are pulling their money out. The institutional investor might become concerned about the district's credit. The individual investor might decide it's time to finally remodel the kitchen. The reason is unimportant. What matters is that municipal bonds are a relatively liquid investment that can easily be sold in the secondary market.

Selling isn't the problem. The complication is on the buy side. Starting in the 1960s and continuing on through the 1980s, two things happened in the muni bond market. Municipal bond deals started getting more and more complex. Besides GO bonds, revenue bonds, which relied on some outside source of funding, started becoming more prevalent. There were multi-family housing bonds, to provide low-cost financing, nursing home bonds, industrial development bonds and variable rate bonds.

At the same time that bonds started becoming more complex, the profile of the typical investor began to shift away from institutions like banks and insurance companies toward private individuals.

During this period, the amount of information available to an investor was pretty sketchy. While big institutions could afford analysts to follow an issuer's credit after the bonds were sold, this information wasn't readily available to the private investor. In fact, the only information that was often available was the original Official Statement.

Unfortunately, the credit rating that appeared so prominently on the front cover of an issue's offering statement might be hopelessly out of date when these same bonds were resold in the secondary market five or 10 years later.

For this reason, the Securities and Exchange Commission stepped in and began requiring annual "secondary market disclosure" for almost all issuers of municipal securities. The SEC has no regulatory power over municipal governments, but it wields a big stick with underwriters.

And wield it the SEC did. At least it tried. In 1994, the SEC amended the regulation (Rule 15c2-12) that governed municipal market disclosure, barring the underwriters of municipal bonds from buying an issuer's securities unless the issuer had agreed, in writing, to provide continuing disclosure. This disclosure must reasonably mirror the disclosure originally included in the issuer's original Official Statement. (In 2008, the MSRB established an Electronic Municipal Market Access [EMMA] system as the sole repository for all continuing disclosure.)

In addition, issuers – that is, districts – must file *event notices* for all material events that might affect their securities. These notices, which must be filed within 10 business days of their occurrence, include payment delinquencies, adverse tax opinions by the IRS, bond calls, rating changes, and anything else that might affect an issuer's credit.

Although a number of districts have tried to ignore the secondary market disclosure requirements, this is a very bad idea. Since the agreement to provide secondary market information is included in the final signed bond documents, failure to comply with this requirement is technically a breach of contract. Although prosecution is unlikely, the SEC has stepped up its investigations into the area, and underwriters are becoming much more concerned about districts that have a history of noncompliance.

Another bad idea is for districts to try to do this by themselves. While the annual filings used to be fairly straightforward, the increased scrutiny of event notices has made this area too complicated and fraught to be handled by most K–14 district staffs. There are numerous qualified firms (including mine) that will handle these filings, and the fees tend to be quite modest.

Chapter
FIFTEEN

....

CONCLUSION

....

"You cannot open a book without learning something."

~ Confucius

"Outside of a dog, a book is man's best friend. Inside of a dog it's too dark to read."

~ Groucho Marx

The victory party was just getting started at a small Mexican restaurant in the middle of town. Each table was decorated with small American flags and set with a bowl of chips and salsa. Campaign volunteers, union representatives, board members, administrators and parents were streaming in, giving each other big hello hugs, shaking their heads in amazement that the bond had actually passed, and then heading for the bar.

The district was located in a midsized working-class city near the heart of Los Angeles County. Even though it had been over a decade since the passage of Prop. 39, it had never placed a bond measure on the ballot. The administrators told me they never thought it could pass, and there had been serious opposition from former board members.

Conclusion

But in 2011, a newly elected board member started pushing to improve the district's schools right after he'd been sworn in. Discussions began. Presentations were made. We ran a poll, and the results looked promising. The superintendent decided the time was ripe. The employees' unions promised support. A quick canvassing of local leaders found most to be in favor. After a lot of hard questions and soul searching, the board decided the voters of the district deserved the right to decide whether or not to raise their taxes to improve local schools.

That was more than a year earlier. I stood off to the side, watching as people continued to pour in, thinking about all that had gone into making this moment possible, and all the work that remained to be done to get the bond into the market. Leading up to the board's final vote to place the bond on the ballot, the district administration had spent hours working with our staff in developing a Project List, analyzing tax rates, reviewing the voter survey and making sure all the documents were in order.

And as the campaign began to pick up steam, more and more volunteers began showing up, wanting to know what they could do to help pass the bond. In the final run-up to Election Day, you could sense people's excitement as they began to see that the bond measure looked as if it would win.

Everyone, that is, except Saul. Saul had been on the board for years and was always the top vote getter. He was a big guy with a wide bristly mustache and hands that showed the years he spent building up his construction business. He was well known and well respected. And he hated taxes.

During the board's initial discussions about the bond, he made no secret of the fact that he was against it. But Saul was also smart enough to see the board's attitude had shifted. He could count his fellow board members' votes and knew he was outgunned. On the night the board voted to place the measure on the ballot, Saul was conveniently out of town on business. The resolution passed 4–0.

Even though he was against the bond, during the campaign he was good enough to keep it to himself. And now here he was at the victory party, leaning against the bar, sipping a Budweiser as he coolly surveyed the crowd. I walked over, stuck out my hand and introduced myself.

"I know who you are," he said with a wry grin. "You're the guy who got us into all this."

"Well," I stammered. "Not really …"

"Ah, don't worry about it," he said, cutting me off. "What's done is done."

He paused and went back to his Bud, lost in thought. The restaurant was now filled to the max, and it was getting hard to hear over the laughter and the high-fives.

"You know," he said, leaning in, "it's not like I was against the bond. I just thought it was …"

"The wrong time?" I suggested.

"Exactly," he nodded. "What with the state raising our taxes and Washington constantly sticking their hand in our pockets, it's killing us. I mean I'm all for improving schools, I just think there ought to be a better way of doing it than raising taxes."

I nodded, as if I knew what he was talking about.

"Besides," he said, "I didn't know a single person who said they were going to vote for this bond. Not one."

He turned and signaled the bartender for a check.

"Guess I must know the wrong people," he laughed, scanning the crowd again. "Then again, maybe people around here are just changing." He stopped and shook his head. "It's kinda like this bond thing of yours got people all revved up and excited, like it was, I don't know …"

"Transformative?" I offered.

Saul shot me a look like I was speaking Urdu. "Whatever," he finally shrugged. He pushed himself back from the bar and dug his car keys out of his coat pocket. "But there's one thing I can tell you and I know it for certain." He paused, taking one last look at the crowd. "If you can pass a bond in this town, you can pass one anywhere."

ACKNOWLEDGEMENTS

My decision to write this book grew out of the controversies that erupted in the summer of 2012 over the General Obligation Capital Appreciation Bonds sold by a number of school and college districts throughout California. Before these bond deals made headlines, the field of school bond finance more often than not occupied a sleepy corner of the nation's securities market. Now suddenly it was front and center, as reporters, politicians, and taxpayer organizations grappled with the ins and outs of this esoteric, usually ignored subject.

Few books are written without the help of many, and *Win-Win* is no exception. Before giving thanks to those involved in the creation of this book, I want to acknowledge a handful of elected officials who – although they had no involvement in the writing of *Win-Win* – jumped into the school-bond scrum as the Capital Appreciation Bond controversy began to explode. Rather than merely sit on the sidelines wringing their hands, each of these officials set to work to restore a touch of sanity to the process of issuing school bonds, a process that had clearly veered out of control. This list includes Dan McAllister, treasurer-tax collector of San Diego County, who was among the first to propose new regulations for school bonds; former Assemblywoman Joan Buchanan (chair of the Assembly Education Committee) and State Senator Ben Hueso, the co-authors of AB 182; and former State Treasurer Bill Lockyer, who was instrumental in AB 182's final form and passage by both the California Assembly and Senate.

Turning back to *Win-Win*, I want to thank the staff of Dale Scott & Company for their help in moving this book from a folder of loose pages to final publication: especially Mark Farrell for his comments and careful

Acknowledgements

reading; and Mary Ellen Kissell and Seija McMillin, for overseeing the arcane and time-consuming process of publishing a book. Thanks to the book's production team for taking the dive into the world of publishing including Joyce Schmidt, Shari Teach, Adam Elwell, Chris Shults and Mike Swenson. I would also like to thank the amazing analysts at DS&C - Joe Crump, Nicole Roberts and Stephen Zhang.

Sandie Arnott, treasurer-tax collector of San Mateo County, deserves special thanks for her time spent in reviewing the *Win-Win* manuscript and making numerous suggestions and edits. Wayne Oetken, retired CBO of the Cajon Valley Union School District, brought a much-appreciated school business official's perspective to the book.

Thanks also to current and former members of the Dale Scott & Company Board of Advisors, including Michael Crilly, Pat Furlong, David Gomez, Marilou Ryder, Phil Pendley, John Rogers, and Dennis Scott for providing both their strong support and valuable professional knowledge. In particular, I want to thank John for providing a better understanding of the impact of Prop. 13 on school budgets, and Dennis and Marilou for their valuable comments on the manuscript.

Finally, warm and loving thanks go to my wife, Hayedeh Scott, for her encouragement, feedback and insights, which I relied on throughout the writing of *Win-Win*.

Dale Scott
San Francisco
October 2019

ABOUT THE AUTHOR

Dale Scott, President of Dale Scott & Company (DS&C) has worked with California's school and community college districts for more than 30 years, serving as a financial advisor and campaign manager on hundreds of California's school and community college district voter-approved GO bond financings and elections. His firm, headquartered in San Francisco, provides financial advisory consulting services throughout the state and is consistently ranked among the leading advisors. Dale is widely viewed within the school bond industry as one of the most innovative thinkers. Dale worked with Jefferson Union High School District in Daly City, California, on the nation's first Teacher-Staff Housing General Obligation Bond. Jefferson Union High School District and DS&C are recipients of the Bond Buyer Small-Issuer Deal of the Year award in December 2018. He holds two patents from the United States Patent and Trademarks Office for financing mechanisms for school district debt. Dale is also a frequent speaker on the subject of school district finance and has appeared before numerous taxpayer organizations and statewide school district symposiums. Dale started his career as an investment banker on Wall Street and, prior to forming DS&C, managed Wells Fargo Bank's Public Finance Department. He is a graduate of Napa High School and Napa Community College, and has a bachelor's degree from San Francisco State University and a master's degree from Harvard University.

dscott@dalescott.com

INDEX

Index

Index